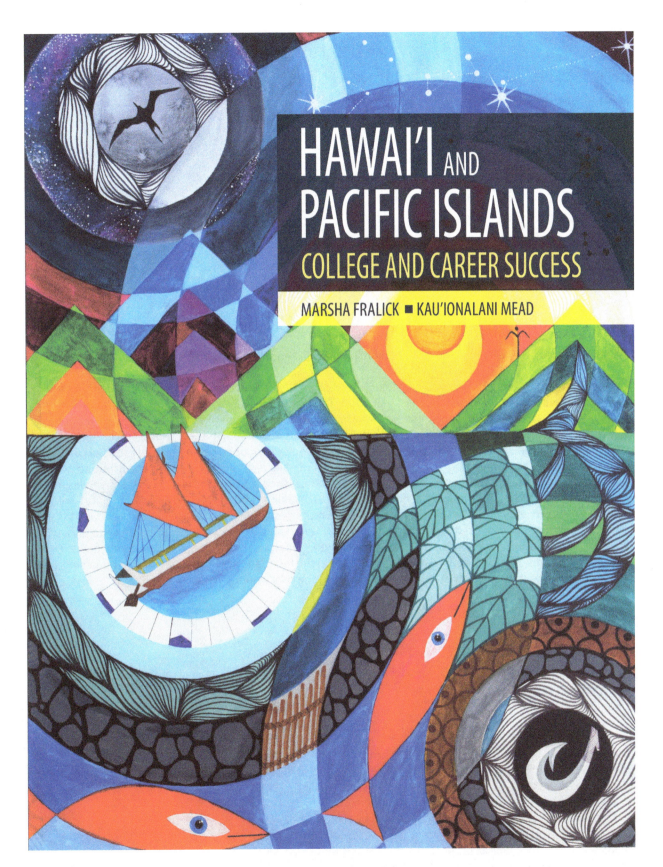

HAWAI'I AND PACIFIC ISLANDS
COLLEGE AND CAREER SUCCESS

MARSHA FRALICK ▪ KAU'IONALANI MEAD

Kendall Hunt
publishing company

Book Team

Chairman and Chief Executive Officer Mark C. Falb
President and Chief Operating Officer Chad M. Chandlee
Vice President, Higher Education David L. Tart
Director of Publishing Partnerships Paul B. Carty
Product/Development Supervisor Lynne Rogers
Vice President, Operations Timothy J. Beitzel
Senior Project Coordinator Stefani DeMoss
Permissions Editor Caroline Kieler
Cover Designer Heather Richman

Cover art courtesy of Nicole Arielle Maka'āhina'ālohilohi Jack. © Kendall Hunt Publishing Company

The cover art for this publication aims to highlight just a few of the many accomplishments of Indigenous Pacific peoples. In recognition of their skills in long distance voyaging and celestial navigation, the Hōkūle'a is featured, sailing within the 32-point star compass that Nainoa Thompson adapted from the Satawalese version taught to him by Mau Piailug. Navigational aids like star constellations, birds, the moon, the sun, winds, and ocean currents are included, as Oceanic navigators cleverly devised how to use them for open ocean sailing. Island people skillfully developed sophisticated agriculture and aquaculture techniques like terraced kalo farming and fishpond wall construction, which enabled them to provide stable food sources for a thriving population. Petroglyph designs symbolize people joined together, exemplifying the customs of laulima and of working as a community—integral values for living on geographically small islands with finite resources. Shown too is the abundance of healthy, natural environments like forested mountains and plentiful waterways, which were the product of Pacific Islanders' successes in applied sustainable living practices. Moving into the future, we can glean from the Indigenous peoples of the Pacific the importance of staying ancestrally rooted in the foundations of the past, but also remaining ever adaptive and flexible to changes that will invariably come in the contemporary age.

Kendall Hunt
publishing company

www.kendallhunt.com
Send all inquiries to:
4050 Westmark Drive
Dubuque, IA 52004-1840

Copyright © 2017 by Kendall Hunt Publishing Company

ISBN 978-1-5249-2325-9

All rights reserved. No part of this publication may be reproduced, stored in a retrieval system, or transmitted, in any form or by any means, electronic, mechanical, photocopying, recording, or otherwise, without the prior written permission of the copyright owner.

Published in the United States of America

BRIEF CONTENTS

Chapter 1 Cultural Identity and Success 1

Chapter 2 Understanding Motivation 15

Chapter 3 Exploring Your Personality and Major 49

Chapter 4 Managing Time and Money 81

Chapter 5 Using Brain Science to Improve Memory 119

Chapter 6 Using Brain Science to Improve Study Skills 141

Chapter 7 Taking Notes, Writing, and Speaking 167

Chapter 8 Test Taking 199

Chapter 9 Thinking Positively about the Future 233

CONTENTS

Preface ix
Features of This Book xi
Acknowledgments xiii
About the Authors xv

1 Cultural Identity and Success 1

Learning Objectives 1
Taking Pride in Your Culture 2
Who Are the Pacific Islanders? 2
    Diversity 4
    Educational Attainment 4
    Hawaiian Values 4
    History of Education in Hawai'i 6
The Revival of Pride in Hawaiian and Pacific Island Culture: The Hokule'a 7
Navigating Different Cultures and Finding a Safe Place 9
Appreciating Island Cultures: The Story of the Kahuli Shells 10

2 Understanding Motivation 15

Learning Objectives 15
What Do I Want from College? 16
What Is the Value of a College Education? 16
Choosing a Major and Career 18
How to Be Motivated 19
    Your Mindset Makes a Difference 19
    Thinking Positively about the Future 20
    Find Something Interesting in Your Studies 22
    Improving Your Concentration and Attention 22
    Intrinsic or Extrinsic Motivation 24
    Locus of Control 25
    Affiliation 27
    Achievement 28
    Using a Reward 28

Success Is a Habit 29
    Eight Steps to Change a Habit 29
Keys to Success: Persistence 31
Appreciating Island Cultures: 'Opae E 32
Notes 36
Exercises 37

3 Exploring Your Personality and Major 49

Learning Objectives 49
Choose a Major That Matches Your Gifts and Talents 50
Understanding Personality Types 50
    Extraversion or Introversion 51
    Sensing or Intuition 54
    Thinking or Feeling 56
    Judging or Perceiving 58
Personality and Career Choice 62
Personality and Preferred Work Environment 62
More on Personality Type 63
Exploring Your Personal Strengths 68
Other Factors in Choosing a Major 69
Keys to Success 72
Appreciating Island Cultures: Tattoos 73
Notes 75
Exercises 76

4 Managing Time and Money 81

Learning Objectives 81
What Are My Lifetime Goals? 82
    A Goal or a Fantasy? 83
The ABCs of Time Management 85
How to Estimate Study and Work Time 87
Schedule Your Success 88
    What Is Your Chronotype? 88
    Using a Schedule 89
    If You Dislike Schedules 90
    Manage Your Time with a Web Application 91

Time Management Tricks 91
   Divide and Conquer 92
   Do the First Small Step 92
   The 80/20 Rule 92
   Aim for Excellence, Not Perfection 93
   Make Learning Fun by Finding a Reward 93
   Take a Break 93
   Learn to Say No Sometimes 94
Dealing with Time Bandits 94
Dealing with Procrastination 95
   Why Do We Procrastinate? 95
   Tips for Dealing with Procrastination 97
Managing Your Money 99
   How to Become a Millionaire 99
   Budgeting: The Key to Money Management 100
   Need More Money? 101
   The Best Ideas for Becoming Financially Secure 103
   Tips for Managing Your Money 103
Keys to Success: Do What Is Important First 104
Notes 106
Exercises 107

5 Using Brain Science to Improve Memory 119

Learning Objectives 119
Improving Your Memory 120
   Memory: Short Term versus Long Term 120
   Forgetting 120
   Minimizing Forgetting 121
Practical Memory Techniques Based on Brain Science 123
   Think Positively about Learning 123
   Develop an Interest 123
   See the Big Picture First 124
   Meaningful Organization 124
   The Magical Number 7 Theory 124
   Visualization 125
   Intend to Remember 126
   Elaboration 126
   Distribute the Practice 126
   Create a Basic Background 127
   Stress and Emotions 127
   Relax While Studying 128
Using Mnemonics and Other Memory Tricks 128
   Acrostics 128
   Acronyms 129
   Peg Systems 129
   Loci Systems 130
   Visual Clues 130
   Say It Aloud 131
   Have a Routine 131
   Write It Down 131
   Remembering Names 131
Optimize Your Brain Power 132
Keys to Success: Positive Thinking 134
Notes 136
Exercises 137

6 Using Brain Science to Improve Study Skills 141

Learning Objectives 141
Neuroscience and Practical Learning Strategies 142
   Visual Learning Strategies 142
   Audio Learning Strategies 143
   Tactile Learning Techniques 144
   Kinesthetic Learning Strategies 144
   Olfactory Learning Strategies 144
   Gustatory Learning Strategies 144
Applying Memory Strategies to Reading 145
   A Study System for Reading a College Textbook: SQ4R 145
   Reading Strategies for Different Subjects 149

Improving Reading Concentration 150
E-Learning Strategies 151
Guidelines for Marking Your Textbook 152
How to Be Successful in Your Math Courses 154
Keys to Success: Create Your Success 158
Appreciating Island Cultures: Tiare Apetahi 159
Notes 161
Exercises 162

7 Taking Notes, Writing, and Speaking 167

Learning Objectives 167
Why Take Notes? 168
The College Lecture 169
How to Be a Good Listener 169
Tips for Good Note Taking 170
Note-Taking Systems 171
    The Cornell Format 171
    The Outline Method 173
    The Mind Map 174
    Taking Notes in Math 175
Improving Note-Taking Efficiency 176
    Telegraphic Sentences 176
    Signal Words 176
How to Review Your Notes 178
Power Writing 179
    Prepare 180
    Organize 182
    Write 183
    Writer's Block 184
    Edit and Revise 185
    Final Steps 187
Effective Public Speaking 187
    Learn to Relax 188
    Preparing and Delivering Your Speech 188
Keys to Success: Be Selective 191

Appreciating Island Cultures: How the 'Ulu Tree Came to Hawai'i 192
Notes 193
Exercises 194

8 Test Taking 199

Learning Objectives 199
Preparing for Tests 200
    Attend Every Class 200
    Distribute the Practice 200
    Schedule a Time and a Place for Studying 201
    Test Review Tools 202
    Reviewing Effectively 202
    Predicting Test Questions 204
    Preparing for an Open-Book Test 204
    Emergency Procedures 204
    Ideas That Don't Work 206
Dealing with Test Anxiety 209
Dealing with Math Anxiety 211
    Math Tests 212
Taking Tests 213
    True-False Tests 213
    Multiple-Choice Tests 215
    Matching Tests 220
    Sentence-Completion or Fill-in-the-Blank Tests 221
    Essay Tests 222
    What to Do When Your Test Is Returned 224
Keys to Success: Be Prepared 225
Appreciating Island Cultures: How Maui Slowed the Sun(Maori) 226
Notes 227
Exercises 228

9 Thinking Positively about the Future 233

Learning Objectives 233
Life Stages 234

  Erik Erikson 234
  Daniel Levinson 235
  Gail Sheehy 236
Thinking Positively about Your Life 239
  Optimism, Hope, and Future-Mindedness 240
  Believe in Yourself 241
  The Self-Fulfilling Prophecy 241
  Positive Self-Talk and Affirmations 242
  Visualize Your Success 243
Successful Beliefs 244

Secrets to Happiness 246
Keys to Success: You Are What You Think 251
Appreciating Island Cultures: Maui and His Magic Fish Hook 251
Notes 253
Exercises 255

Glossary 263

Index 267

PREFACE

Because of my own cultural background, I have always been interested in Indigenous cultures around the world. Growing up on the outskirts of Santa Fe, New Mexico, near several Native American reservations, I had the opportunity to learn about Native American culture and attend school with many Native American students. I was one of the few students in my high school who attended college. I have always wondered why more students did not attend college.

I wrote a textbook, "Native American and First Nations College and Career Success" to help these students to be successful in college. My travels took me to the state of Hawai'i and I could see a parallel with Native American and Native Hawai'ian and Pacific Island students. All of these Indigenous populations are underrepresented in higher education with corresponding lower income and career opportunities.

After working for 35 years as a college counselor and professor at Cuyamaca College in El Cajon, California, I came to realize that success in education begins with a positive self-concept. Students need confidence in their abilities and have a vision of what their life can be in the future. For Indigenous students, positive self-concept includes pride in their cultural background. Sadly, our educational system has focused on assimilation rather than on appreciation of Native cultures. This has resulted in a diminished self-concept for many students and their consequent lack of success in high school and college. It is fortunate that there is a rebirth of interest in Native culture and appreciation of students of diverse cultural backgrounds.

After teaching students for many years to be successful in college and writing a textbook on this topic, *College and Career Success*, I began to think about writing textbooks that incorporated Native cultures. I was encouraged to begin working on this project by Dr. Kelly Withy, Director of the Hawai'i/Pacific Basin Area Health Education Center, who was working on a grant to recruit and retain students in a Pre-Health Career Core at the University of Hawai'i, John A. Burns School of Medicine at Manoa. They were interested in incorporating cultural material along with college and career success skills to increase success for their students. I was able to collaborate with Native Hawai'ian Kau'ionalani Mead, the Outreach and Recruitment Pathways Specialist, to incorporate Hawai'ian and Pacific Island culture with my materials.

The added cultural content includes an introductory chapter, Cultural Identity and Success, that provides the rationale for this edition. It includes information on college success and cultural pride, how island values can be used to increase success, a brief history of higher education in the area, and how to navigate between Native cultures and the culture of higher education. It helps students to understand their history and increase appreciation of their culture as a foundation for their future success.

Each chapter contains Native stories and legends that reflect the island values along with discussion questions that help students connect their culture to success in college and careers.

While the textbook is designed for Native students, all students who live in Hawai'i and the Pacific Islands can benefit from increasing their knowledge and appreciation of the culture of the people where they live.

Hawai'ian and Pacific Island College and Career Success is the first textbook of its type to include island culture as well as college and career success topics. We anticipate future editions of this textbook which will incorporate additional cultural information along with examples of successful Native students who can serve as role models for upcoming students. We look forward to your feedback on the effectiveness of this textbook in improving college success for Hawai'ian and Pacific Island students.

FEATURES OF THIS BOOK

With a Native Hawaiian and Pacific Island Cultural Perspective
The book is based on the premise that education for Native Hawaiian and Pacific Island students begins with a positive self-concept. For these students, positive self-concept includes pride in their cultural background.

Chapters include a section titled "Appreciating Island Cultures" which helps students connect their culture to success in higher education. Discussion questions help students understand traditional stories and how the teachings can be used for success in college, careers, and in life.

Chapter 1, Cultural Identity and Success, contains an overview of Hawaiian history of higher education from colonization to the present day. It helps students understand that taking pride in their culture and appreciating diversity is the foundation for learning. It also helps students in transitioning to college and overcoming common obstacles to their success.

Native Hawaiian and Pacific Island photos are used throughout the text.
Hawaiian values and famous sayings are featured in the margins.

Includes Concepts from Positive Psychology
Concepts from positive psychology are used to help students:

- discover their strengths, interests, and values;
- build on their strengths;
- think positively about themselves and their future;
- clarify what happiness means and work toward attaining it in life.

Helps Students Assume Responsibility for Their Own Success
Topics include motivation, positive thinking, locus of control, mindset, future-mindedness, hope, belief, persistence, emotional intelligence, and learning positive behavior.

Incorporates the Latest Research in Psychology, Education, and Neuroscience
The suggested strategies in this textbook are all based on current research. The latest research in neuroscience is translated into practical strategies for memory and study skills.

Online Career Portfolio
The career material in the online portfolio helps students make an informed choice of their college major and career. It includes the Do What You Are (DWYA) personality assessment and the Multiple Intelligence Advantage assessment. The results of these assessments are linked to the O*Net database of careers for career exploration. They include Indeed.com which helps students find employment.

Increasing Math Success
Since math is the gateway to high-paying careers and is a challenging requirement for graduation, this edition has expanded material on how to study math, take math notes, deal with math anxiety, and how to be successful in math tests.

Tools for Student Engagement

- Interactive activities within the text help students practice the material learned.
- Frequent quizzes and answer keys within the chapters help students with reading comprehension and check understanding of key concepts.

- Journal entries help students think critically and apply what they have learned to their personal lives.
- Individual and group exercises are included at the end of each chapter.

Resources for Faculty and Students at College Success 1

The College Success 1 website at www.collegesuccess1.com has additional materials accompanying this textbook. Student resources include key ideas, Internet links related to each chapter, and Word documents for the journal entries. Resources for faculty include the **Instructor Manual** and **Faculty Resources** for teaching college success courses including over 500 pages of classroom exercises, handouts, video suggestions, Internet links to related material, and much more.

ACKNOWLEDGMENTS

The authors extend their sincere thanks to:

- The volunteers on our Review Board who reviewed the materials and offered suggestions: Gina Tillis, Huston-Tillotson University; Bonnyjean Manini, University of Hawaii, Manoa; Wiliama Sanchez, Oregon State University; Christine Floether, Centenary College; Olu Ariyo, Vance-Granville Community College; Winnie Tang, University of Hawaii, Manoa; Rajone Lyman, Houston Community College; Lisa Gillis-Davis, Windward Community College; Joseph Yoshida, Windward and Kapiolani Community Colleges; Cara Chang, University of Hawaii; William Dressler, Kauai Community College; Makanani Sala, Windward Community College; Charlene Akina, Windward Community College; Kaahu Alo, Windward Community College; Danny Wyatt, Leeward Community College; Erin Kahunawai Wright, University of Hawaii, Manoa; Michelle Tuitupou, Salt Lake Community College; Claudia Gutierrez-Sanchez, Salt Lake Community College.

- Nicole Arielle Maka'āhina'ālohilohi Jack, the talented artist who created the artwork, "The Hōkūle'a," which highlights just a few of the many accomplishments of Indigenous Pacific peoples.

© 2017 Aaron Mizushima

Nicole Arielle Maka'āhina'ālohilohi Jack was born and raised in Kapahulu on the island of O'ahu. She will graduate from the University of Hawai'i at Manoa with a degree in Pacific Islands Studies in 2017. She spends much of her life in and around the Pacific Ocean and so, the sea has had an enormous influence on many of the things she creates. Growing up, she was always fond of hearing the stories of her people. The myths, folktales, and legends from kawākahiko, or the days of old, therefore, inform many of her paintings and other creations. Viewers can construct ideas and interpretations of her artwork in many different ways because symbolism, metaphor, and layered meaning are hallmarks of her pieces. She enjoys working with various forms of tangible artistic expression and bouncing from one medium to the next. Whether in bone carving, ceramic sculpting, photography, painting, or constructing wearable art, she aims to channel her strong cultural connection and the historic traditions of her homeland into new avenues for telling her own stories.

The overall design flow of the cover art is meant to be reminiscent of ripples, like when a stone is cast into still water. Ripples represent the effects that the things one does as an individual has on the environment and people around them. The way the generations who have come before us pass down knowledge in a way that ripples out from them to the next generation also falls within this symbolism. Metaphorically, our many islands in the Pacific may be seen as central points where ideas and people ripple outwards towards other islands, intersect and blend together, and then bounce back home again. As physical energy, ripples act in ways that create connections and affect change, which is what a successful student should aim for, too.

ABOUT THE AUTHORS

Used with permission. © Lifetouch, Inc.

Dr. Marsha Fralick is the author of *College and Career Success*, which has been used to improve student success and retention across the country since 2000. This specialized edition includes material from this textbook with added Hawaiian and Pacific Island cultural content. Dr. Fralick grew up near Santa Fe, New Mexico and has always been interested in Indigenous cultures and student success. She is also the author of Native American and First Nations College and Career Success. She has 48 years of experience working in a variety of roles in education including Spanish teacher, high school counselor, college counselor, college professor, and administrator.

Dr. Fralick believes that education is important because it provides a means for accomplishing a person's dreams. Based on her experience, she believes that a positive self-concept is the foundation for success in education. This positive self-concept is enhanced when students know about their culture and take pride in it. Students need to think positively, believe in themselves, and then take the steps needed to complete their education.

In 1978, Dr. Fralick began working as a college counselor and started teaching college success courses at Cuyamaca College in El Cajon, California where she was one of the founding faculties of the college. She wrote the curriculum, trained faculty, and developed a college success program that increased student success and retention, becoming part of the culture of the college. Dr. Fralick also published numerous research articles on student success, retention, and career development. Her program was recognized as an Exemplary Program by the California Community College Board of Governors. Upon her retirement in 2007, she was awarded Professor Emeritus status for her contributions to the development of the college and the student success program at Cuyamaca College. She was also recognized by the students of the college with the Golden Rainbow Award for Outstanding Service to the Students of Cuyamaca College.

After retiring, Dr. Fralick continues as an author and educational consultant working with faculty across the country to improve their student success programs. Based on her work with students and faculty in the development of student success programs, Dr. Fralick was recognized as the 2011 Outstanding First-Year Student Advocate by the National Resource Center for the First-Year Experience and Students in Transition from the University of South Carolina.

Dr. Fralick attended the University of New Mexico and Arizona State University where she completed her bachelor's degree in Spanish and English. After working as a high school Spanish teacher for several years, she returned to school to earn a master's degree in counseling from the University of Redlands in California. She later earned her doctorate degree from the University of Southern California in Los Angeles.

© 2017 Kau'ionalani Mead

Introducing Coauthor: Kau'ionalani Mead

Kau'ionalani Mead is a Hawai'i Native, born on the island of O'ahu. Since she was a child, her parents instilled in her the desire to pursue higher education, meaning that going to college was the only option. Her desire to succeed led her to be the first in her immediate family to receive her Bachelor of Arts with an emphasis on Vocal performance and later a Master's in Educational Leadership with an emphasis on Educational Foundations and Multi-Cultural Diversity in Education, both from the University of Hawai'i at Manoa. Growing up in her faith-based community, Kau'i began teaching at the age of 18 through her church. Her passion for children has continued to blossom and grow. It became her passion to help children succeed and eventually become contributing members to their communities.

Kau'i's mother had the desire for all of her children to understand their identities as Hawaiians and she enrolled her daughter in Hula at the age of 4. This imbedded a deep love for Hawaiian music and language. However, it wasn't until she went to the University of Hawai'i that Kau'i began to speak the language. Enrolling in Hawaiian language classes as a freshman, she had a community of people surrounding her who would speak only Hawaiian and so her ability to converse grew over time. With her love for music and culture and her Bachelor's degree, Kau'i began her journey in the educational system, first as a Pre-School through eighth grade music teacher, and then as a Kindergarten to eighth grade Hawaiian Language and Culture Specialist and currently as an Outreach and Recruitment Pathways Specialist at the Hawaii and Pacific Basin Area Health Education Center in Honolulu, Hawai'i at the John A. Burns School of Medicine.

Kau'i's newest endeavor is Ho'ola Music and Cultural Arts, a nonprofit Music Mentorship program using Hawaiian Values as its core. She will be partnering with many different community organizations that work with Native Hawaiian populations offering classes for students to participate in and learn about the values of their people, urging them to make a difference in their communities, perpetuating the music, language, and culture of the Hawaiian people.

Kau'i has been gifted the opportunity to work in collaboration with Dr. Marsha Fralick, assisting with adding Hawai'i and Pacific Island cultural material to the already successful College and Career Success curriculum. She looks forward to expanding her borders by now working with college students, helping them to be successful by gaining a better understanding and appreciation of who they are and how important they are in the communities of Hawai'i.

CHAPTER 1

Cultural Identity and Success

Learning Objectives

Read to answer these key questions:

- How is college success related to cultural pride?

- Who are the Hawaiian and Pacific Islanders?

- How can Hawaiian and Pacific Islanders increase education and income?

- What island values can empower me to succeed in college, my career, and life?

- What is the history of higher education in Hawai'i and other Pacific Islands?

- How does the Hokule'a increase pride in Hawaiian and Pacific Island cultures?

- How can I successfully navigate my culture and the culture of higher education?

- What are some tips for success?

Taking Pride in Your Culture

Welcome to college! This textbook is designed to help you to be successful in college, your career, and your life. It is based on the premise that students are more successful if they take pride in themselves and their culture, so it incorporates cultural material relevant to students in Hawai'i and the Pacific Islands. Even if you are not of Hawaiian or Pacific Island heritage, your college experience will be enriched by increasing your knowledge of the culture in which you live and study.

© Joseph Sohm/Shutterstock.com

> A'ohe Hana Nui Ka Alu 'ia: No task is too big when done together.

Having pride in yourself is the basis of good self-esteem and the foundation for good mental health and success in life. Sonia Nieto did research on a group of successful students. These students had good grades, enjoyed school, had plans for the future and described themselves as successful. She found that "one of the most consistent, and least expected, outcomes to emerge from these case studies has been a resoluteness with which young people maintain pride and satisfaction in their culture and the strength they derive from it."[1] Having pride in yourself and your culture is an important part of good self-esteem and can help you to become a better student and worker. Having good self-esteem provides the confidence to accept and care for others. The best schools and workplaces provide an environment where people value their own culture as well as appreciate the differences and values of other cultures. With respect among different cultures, ideas can be freely exchanged and the door is open to creativity and innovation.

Photo courtesy of Lilieni Tuitupou, Salt Lake Community College

Who Are the Pacific Islanders?

The Pacific Islands are home to the most diverse group of Indigenous people in the world. They include many different cultural groups from Polynesia, Melanesia, and Micronesia in the Pacific Ocean. Polynesia means "many islands" and forms a triangle between Hawai'i, the Easter Islands, and New Zealand. The islands of Hawai'i, Samoa, and Tahiti are located in Polynesia. Melanesia includes Fiji, Papua New Guinea, the Solomon Islands, the Vanuatu Islands, and New Caledonia. Micronesia has eight territories including Guam, Kiribati, and the Marshall Islands. There are over 25,000 islands, atolls, and islets in the Pacific Ocean. Pacific Islanders speak at least 39 different languages as a second language. The largest group of Pacific Islanders in the United States includes Hawaiians, Samoans, and Guamanians.[2]

Photo courtesy of Lilieni Tuitupou, Salt Lake Community College

Diversity

Hawai'i is known for its Aloha spirit where many different groups of people live in harmony. Hawai'i is one of the most diverse states in the United States with no racial or ethnic group as the majority. The minority population, which the U.S. Census Bureau defines as other than non-Hispanic White, is 77.1% of the population of the state of Hawai'i. Hawai'i has more mixed race residents than any other state. The latest census data show the following:[3]

55.9% Asian
43.7% White
23% Mixed Race
26% Native Hawaiians and Other Pacific Islanders
2.6% Black or African American

> Aloha is one of the most common Hawaiian words. It is used when saying hello or goodbye, but its true meaning is love. The "Aloha Spirit" is a guideline for treating people with love and compassion.

Journal Entry #1

What is your cultural background? Write at least one sentence about being proud of who you are. Remember that you can be empowered by taking pride in yourself and your community. You may be asked to share this information with students in your class.

Educational Attainment

College enrollment and degree completion are important to improve the lives of all Native Hawaiian and Pacific Islanders. They have lower rates of educational attainment and corresponding higher rates of poverty and unemployment as compared to national statistics.[4]

- About 28% of the general population of the United States has a bachelor's degree while only 15% of Native Hawaiians and Pacific Islanders have a bachelor's degree.
- Only 29% of Pacific Islanders between the age of 18 and 24 are enrolled in college as compared to 39% of non-Hispanic whites and 57% of Asians.
- About 18% of Native Hawaiian and Pacific Islanders live below the poverty rate as compared to 12% for the total U.S. population.

Journal Entry #2

You have just read about the low college completion rates for Native Hawaiian and Pacific Island students. You have made the courageous decision to attend college. What steps can you take to be one of the students who successfully completes his or her education?

> 'A`ohe pu`uki`eki`e ke ho`a`oia e pi'i. No cliff is so tall it cannot be climbed.

Hawaiian Values

The values of the Hawaiian people are timeless and passed on throughout generations. Hawaiians lived less by what they said and more by what they did. Aloha is the root of all other values that lead to success in life and can be applied to education and careers. Aloha means love, but goes beyond that. To have Aloha is to know how to treat others with love and to show respect. It begins with loving ourselves and spreading this love to others. The Hawaiians were and continue to be humble people with Aloha; Aloha for their 'aina (land), 'ohana (family), kanaka (the people), and mo'omeheu (culture). This Aloha is what transcends and connects them to the past, pushing them forward into the future. Some Hawaiian values are:[5]

> Be the aloha you wish to see in the world.

Ma kahanaka ʻike: By working, you learn.

Pono: This value represents goodness, uprightness, moral qualities, excellence, virtue, fairness, and being correct.

When we are "pono," we are right all the way around. We are right in the things we say, in the actions we take, and in our thoughts and emotions. Being "pono" is more than just an act, it is a way of living.

ʻImiNaʻauao: This is the value of seeking wisdom.

Knowledge is something that can be found when looking, researching, and reading. Wisdom is something that goes deeper. Wisdom is knowing all of the facts, but being able to take it to the next level, looking into the character of people or the heart of situations, past the facts. The Hawaiian people are wise and understanding, often seeing things past the surface of what is presented.

Aloha Kekahi I Kekahi: This is the value of love, from one to another. Hawaiians are people filled with love, but not in just giving love, but also in receiving love. When we show love, we receive love in return and are open to being loved by others. Love often goes past the emotion and into respect. If we have aloha for something, we respect everything about it, even if we don't agree with the lifestyle or choices and in return we are able to receive aloha from respect.

Kulia I Ka Nuʻu: This is the value of striving for excellence.

Kuleana: This is the value of responsibility. Kuleana or responsibility in the sense that you don't leave things for others to do; you take responsibility for them yourself. For example, if I see something on the ground that I didn't put there, do I leave it there and not pick it up? Even though I did not place it there, it is still my kuleana to pick it up so the next person behind me does not have to stop and do it. Kuleana is responsibility and as Hawaiians, it is our kuleana to care for the land, to care for our people, to care for our culture, and to care for our language, making sure that the values of our kupuna, our ancestors, live on from generation to generation.

Lōkahi: This is the value of unity which is the state of being one.

Lōkahi is the concept that we are one with our creator, the creation and with one another; each goes hand in hand. If the land is hurting or desolate, there are no resources for the people, yet if the people do not tend to the land and care for it, it will die. Each goes hand in hand. Lokahi, we are all one.

Mālama: This term means to care for or to take care of, to tend, preserve, save, and honor.

ʻAʻohe pau ka ʻike I ka hālau hoʻokahi: "Not all knowledge is taught in just one school."

This is an ʻolelo noʻeau, or wise saying, meaning there are many sources of knowledge, that are each different, yet valuable and we are not able to learn everything from one source. Each source can contribute to our learning and our experiences in both negative and positive ways, but without each of them individually, there would be no growth. For example, when we first enter school at five years of age, would we be able to stay in one class with the same teacher until we are 18 and ready to graduate? Would that teacher then go on to give us the skills we need for a college education? No. Each teacher comes with his or her own experiences that shaped their lives and the knowledge they gathered from their studies. Their perspectives give us one understanding of things, but they each teach us the skills to go out and explore those perspectives for ourselves, gathering our own information, and learning what makes us successful. We were created to learn differently, see differently, and experience things differently.

Ahupuaʻa: This term refers to land division, usually extending from the uplands to the sea containing all the resources needed for that particular community. Literally, ahu means "altar" and "puaʻa" means pig. Ahupuaʻa is the altar upon which the pig was laid as payment to the chief for the use of their land. The ahu is a stone foundation made into a big wall marking the separation from one ahupuaʻa to the next. Throughout every ahupuaʻa, there were diverse roles and contributions and collaborations which led to the sustainability of the people. Throughout the ahupuaʻa, everyone knew what it meant to work together, each decision to do or not do affected everyone.

> **Journal Entry #3**
>
> Values are simply what is important in your life. We often learn these values from our parents, culture, and community. What are some values you have learned in your family? How can island values be used to create your success in college, your career, and your life? How can these values make the world a better place?

History of Education in Hawai'i

Taking pride in your culture is important because it serves as a foundation for learning. You are more likely to be successful if you approach learning with an understanding of yourself which includes a sense of belonging to your family and an understanding and appreciation of your culture and history. Since colonial times, the story of the Native Hawaiian and Pacific Island experience has been a sad one in which the colonizers attempted to destroy Native culture, language, and religious practices and assimilate these groups into the dominant culture. Fortunately, there is a cultural renaissance beginning to take hold in Hawai'i and the Pacific Islands.

> 'Ohana means family. Family means nobody gets left behind or forgotten.

Early Hawaiian education consisted of stories, legends, chants, songs, poems, and dance. There was no written language or books and children learned by observing their family members and then trying out their new skills. The extended family included grandparents, aunts, uncles, and people of the village. Family members looked after one another, respected their elders, and shared resources with the village.

History changed dramatically when Captain Cook arrived on the Hawaiian Islands in 1778 and claimed the land for England. The Native population was estimated to be 400,000–800,000. Native Hawaiians were quickly decimated by diseases brought by the sailors accompanying Captain Cook including tuberculosis, venereal diseases, measles, and influenza. The Native people had no immunity to these diseases and population decreased by 80% or more. Cook's legacy is varied from different cultural perspectives, from great explorer to the destroyer of Indigenous people and cultures.

American missionaries came to Hawai'i in 1820. This was a time of great change in Hawai'i in which Ka'ahumanu had recently abolished the kapu system of rules that dictated religious, social, and political laws affecting all aspects of Hawaiian life. The kapu were rules that were made by the gods and interpreted by the ali'i who were hereditary rulers thought to possess mana or spiritual powers from the gods. Some examples of the kapu were:

- Men and women had to eat separately.
- Women could not eat certain foods including pork, bananas, coconuts, and certain types of fish.
- A commoner would be sentenced to death if his shadow fell on an ali'i house.

Those who broke the kapu were killed unless they could reach a place of refuge before they were caught.

The missionaries were able to capitalize on this major societal change to bring in Christianity. They considered the Hula dance as immoral and against their religion. They were influential in changing Hawaiian law to match Christian doctrine and converted the Hawaiian language into a written language to share the Bible with the Indigenous population. They introduced printing presses to produce Bibles and newspapers. Missionary schools taught Hawaiians to "abandon their culture for 'civilized' Western ways."[6] Children went to school to learn about God and to read and write. It is interesting to note that Hawaiians became among the most literate nations in the world during this period in history.

After the overthrow of King Kamehameha III, using the Hawaiian language in schools was banned in 1896 and students were punished for using their Native language. As a result, there was growing concern that the Hawaiian language would be lost. Hawaiians resisted the change to their culture. In 1901, the "Home Rule Party, passed rules promoting the growing of taro, the use of the Hawaiian language, and the honoring of their then-deposed queen, Lili'uokalani."[7] Mary Abigail Pukui (1895–1985) taught the Hawaiian language, contributed to the Hawaiian–English Dictionary and began translating and preserving chants, stories, words, and sayings to preserve them for the future.

It was not until the 1960s that there was a revival of interest in the Hawaiian language and culture. Communities began demanding the teaching of music, Hula, culture, and language. In 1978 The Hawai'i State Constitution was amended to include "the study of Hawaiian, culture, history and language . . . using the community expertise as a suitable and essential means in furtherance of Hawaiian education."[8]. It also recognized Hawaiian as the official language of the state. Hawaiian studies programs and language immersion programs have followed.

The Revival of Pride in Hawaiian and Pacific Island Culture: The Hokule'a

The Hokule'a, the double-hulled Hawaiian Canoe that has been traveling the world, has become a symbol of hope for the revival of Pacific Island and Hawaiian culture. It has resulted in increased interest in preserving the Hawaiian language and maintaining Hawaiian identity and culture. This revival is represented graphically on the cover of this textbook.

Although the origins of the Hawaiian people are still being studied, the most recent archeological research shows that the Hawaiian Islands were settled about 1,000 years ago. While it is commonly assumed that the residents came from Samoa, recent research on linguistics indicates that the settlers came from East Polynesia, a distance of about 2,500 miles from the Hawaiian Islands. A later wave of immigration came from Tahiti.[9] These voyages are considered among the greatest accomplishments of humanity. Herb Kane, a historian and artist has stated that almost every island in the Pacific was discovered before European settlers came and that "their voyaging canoes were the spaceships of the Stone Age."[10]

These early explorers were able to navigate great distances by using wayfinding, a method of navigation using the stars and being aware of nature and the ocean environment. Wayfinding is a complex skill using a memorized star compass with houses of stars and knowing where they rise and set. The star compass is also used to understand the direction of waves and the flight of birds. Using the star compass involves memorizing your point of departure, direction, and time, without the use of mechanical devices. It requires careful observation of natural phenomena such as the rise and setting of the sun. There are different names for the colors and widths of the sun's passage over the water from sunrise to sunset. On cloudy days, navigators rely on different wave patterns that show the direction of the canoe. These wave patterns and the behavior of dolphins and sea birds change when approaching an island.[11]

Copyright Herbert K. Kane, LLC.

The Hawaiian ancestors told stories about voyaging canoes that set off across the vast ocean and brave explorers who were compared to modern day astronauts. However, the canoes used in the original voyages had not been seen for 600 years, and the legacy of exploration was about to disappear. In 1976, the first Hokule'a voyage took place. The Polynesian Voyaging Society calls the Hokule'a "a story of survival, rediscovery, and the restoration of pride and dignity. It is a story of a society revaluing its relationship to its island home. It is a story that is crucially important as the world's populations struggle with the ability to live in balance with our island that we call earth. It is a story that is still being written for our children and all future generations."[12]

> Hokule'a means "Star of Joy" after a star, Arcturus, that hangs over the islands.

© 2014 Polynesian Voyaging Society and ʻŌwi TV. Photo courtesy of *Nāʻālehu Anthony*.

The first voyage of the Hokule'a was challenging because there were no Native navigators left from Polynesia or Hawai'i. The Voyaging Society found a navigator, Mau Piailug, from a small island in Satawal, Micronesia. This navigator guided the original voyage from Hawai'i to Tahiti to prove the theory that the ancient Hawaiians had successfully traveled great distances to settle on the Hawaiian Islands. Finding Tahiti from Hawai'i is a difficult task without modern navigation. When the Hokule'a arrived in Pape'ete Harbor, Tahiti, it was met by 17,000 people, which demonstrated much interest in the cultural revival. In 1978, the voyage was attempted again, but the canoe capsized in stormy waters off Moloka'i. Fortunately, the crew was rescued by Eddie Aikau who left on a surfboard and was able to summon help and rescue the adventurers. In 1979, Mau Piailug shared his navigation skills with Nainoa Thompson and they were successful in navigating from Tahiti to Hawai'i, which was the first voyage of its kind in 600 years.

Nainoa Thompson has become a spokesperson for the revival of Hawaiian and Pacific Island culture.

> Nainoa recalls his conflicted youth, when his grandmother spoke with pride of her own grandfather, an independent fisherman, and then averted her eyes as she discussed the more recent Hawaiian period, when people were beaten with sticks for simply being Hawaiian. "Hawaiian had a negative connotation," adds Nainao. "People tried to wash the brown off their skin." Young Nainoa came under the influence of an artist, Herb Kane, who was obsessed with images of the great open-hulled canoes that the ancients must have used to cross the oceans. Kane instilled in Thompson and others the dream of building such a canoe, re-creating the voyages, and raising the pride of the people over the feats involved in these monumental voyages and the many skills required to make them. The ocean is a severe and unforgiving adversary for anyone who ventures out unprepared. "We dreamed that the voyages would bring dignity to people," says Nainoa. "We could take our anger about our self-image and put it to a positive use. Our language and culture were asleep, but perhaps the re-created voyages would wake us all up."[13]

> You will know the expert navigators when it comes to a rough time in the ocean.—Tongan Proverb

The Hokule'a completed a two-year voyage to Aotearoa from 1985 to 1987, and in 1999, a voyage to Rapa Nui, one of the most isolated islands on earth located at the far southeastern corner of the Polynesian Triangle.[14] Since 1976, there have been 25 voyages around the world as people are drawn to experience the ancient ways and challenges of navigation. The Hokule'a has visited the South Pacific, Indonesia, the Indian Ocean, the Cape of Good Hope in South Africa, Brazil, Chesapeake Bay, and the Panama Canal. A new generation is planning future voyages.

At each stop the canoe is greeted by Indigenous people and organizations concerned about climate change and keeping the ocean clean. Voyages continue to "spread the message about what the world could learn from island people about how to live sustainably and care for the ocean."[15] The message delivered by the Hokule'a is called Malama Honua, which means taking care of Island Earth. This message is particularly important to the inhabitants of the Pacific region concerned about rising sea levels, extreme weather, flooding, coastal erosion, coral reef bleaching, ocean acidification, loss of sensitive habitat, and the contamination of fresh water by sea water.[16]

The Hokule'a has connected the Indigenous populations of the world. The search for traditional Koa wood to build the Hawai'iloa, the second voyaging canoe, was unsuccessful because of deforestation of the islands. The SeAlaska Corporation owned by the

Tlingit, Haida, and Tshimshian tribes of Southeast Alaska volunteered to donate Large Sitka spruce logs.

> Byron Maillot, the CEO of SeAlaska, explained the connection between the native peoples of Hawai'i and Alaska: "Both the reality and the symbolism of the [Hawai'iloa] project breathe hope and inspiration into all peoples seeking to maintain their traditions, heritage and culture in a society that does not place a high priority on such things except when they may touch a nerve or help nurture shared values through an expression of such vision, initiative and sheer innate beauty that all can feel ennobled by it. . . . You do it for the Hawaiian people, but it reaches far beyond. In your canoe you carry all of us who share your vision and aspiration for a people to live and prosper with their future firmly built on the knowledge of their heritage and tradition."[17]

The Hokule'a project is helping students around the world to take pride in their culture and view the world in a different way, inspiring students to organize beach clean-ups, school beautification, and discourage pollution and littering. The crew share the information about life on the ocean with students around the world.

The Hokule'a has received worldwide attention from the United Nations when past Secretary Ban Ki-moon boarded the canoe in Samoa and delivered a gift in a bottle, a message pledging worldwide support for ocean protection.[18]

Malama Honua: taking care of the Island Earth.

Journal Entry #4

How has the Hokule'a contributed to a revival of Hawaiian and Pacific Island culture?

Navigating Different Cultures and Finding a Safe Place

The world is constantly changing and we have to constantly adapt to new situations. It is difficult to balance "fitting in" and maintaining our own cultural identities. Researchers describe a process called **transculturation**, in which a person adapts to a different culture without sacrificing individual cultural identity.

Successful Native and Indigenous students are those who are able to navigate the terrain of two distinct worlds as they bridge the gap between their own culture and that of the college/university setting. We also know that those students with confidence in self and strong feelings of culture have an anchor from which they can draw strength.

According to Dr. Mario E. Aguilar, in a research study he conducted called *The Ritual of Kindness*, he suggests that a healthy aspect of this transculturation is to learn to create your own unique Third Space, a safe space. He explains that the First Space is where you live or where you have come from, and the Second Space is where you must learn to negotiate [college].[19] Learning to adapt as needed within the two realms can be challenging, but with practice and introspection, you can develop a healthy place that he calls the Third Space.

Give some thought to how you will create your own safe place between your own culture and that of the university environment. Once you learn to trust in your culture and gain strength from knowing who you are in this world and why you are in college, you will be invigorated and increase your chances of success.

Photo courtesy of Lilieni Tuitupou, Salt Lake Community College

> **Journal Entry #5**
>
> What do you think you need to do to be able to navigate two world views: your own culture and that of the institutional culture? Think about how you can create your Third Space, your safe space. What will you draw upon from your culture, your spirituality, and the universe during those times when you must travel the first and second spaces of your world?

Tips for Success

Celebrate your culture. Taking pride in yourself, your family, and your culture is the basic building block of self-confidence that can empower you to be successful. Traditional island values can help you to be successful in college, your career, and your life.

Your ohana (family) is a source of strength, support, identity, and confidence. Maintain a support network at home with family and community. It is like going back for nurturance, especially during those challenging times when cultural conflicts arise. Your task will be to find ways to include your family in your college experience, explaining to them the experiences and challenges you face as you move through college.

Learn about other cultures. Every culture has a different perspective that can be of value in solving the problems of the world.

In college, you will have the opportunity to learn from your professors and other students who are different from yourself. You may have professors with very different personality styles and teaching styles. Your success will depend on being aware of the differences and finding a way to adapt to the situation. Also, each student in your classes will come from a different perspective and has valuable ideas to add to the class.

It is through networking with other people that most people find a job. You are likely to find a job through someone you know, such as a college professor, a student in one of your classes, a community member or a referral from a previous employer. Once you have the job, you will gain proficiency by learning from others. The best managers are also open to learning from others and help different people to work together as a team.

Be an advocate for the value of Malama, protecting and caring for the earth, to improve the lives and futures of all the earth's inhabitants.

Appreciating Island Cultures:
The Story of the Kahuli Shells

Located at the end of each chapter are traditional stories of Hawai'i and the Pacific Islands. These stories are presented as a way to learn about island culture and values and to connect them to success in college, careers, and life. Here is the story of the kahuli shells.

Long ago when the forests of Hawai'i were uninhabited by other animals, there lived these tiny, beautiful shells called kahuli, or pupukani 'oe (shell with the long sound). They were said to sing as their shells moved from side to side while the wind blew through them.

These beautiful shells lived either high up in the hau tree or on the leaves of the ki, or ti, leaf plants. They were beautiful and their shells were made up of different, delicate colors: yellow, green, and pink. They were said to have inhabited the forests of Hawai'i by the millions. The kahuli would often be found coming down from the tree tops to search along the streams of the mountain for the nectar of the 'akolea fern, which had beautiful bright red blossoms. The blossoms were filled with nectar that they loved to eat and fill their 'opu, or stomach. Once they were pau, or finished eating, they would climb back up into their trees and fall asleep.

One day, there were foreign animals brought over on the different ships from other lands. These cows, horses and many other large animals came and invaded the forests. This scared the kahuli shells and kept their 'opu empty because they were too afraid to go down to get the nectar from the 'akolea blossoms thinking that if they left the trees to walk along the forest floor, the animals would trample and kill them. After a time, they could not take being hungry any longer. They decided to have a council meeting with their elders high up in the tree tops. They were asking one another "What should we do? How will we get the 'akolea nectar to eat again?"

© NadinaS/Shutterstock.com

As they were talking, their friends, the kolea birds, were sitting in the branches of the tree. They heard everything and knew they wanted to help the kahuli. They looked at the sad little shells and said "Little shells, little shells! We are your friends; we want to help you. We know how! We can fly down to the streams and gather the nectar from the 'akolea blossoms and carry it back to you in our beak and feed you. How does that sound?" The kahuli were so excited that they cheered! "Yes, friends! Mahalo NUI (Thank you SO MUCH!) Now we don't have to be hungry!!"

The pacific Golden Plover or Kolea bird of Hawai'i.
© Doug Oglesby/Shutterstock.com

The very wise snail thought and said "Since they are doing this for us, we should also think of something to do for them." So they sat and thought for a while. Suddenly, a tiny little voice came from under a leaf. It was the tiniest of all the kahuli snails! "I know what we can do! We can promise to sing to them every night when the moon is full!" The wise snail smiled and looked at the kolea bird asking, "How does that sound?" The kolea loved that idea because they loved to hear the sweet notes of the kahuli shells as the wind blew and their singing filled the forest. "We agree!" they shouted. "We will fly down to gather the nectar in our beaks and fly it back up to you in the trees so you do not have to go hungry. In return, you will sing to us every night when the moon is full!"

Since that day, the kahuli snails and the kolea birds have kept their promise. Every night when the moon is full, the forests of Hawai'i are filled with the kahuli shells singing to their friends, the kolea birds.

Here is their song:

KaHuliAku, Kahuli Mai	Turn little shell, turn this way
Kahuli lei 'ula _____	The tree shell is a red ornament
Lei 'akolea	In the lei of the 'akolea fern
Kolea, Kolea	Little Kolea, Little Kolea
Ki'i I kawai	Go down to the stream
Wai 'akolea, wai 'akolea	Sip the sweet nectar from the 'akolea fern
Lulu lulululuLulululululu	

Cultural Identity and Success

'Akolea: Type of fern
Hau: Type of tree
Huli: Turn
Ka: The
Kani: Sound
Ki: Ti Leaf
Kolea: Golden plover
Mahalo Nui: Thank you very much
'Opu: Stomach
Pupukani 'oe: Shell with the long sound
'Akolea: Type of fern

Questions

1. What struggle did the kahuli shells have?
2. Did their struggle stem from something that was already there or was it something that was introduced to them?
3. How was the problem solved? What made the kahuli shells successful?
4. Does it make a difference when there are others trying to help you succeed?
5. Did the kahuli shells just take what their friends, the kolea birds offered them, or did they prepare to give something in return? Why is that an important thing to do?

Notes

1. Sonia Nieto, *Affirming Diversity: The Sociopolitical Context of Multicultural Education*, (New York: Longman, 1996), p. 283.

2. Pacific Islander Diversity Cultural Information, BYU David O. McKay School of Education accessed from http://education.byu.edu/diversity/culture/pacificislander.html

3. Department of Business, Economic Development & Tourism Census, Hawai'i Population Characteristics 2015 accessed from http://files.hawaii.gov/dbedt/census/popestimate/2015_county_char_hi_file/Pop_char_hi_2015_final.pdf, January, 2017.

4. White House Initiative on Asian Americans & Pacific Islanders (WHIAAPI) Fact Sheet: What You Should Know about Native Hawaiians and Pacific Islanders (NHPI's) accessed from https://www2.ed.gov/about/inits/list/asian-americans-initiative/what-you-should-know.pdf

5. Mary KawenaPukui, *Hawaiian Proverbs & Poetical Sayings*, Bernice P. Bishop Museum Special Publication No. 71, Bishop Museum Press, Honolulu, Hawai'i, 1983.

6. " Hawai'i Alive" from the Bishop Museum, Honolulu, Hawai'i. Accessed from http://www.hawaiialive.org/topics.php?sub=Unification+and+Monarchy&Subtopic=45, January 2017.

7. Ibid.

8. "History of Hawaiian Education." Accessed from http://www.hawaiipublicschools.org/TeachingAndLearning/StudentLearning/HawaiianEducation/Pages/History-of-the-Hawaiian-Education-program.aspx, January 2017.

9. Stewart, Colin. "Scholar Tracks Origins of Hawaii's Ancestors," accessed from http://hawaiitribune-herald.com/sections/news/local-news/scholar-tracks-origins-hawaii%E2%80%99s-ancestors.html, January, 2017.

10. Borreca, Richard. "South Polynesian Seafarers Settled Hawaiian Isles in Two Migrant Tides." Accessed from http://archives.starbulletin.com/1999/05/05/millennium/index.html, January, 2017.

11. Thompson, Nainoa. "On Wayfinding" accessed from http://pvs.kcc.hawaii.edu/ike/hookele/on_wayfinding.html, January 2017.

12. "The Story of Hokule'a" by the Polynesian Voyaging Society, accessed from http://www.hokulea.com/voyages/our-story/, January 2017.

13. " Hawaii's Hokulea Canoe Tells Story of Polynesian Voyage" accessed from http://www.fostertravel.com/hawaiis-hokulea-canoe-tells-story-of-polynesian-voyage/, January 2017.

14. "The Story of Hokule'a" by the Polynesian Voyaging Society, accessed from http://www.hokulea.com/voyages/our-story/, January 2017.

15. Goo, Sara Kehaulani. "Hokule'a, The Hawaiian Canoe Traveling the World By a Map of the Stars" accessed from http://www.npr.org/sections/codeswitch/2016/05/27/479468130/hokulea-the-hawaiian-canoe-traveling-the-world-by-a-map-of-the-stars, January, 2017.

16. "Climate Change in the Pacific Region, U.S. Fish & Wildlife, accessed from https://www.fws.gov/Pacific/Climatechange/changepi.html, January 2017.

17. Hawaiian Voyaging Traditions, The Building of the Hawai'iloa, http://pvs.kcc.hawaii.edu/ike/kalai_waa/hawaiiloa.html, January 2015.

18. Hokule'a Voyage Makes Impact on Hawai'i Students, January 2015, accessed from http://www.staradvertiser.com/2015/01/16/hawaii-news/hokulea-voyage-makes-impact-on-hawaii-students/, January, 2017.

19. Mario E. Aguilar, "The Rituals of Kindness," Claremont Graduate University and San Diego State University, 2009, 166–183.

CHAPTER 2

Understanding Motivation

Learning Objectives

Read to answer these key questions:

- What do I want from college?

- What is the value of a college education?

- How do I choose my major and career?

- How can I motivate myself to be successful?

- How can I begin habits that lead to success?

- How can I be persistent in achieving my goal of a college education?

Most students attend college with dreams of making their lives better. Some students are there to explore interests and possibilities, and others have more defined career goals. Being successful in college and attaining your dreams begin with motivation. It provides the energy or drive to find your direction and to reach your goals. Without motivation, it is difficult to accomplish anything.

Not everyone is successful in college. Unfortunately, about one-third of college students drop out in the first year. Forty percent of students who start college do not finish their degrees. Having a good understanding of your personal strengths, reasons for attending college, career goals, and how to motivate yourself will help you to reach your dreams.

What Do I Want from College?

Succeeding in college requires time and effort. You will have to give up some of your time spent on leisure activities and working. You will give up some time spent with your friends and families. Making sacrifices and working hard are easier if you know what you want to achieve through your efforts. One of the first steps in motivating yourself to be successful in college is to have a clear and specific understanding of your reasons for attending college. Are you attending college as a way to obtain a satisfying career? Is financial security one of your goals? Will you feel more satisfied if you are living up to your potential? What are your hopes and dreams, and how will college help you to achieve your goals?

When you are having difficulties or doubts about your ability to finish your college education, remember your hopes and dreams and your plans for the future. It is a good idea to write these ideas down, think about them, and revise them from time to time.

What Is the Value of a College Education?

Many college students say that getting a satisfying job that pays well and achieving financial security are important motivators for attending college. As a result of the rising cost of higher education, students have started to question whether a college education is still a good investment. Recent analyses by the Federal Reserve Bank have shown that the benefits still outweigh the cost for both an associate's and a bachelor's degree. These degrees have a 15% return, which is considered a good investment.[1] By getting a degree, you can get a job that pays more per hour, work fewer hours to earn a living, and have more time for leisure activities. In addition, you can spend your time at work doing something that you enjoy. A report issued by the Census Bureau in 2014 listed the following education and income statistics for all races and both genders throughout the United States.[2] Lifetime income assumes that a person works 30 years before retirement.

Average Earnings Based on Education Level

Education	Yearly Income	Lifetime Income
High-school graduate	34,736	1,042,080
Some college, no degree	38,532	1,155,960
Associate's degree	41,184	1,235,520
Bachelor's degree	57,252	1,717,560
Master's degree	68,952	2,068,560
Professional degree	85,228	2,556,840

Notice that income rises with educational level. Over a lifetime, a person with a bachelor's degree earns about 61% more than a high-school graduate. Of course, these are average figures across the nation and some individuals earn higher or lower salaries. People fantasize about winning the lottery, but the reality is that the probability of winning the lottery is very low. In the long run, you have a better chance of increasing your income by going to college.

Let's do some further comparisons. A high-school graduate earns an average of $1,042,080 over a lifetime. A college graduate with a bachelor's degree earns $1,717,560 over a lifetime. A college graduate earns $675,480 more than a high-school graduate does over a lifetime. So how much is a college degree worth? It is worth $675,480 over a lifetime. Would you go to college and finish your degree if someone offered to pay you $675,480? Here are some more interesting figures we can derive from the above table:

Completing one college course is worth $16,887.
($675,480 divided by 40 courses in a bachelor's degree)

Going to class for one hour is worth $352.
($16,887 divided by 48 hours in a semester class)

Would you take a college course if someone offered you $16,887? Would you go to class today for one hour if someone offered you $352? Of course, if this sounds too good to be true, remember that you will receive these "payments" over a working lifetime of 30 years.

While college graduation does not guarantee employment, it increases your chances of finding a job. In 2014, high-school graduates had an unemployment rate of 6% as compared to college graduates who had an unemployment rate of 3.5%.[3] Increase your chances of employment by continuing your education.

Employment and earning are only some of the values of going to college. College helps develop your potential and increase your confidence, self-esteem, and self-respect. It increases your understanding of the world and prepares you to be an informed citizen.

Journal Entry #1

What are your dreams for the future? Write a paragraph about what you hope to accomplish by going to college.

Choosing a Major and Career

© iQoncept/Shutterstock.com

Having a definite major and career choice is a good motivation for completing your college education. It is difficult to put in the work necessary to be successful if you do not have a clear picture of your future career; however, three out of four college students are undecided about their major. For students who have chosen a major, 30 to 75 percent of a graduating class will change that major two or more times.[4] Unclear or indefinite career goals are some of the most significant factors that identify students at risk of dropping out of college.[5] Choosing an appropriate college major is one of the most difficult and important decisions that college students can make.

How can you choose the major that is best for you? The best way is to first understand yourself: become aware of your personality traits, interests, preferred lifestyle, values, gifts, and talents. The next step is to do career research to determine the career that best matches your personal characteristics. Then, plan your education to prepare for your career. Here are some questions to help you understand yourself and what career and major would be best for you.

To learn about yourself, explore these areas:

- **What is my personality type?** Assessing your personality type will help you to become more aware of your individual gifts and talents and some careers that will give you satisfaction.
- **What are my aptitudes?** Focus on your strengths by identifying your multiple intelligences.
- **What are my interests?** Knowing about your interests is important in choosing a satisfying career.
- **What kind of lifestyle do I prefer?** Think about how you want to balance work, leisure, and family.
- **What are my values?** Knowing what you value (what is most important to you) will help you make good decisions about your life.

To learn about career possibilities, research the following:

- **What careers match my personality, aptitudes, interests, lifestyle, and values?** Learn how to do career research to find the best career for you. Find a career that has a good outlook for the future.
- **How can I plan my education to get the career I want?** Once you have identified a career that matches your personal strengths and interests, consult your college catalog or advisor to make an educational plan that matches your career goals.

By following the above steps, you can find the major that is best for you and minimize the time you spend in college.

> **Journal Entry #2**
>
> Write a paragraph about deciding on your ideal major and career. Use any of these questions to guide your thinking: If you have chosen a major, why is it the best major for you? How does it match your interests, aptitudes, and values (what is most important to you)? Does this major help you to live your preferred lifestyle? If you have not chosen a major, what are some steps in choosing the right major and career? What qualities would you look for in an ideal career? Can you describe some of your interests, aptitudes, and values? What is your preferred lifestyle?

How to Be Motivated

There are many ways to be motivated to be successful in college and in your future career. Set the stage with a positive mindset, think positively about the future, find something interesting in your studies, and learn new ways to improve your attention and concentration. Apply some concepts from psychology including intrinsic motivation, locus of control, affiliation, achievement, and simply using a reward. We will examine each of these concepts in more detail. As you read through them, think about how you can apply them to your personal life.

> "The purpose of our lives is to give birth to the best which is within us."
> Marianne Williamson

Your Mindset Makes a Difference

Did you know that your mindset has a powerful effect on learning and college success? Mindset is related to your self-image as a learner. It affects the effort you put into your studies and how you deal with challenges and setbacks. A positive mindset can even make you smarter as you learn new material and exercise your brain. Scientists have identified a **growth mindset** that leads to success.[6] It includes the belief that

- Intelligence is increased as you learn new knowledge.
- Through practice and effort, skills can be improved.
- Learning and self-improvement continue over a lifetime.
- Challenges are a way to be tested and improve performance.
- Failure is an opportunity to learn.
- Constructive criticism improves performance.
- The success of others is an inspiration.

© Aliwak/Shutterstock.com

In contrast, the **fixed mindset** is an obstacle to success. It includes these beliefs:

- Intelligence is fixed at birth.
- Increased effort does not lead to success.
- There is a limit to what we can accomplish.
- Roadblocks or obstacles are an excuse to be absent.
- It is best to take on only easy tasks in which success is guaranteed.
- Constructive criticism is a personal attack.
- The success of others makes me look bad.
- Hard work is unpleasant.
- The amount of work needed to be successful is underestimated.

The good news is that you can learn to identify and change your mindset so that you can be successful in college, in your career, and in your personal life. If you believe that effort can produce rewards, you are on your way to success.

Thinking Positively about the Future

You can motivate yourself to complete your education by thinking positively about the future. If you believe that your chances of graduating from college are good, you can be motivated to take the steps necessary to achieve your goals. Conversely, if you think that your chances of graduating are poor, it is difficult to motivate yourself to continue. The degree of optimism that you possess is greatly influenced by past experiences. For example, if you were a good student in the past, you are likely to be optimistic about the future. If you struggled with your education, you may have some negative experiences that you will need to overcome. Negative thoughts can often become a self-fulfilling prophecy: what we think becomes true.

How can you train yourself to think more optimistically? First, become aware of your thought patterns. Are they mostly negative or positive? If they are negative, make a conscious decision to change them to positive thoughts. Here is an example.

Pessimism

I failed the test. I guess I am just not college material. I feel really stupid. I just can't do this. College is too hard for me. My (teacher, father, mother, friend, boss) told me I would never make it. Maybe I should just drop out of college and do something else.

Optimism

I failed the test. Let's take a look at what went wrong, so I can do better next time. Did I study enough? Did I study the right material? Maybe I should take this a little slower. How can I get help so that I can understand? I plan to do better next time.

> "Life is very interesting. In the end, some of your greatest pains become your greatest strengths."
> Drew Barrymore

> "There is nothing good or bad, but thinking makes it so."
> Shakespeare's Hamlet

© kentoh/Shutterstock.com

Can a person be too optimistic? In some circumstances, this is true. There is a difference between optimism and wishful thinking, for example. Wishful thinking does not include plans for accomplishing goals and can be a distraction from achieving them. Working toward unattainable goals can be exhausting and demoralizing, especially when the resources for attaining them are lacking. Goals must be realistic and achievable. Psychologists recommend that "people should be optimistic when the future can be changed by positive thinking, but not otherwise."[7] Using optimism requires some judgment about possible outcomes in the future.

There are some good reasons to think more positively. Psychologists have done long-term studies showing that people who use positive thinking have many benefits over a lifetime, including good health, longevity, happiness, perseverance, improved problem solving, and enhanced ability to learn. Optimism is also related to goal achievement. If you are optimistic and believe a goal is achievable, you are more likely to take the steps necessary to accomplish the goal. If you do not believe that a goal is achievable, you are likely to give up trying to achieve it. Being optimistic is closely related to being hopeful about the future. If you are hopeful about the future, you are likely to be more determined to reach your goals and to make plans for reaching them. Be optimistic about graduating from college, find the resources necessary to accomplish your goal, and start taking the steps to create your success.

ACTIVITY

Are you generally an optimist or pessimist about the future? Read the following items and rate your level of agreement or disagreement:

Rate the following items using this scale:

5   I definitely agree
4   I agree
3   I neither agree or disagree (neutral)
2   I disagree
1   I strongly disagree

_____   My chances of graduating from college are good.

_____   I am confident that I can overcome any obstacles to my success.

_____   Things generally turn out well for me.

_____   I believe that positive results will eventually come from most problem situations.

_____   If I work hard enough, I will eventually achieve my goals.

_____   Although I have faced some problems in the past, the future will be better.

_____   I expect that most things will go as planned.

_____   Good things will happen to me in the future.

_____   I am generally persistent in reaching my goals.

_____   I am good at finding solutions to the problems I face in life.

Add up your total points and multiply by two. My total points (× 2) are _____.

90–100	You are an excellent positive thinker.
80–89	You are a good positive thinker.
70–79	Sometimes you think positively, and sometimes not. Can you re-evaluate your thinking?
60 and below	Work on positive thinking.

Understanding Motivation

> **Journal Entry #3**
>
> Write five positive statements about your college education and your future.

Find Something Interesting in Your Studies

If you can think positively about what you are studying, it makes the job easier and more satisfying. Begin your studies by finding something interesting in the course and your textbook. Contrast these two ideas:

I have to take economics. It is going to be difficult and boring. What do I need economics for anyway? I'll just need to get through it so I can get my degree.

I have to take economics. I wonder about the course content. I often hear about it on the news. How can I use this information in my future? What can I find that is interesting?

Make sure to attend the first class meeting. Remember that the professor is very knowledgeable about the subject and finds the content interesting and exciting. At the first class meeting, the professor will give you an overview of the course and should provide some motivation for studying the material in the course. Look at the course syllabus to find what the course is about and to begin to look for something that could be interesting or useful to you.

Skimming a textbook before you begin a course is a good way to find something interesting and to prepare for learning. Skimming will give you an organized preview of what's ahead. Here are the steps to skimming a new text:

1. **Quickly read the preface or introduction.** Read as if you were having a conversation with the author of the text. In the preface or introduction, you will find out how the author has organized the material, the key ideas, and his or her purpose in writing the text.

2. **Look at the major topics in the table of contents.** You can use the table of contents as a window into the book. It gives a quick outline of every topic in the text. As you read the table of contents, look for topics of special interest to you.

3. **Spend five to 15 minutes quickly looking over the book.** Turn the pages quickly, noticing boldfaced topics, pictures, and anything else that catches your attention. Again, look for important or interesting topics. Do not spend too much time on this step. If your textbook is online, skim through the website.

4. **What resources are included?** Is there an index, glossary of terms, answers to quiz questions, or solutions to math problems? These sections will be of use to you as you read. If your book is online, explore the website to find useful features and content.

Skimming a text or website before you begin to read has several important benefits. The first benefit is that it gets you started in the learning process. It is an easy and quick step that can help you avoid procrastination. It increases motivation by helping you notice items that have appeal to you. Previewing the content will help you to relax as you study and remember the information. Early in the course, this step will help you verify that you have chosen the correct course and that you have the prerequisites to be successful in the class.

Improving Your Concentration and Attention

You cannot learn without concentrating and paying attention, so how can you improve this skill? Have you ever watched lion tamers concentrate? If their attention wanders, they are likely to be eaten, so **they are motivated to pay attention**. Skilled athletes, musicians,

> "No pessimist ever discovered the secrets of the stars, or sailed to an uncharted land, or opened a new doorway for the human spirit."
> Helen Keller

> "A pessimist sees the difficulty in every opportunity; an optimist sees the opportunity in every difficulty."
> Winston Churchill

© Eugenio Maronqiu/Shutterstock.com

and artists don't have any trouble concentrating. Think about a time when you were totally focused on what you were doing. You were motivated to continue. You can set the stage for paying attention by focusing on your goals, getting some exercise, and being well-rested and alert. Here are some additional ways to improve concentration, attention, and motivation.

Avoid multi-tasking. Paying attention is not multi-tasking. Often students try to study with many distractions including cell phones and other electronic interruptions. It is a common myth that the brain is able to multi-task and pay attention to several inputs at once. However, the brain cannot multi-task; it pays attention to one input at a time. Research shows the following:[8]

- A person who is interrupted takes 50% longer to complete a task.
- The interruptions results in 50% more errors.

A good example of the problems with multi-tasking is driving while talking on the phone. The brain constantly switches between paying attention to the phone and driving. If you are talking on a cell phone, you are half a second slower in stepping on the brake. At 70 mph, the car travels 51 feet in half a second. In addition, drivers miss 50% of the visual clues noticed by drivers who are not trying to multi-task. Driving while using a cell phone is like driving drunk.[9] While studying, cell phones and other distractions reduce productivity and increase the chance for errors. Focusing on one task at a time saves time and improves the quality of work.

Manage your external environment. Find an environment that minimizes distractions. One idea is to study in the library where there are many cues that remind you to study. There are books and learning resources and other people studying. Concentration and motivation can be increased by varying the places where you study. You may be able to set up a learning environment in your home where you can place a desk or table, your computer, and your materials for learning. Vary your routine by finding a quiet place outside to study or any place where you can focus your attention. Avoid studying in the kitchen, in your bed, or in front of the TV where you will be distracted by food, sleep, or an interesting program on TV.

Manage your internal distractions.

1. **Vary the content and subjects that you are studying.** Athletes maintain concentration and motivation by including strength, speed, and skill practice in each

> **Managing Internal Distractions**
>
> 1. Be here now
> 2. Spider technique
> 3. Worry time
> 4. Checkmark technique
> 5. Increase activity
> 6. Find an incentive
> 7. Change topics

workout. Musicians practice scales, different musical pieces, and rhythm exercises in one practice session. In your studies, you can do the same. For example, when studying a foreign language, spend some time on reading, some time on learning vocabulary, and some practice in speaking the language. Then do some problems for your math class.

2. **Be here now.** Choose where you will place your attention. Your body can be attending a lecture or be at the desk reading, but your mind can be in many different and exciting places. You can tell yourself, "Be here now." You cannot force yourself to pay attention, but when your mind wanders, notice that you have drifted off and gently return your attention to your lecture or reading. This will take some practice, since attention tends to wander often.

3. **The spider technique.** If you hold a tuning form to a spider web, the web vibrates and the spider senses that it has caught some tasty food and goes looking for it. After a while the spider discovers that there is no food and learns to ignore the vibrations caused by the tuning fork. When you are sitting in the library studying and someone walks in talking and laughing, you can choose to pay attention either to the distraction or to the studying. Decide to continue to pay attention to the studying.

4. **Set up a worry time.** Many times, worries interfere with concentration. Some people have been successful in setting up a worry time. Here's how it works:

    a. Set a specific time each day for worrying.

    b. When worries distract you from your studies, remind yourself that you have set aside time for worrying.

    c. Tell yourself, "Be here now."

    d. Keep your worry appointment.

    e. During your worry time, try to find some solutions or take some steps to resolve the things that cause you to worry.

5. **Take steps to solve personal problems.** If you are bothered by personal problems, take steps to solve them. See your college counselor for assistance. Another strategy is to make a plan to deal with the problem later so you can study now.

6. **Use the checkmark technique.** Use the checkmark technique. When you find yourself distracted from a lecture or from studying, place a checkmark on a piece of paper and refocus your attention on the task at hand. You will find that your checkmarks decrease over time.

Intrinsic or Extrinsic Motivation

Intrinsic motivation comes from within. It means that you do an activity because you enjoy it or find personal meaning in it. With intrinsic motivation, the nature of the activity itself or the consequences of the activity motivate you. For example, let's say that I am interested in learning to play the piano. I am motivated to practice playing the piano because I like the sound of the piano and feel very satisfied when I can play music that I enjoy. I practice because I like to practice, not because I have to practice. When I get tired or frustrated, I work through it or put it aside and come back to it because I want to learn to play the piano well.

You can be intrinsically motivated to continue in college because you enjoy learning and find the college experience satisfying. Look for ways to enjoy college and to find some personal satisfaction in it. If you enjoy college, it becomes easier to do the work required to be successful. Think about what you say to yourself about college. If you are saying negative things such as "I don't want to be here," it will be difficult to continue.

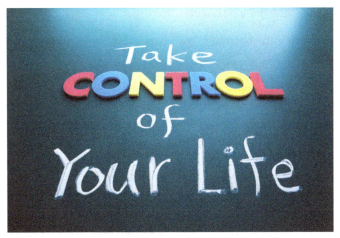
© Arson0618/Shutterstock.com

Extrinsic motivation comes as a result of an external reward from someone else. Examples of extrinsic rewards are certificates, bonuses, money, praise, and recognition. Taking the piano example again, let's say that I want my child to play the piano. The child does not know if he or she would like to play the piano. I give the child a reward for practicing the piano. I could pay the child for practicing or give praise for doing a good job. There are two possible outcomes of the extrinsic reward. After a while, the child may gain skills and confidence and come to enjoy playing the piano. The extrinsic reward is no longer necessary because the child is now intrinsically motivated. Or the child may decide that he or she does not like to play the piano. The extrinsic reward is no longer effective in motivating the child to play the piano.

You can use extrinsic rewards to motivate yourself to be successful in college. Remind yourself of the payoff for getting a college degree: earning more money, having a satisfying career, being able to purchase a car and a house. Extrinsic rewards can be a first step in motivating yourself to attend college. With experience and achievement, you may come to like going to college and may become intrinsically motivated to continue your college education.

If you use intrinsic motivation to achieve your goal, you will be happier and more successful. If you do something like playing the piano because you enjoy it, you are more likely to spend the time necessary to practice to achieve your goal. If you view college as something that you enjoy and as valuable to you, it is easier to spend the time to do the required studying. When you get tired or frustrated, tell yourself that you are doing a good job (praise yourself) and think of the positive reasons that you want to get a college education.

Locus of Control

Being aware of the concept of locus of control is another way of understanding motivation. The word **locus** means place. The locus of control is where you place the responsibility for control over your life. In other words, who is in charge? If you place the responsibility on yourself and believe that you have control over your life, you have an internal locus of control. If you place the responsibility on others and think that luck or fate determines your future, you have an external locus of control. Some people use the internal and external locus of control in combination or favor one type in certain situations. If you favor an internal locus of control, you believe that to a great extent your actions determine your future. **Studies have shown that students who use an internal locus of control are likely to have higher achievement in college**.[10] The characteristics of students with internal and external locus of control are listed below.

> "Ability is what you're capable of doing. Motivation determines what you do. Attitude determines how well you do it."
> — Lou Holtz

Students with an internal locus of control:

- Believe that they are in control of their lives.
- Understand that grades are directly related to the amount of study invested.
- Are self-motivated.
- Learn from their mistakes by figuring out what went wrong and how to fix the problem.
- Think positively and try to make the best of each situation.
- Rely on themselves to find something interesting in the class and learn the material.

ACTIVITY

Internal or External Locus of Control

Decide whether the statement represents an internal or external locus of control and put a checkmark in the appropriate column.

Internal	External		
_____	_____	1.	Much of what happens to us is due to fate, chance, or luck.
_____	_____	2.	Grades depend on how much work you put into it.
_____	_____	3.	If I do badly on the test, it is usually because the teacher is unfair.
_____	_____	4.	If I do badly on the test, it is because I didn't study or didn't understand the material.
_____	_____	5.	I often get blamed for things that are not my fault.
_____	_____	6.	I try to make the best of the situation.
_____	_____	7.	It is impossible to get a good grade if you have a bad instructor.
_____	_____	8.	I can be successful through hard work.
_____	_____	9.	If the teacher is not there telling me what to do, I have a hard time doing my work.
_____	_____	10.	I can motivate myself to study.
_____	_____	11.	If the teacher is boring, I probably won't do well in class.
_____	_____	12.	I can find something interesting about each class.
_____	_____	13.	When bad things are going to happen, there is not much you can do about it.
_____	_____	14.	I create my own destiny.
_____	_____	15.	Teachers should motivate the students to study.
_____	_____	16.	I have a lot of choice about what happens in my life.

As you probably noticed, the even-numbered statements represent internal locus of control. The odd-numbered statements represent external locus of control. Remember that students with an internal locus of control have a greater chance of success in college. It is important to see yourself as responsible for your own success and achievement and to believe that with effort you can achieve your goals.

Students with an external locus of control:

- Believe that their lives are largely a result of luck, fate, or chance.
- Think that teachers give grades rather than students earning grades.
- Rely on external motivation from teachers or others.
- Look for someone to blame when they make a mistake.
- Think negatively and believe they are victims of circumstance.
- Rely on the teacher to make the class interesting and to teach the material.

Affiliation

Human beings are social creatures who generally feel the need to be part of a group. This tendency is called affiliation motivation. People like to be part of a community, family, organization, or culture. You can apply this motivation technique in college by participating in student activities on campus. Join an athletic team, participate in a club, or join the student government. In this way, you will feel like you are part of a group and will have a sense of belonging. College is more than going to class: it is participating in social activities, making new friends, and sharing new ideas. Twenty years after you graduate from college, you are more likely to remember the conversations held with college friends than the detailed content of classes. College provides the opportunity to become part of a new group and to start lifelong friendships.

> "I am a great believer in luck, and I find that the harder I work, the more I have of it."
> Thomas Jefferson

QUIZ

Motivation, Part I

1. To increase your chance of accomplishing your goals,
   a. think positively and work step by step to achieve your goals.
   b. use wishful thinking.
   c. set high goals that may not be possible to achieve.

2. You can increase your motivation for studying by
   a. taking the required courses.
   b. reminding yourself that you have to do it.
   c. finding something interesting in your studies.

3. Intrinsic motivation
   a. comes from within.
   b. is the result of an external reward.
   c. involves higher pay or recognition for a job well done.

4. To be successful in college, it is best to use
   a. an external locus of control.
   b. extrinsic motivation.
   c. intrinsic motivation.

5. A person who is multitasking:
   a. Uses time efficiently.
   b. Takes 50% longer to complete a task.
   c. Minimizes errors.

How did you do on the quiz? Check your answers: 1. a, 2. c, 3. a, 4. c, 5. b

Achievement

Some students are motivated by achievement. Individuals who are achievement-motivated have a need for success in school, sports, careers, and other competitive situations. These individuals enjoy getting recognition for their success. They are often known as the best student, the outstanding athlete, or the employee of the year. These people are attracted to careers that provide rewards for individual achievement, such as sales, law, architecture, engineering, and business. They work hard in order to enjoy the rewards of their efforts. In college, some students work very hard to achieve high grades and then take pride in their accomplishments. One disadvantage of using this type of motivation is that it can lead to excess stress. These students often need to remember to balance their time between work, school, family, and leisure so that they do not become too stressed by the need to achieve.

Using a Reward

You can use rewards to manage your own behavior. If you want to increase your studying behavior, follow it by a positive consequence or a reward. Think about what is rewarding to you (watching TV, playing sports, enjoying your favorite music). You could study (your behavior) and then watch a TV program (the reward). The timing of your reward is important. To be effective, it must immediately follow the behavior. If you watch TV and then study, you may not get around to studying. If you watch the TV program tomorrow or next week, it is not a strong reinforcement because it is not an immediate reward.

Be careful about the kinds of rewards you use so that you do not get into habits that are detrimental to your health. If you use food as a reward for studying, you may increase your studying behavior, but you may also gain a few pounds. Using alcohol or drugs as a reward can start an addiction. Buying yourself a reward can ruin your budget. Good rewards do not involve too many calories, cost too much money, or involve alcohol or drugs.

As a college student, you can use a reward as a powerful motivator. Praise yourself and think positively about your achievements in college even if the achievements come in small steps.

© Andy Dean/Shutterstock.com

Journal Entry #4

Write a paragraph with at least three ideas about how you can motivate yourself to be successful in college. Include any of these ideas: mindset, positive thinking, finding interest, concentration, attention, intrinsic motivation, locus of control, affiliation, achievement, and using rewards.

Success Is a Habit

We establish habits by taking small actions each day. Through repetition, these individual actions become habits. I once visited the Golden Gate Bridge in San Francisco and saw a cross section of the cable used to support the bridge. It was made of small metal strands twisted with other strands; then those cables were twisted together to make a stronger cable. Habits are a lot like cables. We start with one small action, and each successive action makes the habit stronger. Have you ever stopped to think that success can be a habit? We all have learned patterns of behavior that either help us to be successful or interfere with our success. With some effort and some basic understanding of behavior modification, you can choose to establish some new behaviors that lead to success or to get rid of behaviors that interfere with it.

> "Habits are first cobwebs, then cables."
> — Spanish Proverb

> "We are what we repeatedly do. Excellence, then, is not an act but a habit."
> — Aristotle

Eight Steps to Change a Habit

You can establish new habits that lead to your success. Once a habit is established, it can become a pattern of behavior that you do not need to think about very much. For example, new students often need to get into the habit of studying. Following is an outline of steps that can be helpful to establish new behaviors.

1. **State the problem.** What new habit would you like to start? What are your roadblocks or obstacles? What bad habit would you like to change? Be truthful about it. This is sometimes the most difficult step. Here are two different examples:

   - I need to study to be successful in college. I am not in the habit of studying. I easily get distracted by work, family, friends, and other things I need to do. At the end of the day, I am too tired to study.
   - I need to improve my diet. I am overweight. I eat too much fast food and am not careful about what I eat. I have no time for exercise.

2. **Change one small behavior at a time.** If you think about climbing a mountain, the task can seem overwhelming. However, you can take the first step. If you can change one small behavior, you can gain the confidence to change another. For example:

   - I plan to study at least two hours each day on Mondays through Fridays.
   - I plan to eat more fruits and vegetables each day.

   State the behavior you would like to change. Make it small.

3. **State in a positive way the behavior you wish to establish.** For example, instead of the negative statements "I will not waste my time" or "I will not eat junk food," say, "I plan to study each day" or "I plan to eat fruits and vegetables each day."

4. **Count the behavior.** How often do you do this behavior? If you are trying to establish a pattern of studying, write down how much time you spend studying each day. If you are trying to improve your diet, write down everything that you eat each day. Sometimes just getting an awareness of your habit is enough to begin to make some changes.

5. **Picture in your mind the actions you might take.** For example:

   - I picture myself finding time to study in the library. I see myself walking to the library. I can see myself in the library studying.
   - I see myself in the grocery store buying fruits and vegetables. I see myself packing these fruits and vegetables in my lunch. I see myself putting these foods in a place where I will notice them.

6. **Practice the behavior for 10 days.** In 10 days, you can get started on a new pattern of behavior. Once you have started, keep practicing the behavior for about a month to firmly establish your new pattern of behavior. The first three days are the most difficult.

Seven Steps to Change a Habit

1. State the problem
2. Change one small behavior at a time
3. Be positive
4. Count the behavior
5. Picture the change
6. Practice the behavior
7. Reward yourself

> "The difference in winning and losing is most often . . . not quitting."
> — Walt Disney

> "It's not that I'm so smart; it's just that I stay with problems longer."
> — Albert Einstein

Understanding Motivation

If you fail, don't give up. Just realize that you are human and keep trying for 10 days. Think positively that you can be successful. Write a journal entry or note on your calendar about what you have accomplished each day.

7. **Find a reward for your behavior.** Remember that we tend to repeat behaviors that are rewarded. Find rewards that do not involve too many calories, don't cost too much money, and don't involve alcohol or drugs. Also, rewards are most effective if they directly follow the behavior you wish to reinforce.

8. **Ask yourself, "What am I going to do to maintain the change?"** In the long run, the new behavior has to become part of your lifestyle.

Ten Habits of Successful College Students

Starting your college education will require you to establish some new habits to be successful.

1. **Attend class.**

   College lectures supplement the material in the text, so it is important to attend class. Many college instructors will drop you if you miss three hours of class. After three absences, most students do not return to class. If your class is online, log in frequently.

2. **Read the textbook.**

   Start early and read a little at a time. If you have a text with 400 pages, read 25 pages a week rather than trying to read it all at once.

3. **Have an educational plan.**

   Counselors or advisors can assist you in making an educational plan so that you take the right classes and accomplish your educational goal as soon as possible.

4. **Use college services.**

   Colleges offer valuable free services that help you to be successful. Take advantage of tutoring, counseling, health services, financial aid, the learning resources center (library) and many other services.

5. **Get to know the faculty.**

   You can get to know the faculty by asking questions in class or meeting with your instructors during office hours. Your instructors can provide extra assistance and write letters of recommendation for scholarships, future employment, or graduate school.

6. **Don't work too much.**

   Research has shown that full-time students should have no more than 20 hours of outside employment a week to be successful in college. If you have to work more than 20 hours a week, reduce your college load. If you are working 40 hours a week or more, take only one or two classes.

7. **Take one step at a time.**

   If you are anxious about going to college, remember that each class you attend takes you another step toward your goal. If you take too many classes, especially in the beginning, you may become overwhelmed.

8. **Have a goal for the future.**

   Know why you are in college and what you hope to accomplish. What career will you have in the future? Imagine your future lifestyle.

9. **Visualize your success.**

   See yourself walking across the stage and receiving your college diploma. See yourself working at a job you enjoy.

10. **Ask questions if you don't understand.**

    Asking questions not only helps you to find the answers, but it shows you are motivated to be successful.

QUIZ

Motivation, Part II

1. When you participate in student activities in campus such as athletics, student government, or a club, you will be

   a. distracted from your studies.
   b. using affiliation motivation.
   c. decreasing your chances of success in college.

2. If the behavior is followed by a reward

   a. it is likely to be increased.
   b. it is likely to be decreased.
   c. there will probably be no effect.

3. For rewards to be effective, they must occur

   a. before the behavior.
   b. immediately after the behavior.
   c. either before or after the behavior.

4. If you plan to increase time spent studying, the following statement is most likely to help you to achieve your goal.

   a. I will increase the time I spend studying.
   b. I plan to study for at least two hours each day on Mondays through Fridays.
   c. I will study for five hours on Monday to prepare for the test on Tuesday.

5. To change a habit,

   a. set high goals.
   b. focus on negative behavior.
   c. begin with a concrete behavior that can be counted.

How did you do on the quiz? Check your answers: 1. b, 2. a, 3. b, 4. b, 5. c

KEYS TO SUCCESS

Persistence

There is an old saying that persistence will get you almost anything eventually. This saying applies to your success in life as well as in college. The first two to six weeks of college are a critical time in which many students drop out. Realize that college is a new experience and that you will face new challenges and growth experiences. Make plans to persist, especially in the first few weeks. Get to know a college counselor or advisor. These professionals can help you to get started in the right classes and answer any questions you might have. It is important to make a connection with a counselor or faculty member so that you feel comfortable in college and have the resources to obtain needed help. Plan to enroll on time so that you do not have to register late. It is crucial to attend the first class. In the first class, the professor explains the class requirements and expectations and sets the tone for the class. You may even get dropped from the class if you are not there on the first day. Get into the habit of studying right away. Make studying a habit that you start immediately at the beginning of the semester or quarter. If you can make it through the first six weeks, it is likely that you can finish the semester and complete your college education.

It has been said that 90 percent of success is just showing up. Any faculty member will tell you that the number one reason for students dropping out of college is lack of attendance. They know that when students miss three classes in a row, they are not likely to return. Even very capable students who miss class may find that they are lost when they come back. Many students are simply afraid to return. Classes such as math and foreign languages are sequential, and it is very

(continued)

difficult to make up work after an absence. One of the most important ways you can be successful is to make a habit of consistently showing up for class.

You will also need commitment to be successful. Commitment is a promise to yourself to follow through with something. In athletics, it is not necessarily the one with the best physical skills who makes the best athlete. Commitment and practice make a great athlete. Commitment means doing whatever is necessary to succeed. Like the good athlete, make a commitment to accomplishing your goals. Spend the time necessary to be successful in your studies.

When you face difficulties, persistence and commitment are especially important. History is full of famous people who contributed to society through persistence and commitment. Consider the following facts about Abraham Lincoln, for example.

- Failed in business at age 21.
- Was defeated in a legislative race at age 22.
- Failed again in business at age 24.
- Overcame the death of his sweetheart at age 26.
- Had a nervous breakdown at age 27.
- Lost a congressional race at age 34.
- Lost a congressional race at age 36.
- Lost a senatorial race at age 45.
- Failed in an effort to become vice president at age 47.
- Lost a senatorial race at age 49.
- Was elected president of the United States at age 52.[11]

© Gustavo Frazao/Shutterstock.com

The goal of getting a college education may seem like a mountain that is difficult to climb. Break it into smaller steps that you can accomplish. See your college counselor or advisor, register for classes, attend the first class, read the first chapter, do the first assignment, and you will be on the road to your success. Then continue to break tasks into small, achievable steps and continue from one step to the next. And remember, persistence will get you almost anything eventually.

Journal Entry #5

What will you do if you are tempted to drop out of college? What steps can you take to be persistent in achieving your college goals? Are there times when it is best to change goals rather than to be persistent if your efforts are not working? Write a paragraph about how you will be persistent in reaching your college goals.

Appreciating Island Cultures: 'Opae E

There was a Mele Hawai'i, or Hawaiian song, called 'Opae E that was written by Pilahi Paki and Aunty Irmgard `Âluli. This Mele Hawai'i song was based on a mo'olelo, or story, about the different tiny sea creatures that were asked to help a young boy rescue his sister that he loved dearly. None was brave enough, until he met the tiny 'opihi. Here is what the mo'olelo says.

There was a young girl from Kahakuloa on the island of Maui. She had a younger brother with whom she was very close. One day as the two of them were playing in the ocean, she was kidnapped by a puhi, or eel, and taken to his cave. Her brother was so intent on saving his sister's life from the grips of the puhi that he was willing to do whatever he could to get her back. He went and asked every creature he could to help him!

© HakBak/Shutterstock.com

First, as he was walking, he reached the 'opae, shrimp, and said' "Opae come, come with me. Please. I am going to rescue my sister. Puhi caught her and he is going to eat her. Can you help me?"

© Aleksey Stemmer/Shutterstock.com

The 'Opae looked at the boy in dismay and said "Puhi! What are you thinking? Puhi is so big and I am so small! There is absolutely no way I can help you." And the 'opae turned and swam away.

The boy was sad, but he had to rescue his sister before it was too late, so he kept going. Soon, he came to the pupu, or sea shell. The boy told the sea shell "Pupu, come, come with me. I am going to rescue my sister. Puhi got her and he is going to eat her. Please, please pupu, can you help me?"

© Vaclav Volrab/Shutterstock.com

Understanding Motivation 33

© Noppadon Panpichit/Shutterstock.com

© SARAWUT KUNDEJ/Shutterstock.com

The pupu looked at the boy and said "Puhi! What's the matter with you? Puhi is so big and I am so small! How can I possibly help you? No, I cannot help." And pupu turned and floated away.

The boy was so sad that now, two sea creatures had turned him down. But, he would not let that stop him from rescuing his sister from the puhi's cave. The boy kept going.

As he proceeded, the boy came to the pipipi, the tiny mollusk, and said "Pipipi, come, come with me. I am going to rescue my sister from Puhi's cave. Puhi got her and he is going to eat her. I went to see 'opae and pupu, but they would not help. Will you help me? Please."

Pipipi replied "Are you crazy? You want me to help you rescue your sister from Puhi's cave? Puhi is so big and I am so small! How could I possibly help you? No. I cannot help!" And pipipi turned around and a wave swept him away.

As sad as the boy was, he could not allow himself to be discouraged. So he mustered up the courage to persist. The boy kept going and ran into a kupe'e, a little marine snail.

The boy cried out and said "Kupe'e, kupe'e, please come. Please come with me to help rescue my sister from Puhi. Puhi has her and he is going to eat her. Please help!"

Kupe'e looked at him and said "Puhi! Puhi is SO BIG and I am SO SMALL! I cannot help you!" Kupe'e turned and left.

The boy wondered if there was anyone that would help him. It sure didn't feel like he would get ANY help at all. But he also knew that if he gave up, he wouldn't see his sister ever again.

He stopped for a minute to think about what he could possibly do. Just then, he happened to see an 'opihi, or limpet. He ran to the 'opihi and said' "Opihi! Will you come with me? You are my last hope! I am going to rescue my sister from Puhi. Puhi caught her and he is going to eat her. Can you help me? Please say you can."

The 'opihi, as tiny as he is, looked at the boy and said "Boy, maimaka'u, don't be scared. I know how I can help! I will go with you and cover the eyes of the puhi with my shells. That will make him blind! Then you can get your sister away from him. Together we will rescue your sister from Puhi."

© Lizard/Shutterstock.com

The boy shouted! "Mahalo, 'opihi! Mahalo NUI!" (Thank you, 'opihi! Thanks VERY MUCH!). They went on to the puhi's cave. Once they got there, they found puhi and the boy yelled, "Puhi! Stop!" Puhi got angry and came toward the boy ready to capture him. He did not see the 'opihi there with the boy because he was so tiny. As the puhi came toward the boy, 'opihi jumped on him and clamped himself over puhi's eyes. Puhi struggled and struggled, but the 'opihi's grips were so tight that he could not get him off his eyes.

The boy ran to his sister and rescued her! They each got out safely, including the 'opihi! Once they knew they were safe, the boy looked at 'opihi and said "Mahalo nui, 'opihi! You may be small, but you did something I could never do!" The 'opihi said "Na'ukahau'oli, it was my pleasure." And clung tightly once again to a nearby rock. The boy and his sister were safe!

Questions

1. The little boy's purpose was to make sure his sister was safe and bring her home to her family. What is your purpose in pursuing higher education?
2. As the little boy wandered through the ocean looking for help, he encountered some setbacks. What are some obstacles that you may face on this journey?
3. Because the little boy loved his sister, he did whatever it took to find someone to help him and he rescued her. What obstacles are you facing and what will it take for you to overcome them?
4. On this journey to rescue his sister, the little boy looked for support from others around them. How big a role does your family play in your success?
5. Just as the boy was set on saving his sister, how determined are you to succeed and make a difference for yourself and possibly for your family?

- Kahakuloa: Place on the Island of Maui
- Kupe'e": Small marine snail
- Mahalo Nui: Thank you very much
- Mele: Song
- Mo'olelo: Story
- Na'uKaHau'oli: My pleasure
- 'Opae: Shrimp
- 'Opihi: Limpet
- Pipipi: Small mollusk
- Puhi: Eel
- Pupu: Shell

© Lyudmyla Kharlamova/Shutterstock.com

College Success 1

The College Success 1 website is continually updated with supplementary material for each chapter including Word documents of the journal entries, classroom activities, handouts, videos, links to related materials, and much more. See http://www.collegesuccess1.com/.

Notes

1. Federal Reserve Bank of New York, "Do the Benefits of College Still Outweigh the Costs?," *Current Issues in Economics and Finance* 20, no. 3, 2014. Available at www.newyorkfed.org/research/current-issues
2. U.S Census Bureau, "Earnings and Unemployment by Educational Attainment 2014," retrieved from http://www.bls.gov/emp/ep_chart_001.htm
3. Ibid.

4. W. Lewallen, "The Impact of Being Undecided on College Persistence," *Journal of College Student Development* 34 (1993): 103–112.

5. Marsha Fralick, "College Success: A Study of Positive and Negative Attrition," *Community College Review* 20 (1993): 29–36.

6. Terry Doyle and Todd Zakrajsek, The New Science of Learning (Sterling, Virginia: Stylus), 85–87.

7. Christopher Peterson, *A Primer in Positive Psychology* (New York: Oxford University Press, 2006), 127.

8. John Medina, Brain Rules (Seattle: Pear Press, 2008), 87.

9. Ibid., 87.

10. M.J. Findley and H.M. Cooper, "Locus of Control and Academic Achievement: A Literature Review," *Journal of Personality and Social Psychology* 44 (1983): 419–427.

11. Anthony Robbins, Unlimited Power (New York: Ballantine Books, 1986), 73.

Begin with Self-Assessment

Name _____ Date _____

A good way to begin your success in college is to assess your present skills to determine your strengths and areas that need improvement. Complete the following assessment to get an overview of the topics presented in the textbook and to measure your present skills.

Measure Your Success

The following statements represent major topics included in the textbook. Read the following statements and rate how true they are for you at the present time. At the end of the course, you will have the opportunity to complete this assessment again to measure your progress.

5   Definitely true
4   Mostly true
3   Somewhat true
2   Seldom true
1   Never true

_____ I am motivated to be successful in college.

_____ I know the value of a college education.

_____ I know how to establish successful patterns of behavior.

_____ I can concentrate on an important task until it is completed.

_____ I am attending college to accomplish my own personal goals.

_____ I believe to a great extent that my actions determine my future.

_____ I am persistent in achieving my goals.

_____ **Total points for Motivation**

_____ I can describe my personality type.

_____ I can list careers that match my personality type.

_____ I can describe my personal strengths and talents based on my personality type.

_____ I understand how my personality type affects how I manage my time and money.

_____ I know what college majors are most in demand.

_____ I am confident that I have chosen the best major for myself.

_____ Courses related to my major are interesting and exciting to me.

_____ **Total points for Personality and Major**

Understanding Motivation

_____ I have a list or mental picture of my lifetime goals.
_____ I know what I would like to accomplish in the next four years.
_____ I spend my time on activities that help me accomplish my lifetime goals.
_____ I effectively use priorities in managing my time.
_____ I can balance study, work, and recreation time.
_____ I generally avoid procrastination on important tasks.
_____ I am good at managing my money.
_____ **Total points for Managing Time and Money**

_____ I understand the difference between short-term and long-term memory.
_____ I use effective study techniques for storing information in long-term memory.
_____ I can apply memory techniques to remember what I am studying.
_____ I know how to minimize forgetting.
_____ I know how to use mnemonics and other memory tricks.
_____ I know how to keep my brain healthy throughout life.
_____ I use positive thinking to be successful in my studies.
_____ **Total points for Brain Science and Memory**

_____ I understand the latest findings in brain science and can apply them to studying.
_____ I use a reading study system based on memory strategies.
_____ I am familiar with e-learning strategies for reading and learning online.
_____ I know how to effectively mark my textbook.
_____ I understand how math is different from studying other subjects.
_____ I have the math study skills needed to be successful in my math courses.
_____ I take responsibility for my own success in college and in life.
_____ **Total points for Brain Science and Study Skills**

_____ I know how to listen for the main points in a college lecture.
_____ I am familiar with note-taking systems for college lectures.
_____ I know how to review my lecture notes.
_____ I feel comfortable with writing.
_____ I know the steps in writing a college term paper.
_____ I know how to prepare a speech.
_____ I am comfortable with public speaking.
_____ **Total points for Taking Notes, Writing, and Speaking**

_____ I know how to adequately prepare for a test.
_____ I can predict the questions that are likely to be on the test.
_____ I know how to deal with test anxiety.
_____ I am successful on math exams.
_____ I know how to make a reasonable guess if I am uncertain about the answer.
_____ I am confident of my ability to take objective tests.
_____ I can write a good essay answer.
_____ **Total points for Test Taking**

_____ I understand the theories of life stages.
_____ I can describe my present developmental stage in life.
_____ I have self-confidence.
_____ I use positive self-talk and affirmations.
_____ I have a visual picture of my future success.
_____ I have a clear idea of what happiness means to me.
_____ I usually practice positive thinking.
_____ **Total points for Future**

_____ I am confident of my ability to succeed in college.
_____ I am confident that my choice of a major is the best one for me.
_____ **Total additional points**

Total your points:

_____ Motivation
_____ Personality and Major
_____ Managing Time and Money
_____ Brain Science and Memory
_____ Brain Science and Study Skills
_____ Taking Notes, Writing, and Speaking
_____ Test Taking
_____ Future
_____ Additional Points
_____ **Grand total points**

If you scored

290–261 You are very confident of your skills for success in college. Maybe you do not need this class?

260–232 You have good skills for success in college. You can always improve.

231–203 You have average skills for success in college. You will definitely benefit from taking this course.

Below 202 You need some help to survive in college. You are in the right place to begin.

Use these scores to complete the Success Wheel that follows this assessment. Note that the additional points are not used in the chart.

Success Wheel

Name _____ Date _____

Use your scores from the Measure Your Success assessment to complete the following Success Wheel. Use different colored markers to shade in each section of the wheel.

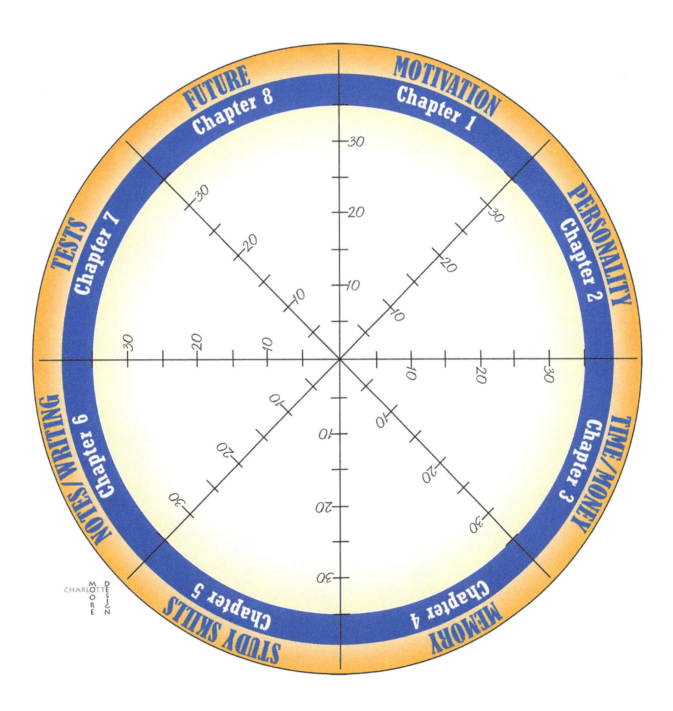

Understanding Motivation   41

1. What are your best areas?

2. What are areas that need improvement?

What Do I Want from College?

Name _____ Date _____

Read the following list and place checkmarks next to your reasons for attending college. Think about why you are attending college and add your own personal reasons to the list.

_____ 1. To have financial security

_____ 2. To find a satisfying career

_____ 3. To explore possibilities provided by college

_____ 4. To expand my options

_____ 5. To become an educated person

_____ 6. To figure out what I want to do with my life

_____ 7. To develop my potential

_____ 8. To become a role model for my children

_____ 9. To make my parents happy

_____ 10. To respect myself

_____ 11. To feel good about myself

_____ 12. To see if I can do it

_____ 13. To meet interesting people

_____ 14. To have something to do and prevent boredom

_____ 15. To become the best I can be

_____ 16. To have better job opportunities

_____ 17. To have no regrets later on

_____ 18. To prepare for a good job or profession

_____ 19. To have job security

_____ 20. To gain confidence in myself

_____ 21. To get a degree

_____ 22. To gain a greater understanding of the world

_____ 23. To have fun

Understanding Motivation

_____ 24. To understand myself

_____ 25. To learn how to think

_____ 26. To enjoy what I do for a living

_____ 27. To reach my potential

_____ 28. Because my parents want me to get a degree

_____ 29. For my own personal satisfaction

_____ 30. To make a difference in other people's lives

_____ 31. To have a position of power

_____ 32. To have respect

_____ 33. To have prestige

_____ 34. To have time and money for travel

_____ 35. To acquire knowledge

_____ 36. _____

_____ 37. _____

What are your top six reasons for attending college? You may include reasons not listed above. If you are tempted to give up on your college education, read this list and think about the reasons you have listed below.

1. _____   4. _____

2. _____   5. _____

3. _____   6. _____

Roadblocks and Pathways to Success

Name _____   Date _____

© IQoncept/Shutterstock.com

Students come to college with a dream of making a better future for themselves. What is your dream? Your instructor may have you share your ideas with other students in the course.

Place a checkmark next to any item that could be a roadblock to your success in college.

_____ Too much work	_____ Family obligations	_____ Lack of study skills
_____ Financial difficulties	_____ Social life	_____ Using time wisely
_____ Lack of confidence	_____ Computer games	_____ Speaking in class
_____ Difficulty with reading	_____ Social media	_____ Negative thinking
_____ Difficulty with writing	_____ Phone use and texting	_____ Lack of motivation
_____ Difficulty with math	_____ Lack of career goals	_____ Learning disabilities
_____ Difficulty with tests	_____ Dislike of homework	_____ Lack of persistence
_____ Difficulty with memory	_____ Dislike of school	_____ Health problems

Understanding Motivation

List any other roadblocks in addition to the items checked above:

What are your top three roadblocks?

1. _____

2. _____

3. _____

Spend 5 minutes skimming through the table of contents in your textbook and looking quickly through the chapters to find ideas that will help you overcome any roadblocks to your success. List 5 topics from the textbook that can help you to be successful in college.

1. _____

2. _____

3. _____

4. _____

5. _____

What are other resources that can help you to overcome your roadblocks? (tutoring, financial aid, advising, family support, self-motivation)

Your instructor will help the class brainstorm ideas for overcoming roadblocks. What is your plan for overcoming the roadblocks to achieve your hopes and dreams for the future?

Textbook Skimming

Name _____   Date _____

Use this text or any new text to answer the following questions. Challenge yourself to do this exercise quickly. Remember that a textbook survey should take no longer than five to 15 minutes. Try to complete this exercise in 15 minutes to allow time for writing. Notice the time when you start and finish.

1. Write two key ideas found in the introduction or preface to the book.

2. Looking at the table of contents, list the first five main ideas covered in the text.

3. Write down five interesting topics that you found in the book.

4. What did you find at the back of the book (e.g., index, glossary, appendixes)?

5. How long did it take you to do this exercise? _____

6. Briefly, what did you think of this textbook skimming exercise?

Understanding Motivation

CHAPTER 3

Exploring Your Personality and Major

Learning Objectives

Read to answer these key questions:

- What is my personality type?

- How is personality type related to choice of a major and career?

- What careers and majors should I consider based on my personality type?

- What are some other factors in choosing a major?

- What is my preferred work environment?

- How does my personality type affect decision making, time management, money management, learning, and meeting the professor's expectations?

- What are my personal strengths or multiple intelligences?

- What are my passions in life?

From *College & Career Success, Concise Version*, Seventh Edition, by Marsha Fralick. Copyright © 2016 by Kendall Hunt Publishing Company. Reprinted by permission.

To assure your success in college, it is important to choose the major that is best for you. If you choose a major and career that match your personal strengths, you will enjoy your studies and excel in your work. It was Picasso who said that you know you enjoy your work when you do not notice the time passing by. If you can become interested in your work and studies, you are on your way to developing passion and joy in your life. If you can get up each morning and enjoy the work that you do (at least on most days), you will surely have one of the keys to happiness.

Choose a Major That Matches Your Gifts and Talents

> "To be what we are, and to become what we are capable of becoming, is the only end of life."
> Robert Louis Stevenson

The first step in choosing the major that is right for you is to understand your personality type. Psychologists have developed useful theories of personality that can help you understand how personality type relates to the choice of major and career. The personality theory used in this textbook is derived from the work of Swiss psychologist Carl Jung (1875–1961). Jung believed that we are born with a predisposition for certain personality preferences and that healthy development is based on the lifelong nurturing of inborn preferences rather than trying to change a person to become something different. Each personality type has gifts and talents that can be nurtured over a lifetime.

While assessments are not exact predictors of your future major and career, they provide useful information that will get you started on the path of career exploration and finding the college major that is best suited to you. Knowledge of your personality and the personalities of others is not only valuable in understanding yourself, but also in appreciating how others are different. This understanding of self and others will empower you to communicate and work effectively with others. Knowledge of your multiple intelligences will help you match your personal strengths with careers.

This textbook includes an online career portfolio to help in choosing your major. See the directions located on the inside front cover of your text to set up your portfolio and complete the career assessments. Complete the Do What You Are personality assessment and the MI Advantage assessment of multiple intelligences before you begin this chapter.

© Andril Kondiuk/Shutterstock.com

Understanding Personality Types

Just as no two fingerprints or snowflakes are exactly alike, each person is a different and unique individual. Even with this uniqueness, however, we can make some general statements about personality. When we make generalizations, we are talking about averages. These averages can provide useful information about ourselves and other people, but it is important to remember that no individual is exactly described by the average. As you read through the following descriptions of personality types, keep in mind that we are talking about generalizations or beginning points for discussion and thoughtful analysis.

As you read through your personality description from Do What You Are and the information in this text, **focus on your personal strengths and talents**. Building on these personal strengths has several important benefits. It increases self-esteem and self-confidence, which contribute to your success and enjoyment of life. Building on your strengths provides the energy and motivation required to put in the effort needed to accomplish any worthwhile task. The assessment also identifies some of your possible weaknesses or "blind spots." Just be aware of these blind spots so that they do not interfere with your success. Being aware of your blind spots can even be used to your advantage. For example, some personality types thrive by working with people. A career that involves much public contact is a good match for this personality type, whereas choosing a career where public contact is limited can lead to job dissatisfaction. Knowing about your personality type can help you make the right decisions to maximize your potential.

Personality type has four dimensions:

1. Extraversion or Introversion
2. Sensing or Intuition
3. Thinking or Feeling
4. Judging or Perceiving

These dimensions of personality will be defined and examined in more depth in the sections that follow.

Extraversion or Introversion

The dimension of extraversion or introversion defines how we interact with the world and how our energy flows. In the general school population, 75 percent of students are usually extraverts and 25 percent are introverts.

> *Extraverts (E) focus their energy on the world outside themselves. They enjoy interaction with others and get to know a lot of different people. They enjoy and are usually good at communication. They are energized by social interaction and prefer being active. These types are often described as talkative and social.*
>
> *Introverts (I) focus their energy on the world inside of themselves. They enjoy spending time alone to think about the world in order to understand it. Introverts prefer more limited social contacts, choosing smaller groups or one-on-one relationships. These types are often described as quiet or reserved.*

We all use the introvert and extravert modes while functioning in our daily lives. Whether a person is an extravert or an introvert is a matter of preference, like being left- or right-handed. We can use our nondominant hand, but it is not as comfortable as using our dominant hand. We are usually more skillful in using the dominant hand. For example, introverts can learn to function well in social situations, but later may need some peace and quiet to recharge. On the other hand, social contact energizes the extravert.

One personality type is not better than the other: it is just different. Being an extravert is not better than being an introvert. Each type has unique gifts and talents that can be used in different occupations. An extravert might enjoy working in an occupation with lots of public contact, such as being a receptionist or handling public relations. An introvert might enjoy being an accountant or writer. However, as with all of the personality dimensions, a person may have traits of both types.

ACTIVITY

Introverts and Extraverts

The list below describes some qualities of introverts and extraverts. **For each pair of items**, quickly choose the phrase that describes you best and highlight or place a checkmark next to it. Remember that one type is not better than another. You may also find that you are a combination type and act like an introvert in some situations and an extravert in others. Each type has gifts and talents that can be used in choosing the best major and career for you. To get an estimate of your preference, notice which column has the most checkmarks.

Introvert (I)

_____ Energized by having quiet time alone
_____ Tend to think first and talk later
_____ Tend to think things through quietly
_____ Tend to respond slowly, after thinking
_____ Avoid being the center of attention
_____ Difficult to get to know, private
_____ Have a few close friends
_____ Prefer quiet for concentration
_____ Listen more than talk
_____ View telephone calls as a distraction
_____ Talk to a few people at parties
_____ Share special occasions with one or a few people
_____ Prefer to study alone
_____ Prefer the library to be quiet
_____ Described as quiet or reserved
_____ Work systematically

Extravert (E)

_____ Energized by social interaction
_____ Tend to talk first and think later
_____ Tend to think out loud
_____ Tend to respond quickly, before thinking
_____ Like to be the center of attention
_____ Easy to get to know, outgoing
_____ Have many friends, know lots of people
_____ Can read or talk with background noise
_____ Talk more than listen
_____ View telephone calls as a welcome break
_____ Talk to many different people at parties
_____ Share special occasions with large groups
_____ Prefer to study with others in a group
_____ Talk with others in the library
_____ Described as talkative or friendly
_____ Work through trial and error

Here are some qualities that describe the ideal work environment. Again, as you **read through each pair of items**, place a checkmark next to the work environment that you prefer.

Introvert (I)

_____ Work alone or with individuals
_____ Quiet for concentration
_____ Communication one-on-one
_____ Work in small groups
_____ Focus on one project until complete
_____ Work without interruption

Extravert (E)

_____ Much public contact
_____ High-energy environment
_____ Present ideas to a group
_____ Work as part of a team
_____ Variety and action
_____ Talk to others

_____ **Total** (from both charts above)   _____ **Total** (from both charts above)

Do these results agree with your personality assessment on the Do What You Are? If your results are the same, this is a good indication that your results are useful and accurate. Are there some differences with the results obtained from your personality assessment? If your results are different, this provides an opportunity for further reflection about your personality type. Here are a couple of reasons why your results may be different.

1. You may be a combination type with varying degrees of preference for each type.
2. You may have chosen your personality type on the Do What You Are based on what you think is best rather than what you truly are. Students sometimes do this because of the myth that there are good and bad personality types. It is important to remember that each personality type has strengths and weaknesses. By identifying strengths, you can build on them by choosing the right major and career. By being aware of weaknesses, you can come up with strategies to compensate for them to be successful.

Look at the total number of checkmarks for extravert and introvert on the two above charts. Do you lean toward being an introvert or an extravert? Remember that one type is not better than the other and each has unique gifts and talents. On the chart below, place an X on the line to indicate how much you prefer introversion or extraversion. If you selected most of the introvert traits, place your X somewhere on the left side. If you selected most of the extravert traits, place your X somewhere on the right side. If you are equally introverted and extraverted, place your X in the middle.

Introvert _____|_____ Extravert

Do you generally prefer introversion or extraversion? In the box below, write **I** for introversion or **E** for extraversion. If there is a tie between **E** and **I**, write **I**.

☐

Notice that it is possible to be a combination type. At times you might prefer to act like an introvert, and at other times you might prefer to act like an extravert. It is beneficial to be able to balance these traits. However, for combination types, it is more difficult to select specific occupations that match this type

> ### Journal Entry #1
>
> Look at the results from Do What You Are and your own self-assessment above. Are you an introvert or an extravert or a combination of these two types? Can you give examples of how it affects your social life, school, or work? Write a paragraph about this preference.

Sensing or Intuition

The dimension of sensing or intuition describes how we take in information. In the general school population, 70 percent of students are usually sensing types and 30 percent are intuitive types.

Sensing (S) persons prefer to use the senses to take in information (what they see, hear, taste, touch, smell). They focus on "what is" and trust information that is concrete and observable. They learn through experience.

*Intuitive (N) persons rely on instincts and focus on "what could be." While we all use our five senses to perceive the world, intuitive people are interested in relationships, possibilities, meanings, and implications. They value inspiration and trust their "sixth sense" or hunches. (Intuitive is designated as **N** so it is not confused with **I** for Introvert.)*

We all use both of these modes in our daily lives, but we usually have a preference for one mode or the other. Again, there is no best preference. Each type has special skills that can be applied to the job market. For example, you would probably want your tax preparer to be a sensing type who focuses on concrete information and fills out your tax form correctly. An inventor or artist would probably be an intuitive type.

ACTIVITY

Sensing and Intuitive

Here are some qualities of sensing and intuitive persons. As you **read through each pair of items**, quickly highlight or place a checkmark next to the item that usually describes yourself.

Sensing (S)

_____ Trust what is certain and concrete

_____ Prefer specific answers to questions

_____ Like new ideas if they have practical applications (if you can use them)

_____ Value realism and common sense

_____ Think about things one at a time and step by step

_____ Like to improve and use skills learned before

_____ More focused on the present

_____ Concentrate on what you are doing

_____ Do something

_____ See tangible results

_____ If it isn't broken, don't fix it

INtuitive (N)

_____ Trust inspiration and inference

_____ Prefer general answers that leave room for interpretation

_____ Like new ideas for their own sake (you don't need a practical use for them)

_____ Value imagination and innovation

_____ Think about many ideas at once as they come to you

_____ Like to learn new skills and get bored using the same skills

_____ More focused on the future

_____ Wonder what is next

_____ Think about doing something

_____ Focus on possibilities

_____ There is always a better way to do it

Sensing (S)

_____ Prefer working with facts and figures
_____ Focus on reality
_____ Seeing is believing
_____ Tend to be specific and literal (say what you mean)
_____ See what is here and now

INtuitive (N)

_____ Prefer working with ideas and theories
_____ Use fantasy
_____ Anything is possible
_____ Tend to be general and figurative (use comparisons and analogies)
_____ See the big picture

Here are some qualities that describe the ideal work environment. Again, as you **read through each pair of items**, place a checkmark next to the work environment that you prefer.

Sensing (S)

_____ Use and practice skills
_____ Work with known facts
_____ See measurable results
_____ Focus on practical benefits
_____ Learn through experience
_____ Pleasant environment
_____ Use standard procedures
_____ Work step-by-step
_____ Do accurate work
_____ **Total** (from both charts above)

INtuitive (N)

_____ Learn new skills
_____ Explore new ideas and approaches
_____ Work with theories
_____ Use imagination and be original
_____ Freedom to follow your inspiration
_____ Challenging environment
_____ Invent new products and procedures
_____ Work in bursts of energy
_____ Find creative solutions
_____ **Total** (from both charts above)

Look at the two charts above and see whether you tend to be more sensing or intuitive. One preference is not better than another: it is just different. On the chart below, place an X on the line to indicate your preference for sensing or intuitive. Again, notice that it is possible to be a combination type with both sensing and intuitive preferences.

Sensing _____|_____Intuitive

Do you generally prefer sensing or intuition? In the box below, write **S** for sensing or **N** for intuitive. If there is a tie between **S** and **N**, write **N**.

☐

Journal Entry #2

Look at the results from Do What You Are and your own self-assessment above. Are you a sensing, intuitive, or combination type? Can you give examples of how it affects your social life, school, or work? Write a paragraph about this preference.

Exploring Your Personality and Major

Thinking or Feeling

The dimension of thinking or feeling defines how we prefer to make decisions. In the general school population, 60 percent of males are thinking types and 40 percent are feeling types. For females, 60 percent are feeling types and 40 percent are thinking types.

Thinking (T) individuals make decisions based on logic. They are objective and analytical. They look at all the evidence and reach an impersonal conclusion. They are concerned with what they think is right.

Feeling (F) individuals make decisions based on what is important to them and matches their personal values. They are concerned about what they feel is right.

We all use logic and have feelings and emotions that play a part in decision making. However, the thinking person prefers to make decisions based on logic, and the feeling person prefers to make decisions according to what is important to self and others. This is one category in which men and women often differ. Most women are feeling types, and most men are logical types. When men and women are arguing, you might hear the following:

Man: "I think that . . ."

Woman: "I feel that . . ."

By understanding these differences, it is possible to improve communication and understanding. Be careful with generalizations, since 40 percent of men and women would not fit this pattern.

When thinking about careers, a thinking type would make a good judge or computer programmer. A feeling type would probably make a good social worker or kindergarten teacher.

ACTIVITY

Thinking and Feeling

The following chart shows some qualities of thinking and feeling types. As you **read through each pair of items**, quickly highlight or place a checkmark next to the items that usually describe yourself.

Thinking (T)

_____ Apply impersonal analysis to problems

_____ Value logic and justice

_____ Fairness is important

_____ Truth is more important than tact

_____ Motivated by achievement and accomplishment

_____ Feelings are valid if they are logical

_____ Good decisions are logical

Feeling (F)

_____ Consider the effect on others

_____ Value empathy and harmony

_____ There are exceptions to every rule

_____ Tact is more important than truth

_____ Motivated by being appreciated by others

_____ Feelings are valid whether they make sense or not

_____ Good decisions take others' feelings into account

Thinking (T)

_____ Described as cool, calm, and objective
_____ Love can be analyzed
_____ Firm-minded
_____ More important to be right
_____ Remember numbers and figures
_____ Prefer clarity
_____ Find flaws and critique
_____ Prefer firmness

Feeling (F)

_____ Described as caring and emotional
_____ Love cannot be analyzed
_____ Gentle-hearted
_____ More important to be liked
_____ Remember faces and names
_____ Prefer harmony
_____ Look for the good and compliment
_____ Prefer persuasion

Here are some qualities that describe the ideal work environment. As you **read through each pair of items**, place a checkmark next to the items that usually describe the work environment that you prefer.

Thinking (T)

_____ Maintain business environment
_____ Work with people I respect
_____ Be treated fairly
_____ Fair evaluations
_____ Solve problems
_____ Challenging work
_____ Use logic and analysis
_____ **Total** (from both charts above)

Feeling (F)

_____ Maintain close personal relationships
_____ Work in a friendly, relaxed environment
_____ Be able to express personal values
_____ Appreciation for good work
_____ Make a personal contribution
_____ Harmonious work situation
_____ Help others
_____ **Total** (from both charts above)

While we all use thinking and feeling, what is your preferred type? Look at the charts above and notice whether you are more the thinking or feeling type. One is not better than the other. On the chart below, place an X on the line to indicate how much you prefer thinking or feeling.

Thinking _____|_____ Feeling

Do you generally prefer thinking or feeling? In the box below, write **T** for thinking or **F** for feeling. If there is a tie between **T** and **F**, write **F**.

Journal Entry #3

Look at the results from Do What You Are and your own self-assessment above. Are you a thinking, feeling, or combination type? Can you give examples of how it affects your social life, school, or work? Write a paragraph about this preference.

Exploring Your Personality and Major

Judging or Perceiving

The dimension of judging or perceiving refers to how we deal with the external world. In other words, do we prefer the world to be structured or unstructured? In the general school population, the percentage of each of these types is approximately equal.

Judging (J) types like to live in a structured, orderly, and planned way. They are happy when their lives are structured and matters are settled. They like to have control over their lives. **Judging does not mean to judge others.** Think of this type as being orderly and organized.

Perceptive (P) types like to live in a spontaneous and flexible way. They are happy when their lives are open to possibilities. They try to understand life rather than control it. **Think of this type as spontaneous and flexible.**

Since these types have very opposite ways of looking at the world, there is a great deal of potential for conflict between them unless there is an appreciation for the gifts and talents of both. In any situation, we can benefit from people who represent these very different points of view. For example, in a business situation, the judging type would be good at managing the money, while the perceptive type would be good at helping the business to adapt to a changing marketplace. It is good to be open to all the possibilities and to be flexible, as well as to have some structure and organization.

ACTIVITY

Judging and Perceptive

As you **read through each pair of items**, quickly highlight or place a checkmark next to the items that generally describe yourself.

Judging (J)

- _____ Happy when the decisions are made and finished
- _____ Work first, play later
- _____ It is important to be on time
- _____ Time flies
- _____ Feel comfortable with routine
- _____ Generally keep things in order
- _____ Set goals and work toward them
- _____ Emphasize completing the task
- _____ Like to finish projects
- _____ Meet deadlines
- _____ Like to know what I am getting into
- _____ Relax when things are organized
- _____ Follow a routine
- _____ Focused
- _____ Work steadily

Perceptive (P)

- _____ Happy when the options are left open; something better may come along
- _____ Play first, do the work later
- _____ Time is relative
- _____ Time is elastic
- _____ Dislike routine
- _____ Prefer creative disorder
- _____ Change goals as new opportunities arise
- _____ Emphasize how the task is done
- _____ Like to start projects
- _____ What deadline?
- _____ Like new possibilities and situations
- _____ Relax when necessary
- _____ Explore the unknown
- _____ Easily distracted
- _____ Work in spurts of energy

Here are some qualities that describe the ideal work environment. Again, as you **read through each pair of items**, place a checkmark next to the work environment that you prefer.

Judging (J)	Perceptive (P)
_____ Follow a schedule	_____ Be spontaneous
_____ Clear directions	_____ Minimal rules and structure
_____ Organized work	_____ Flexibility
_____ Logical order	_____ Many changes
_____ Control my job	_____ Respond to emergencies
_____ Stability and security	_____ Take risks and be adventurous
_____ Work on one project until done	_____ Juggle many projects
_____ Steady work	_____ Variety and action
_____ Satisfying work	_____ Fun and excitement
_____ Like having high responsibility	_____ Like having interesting work
_____ Accomplish goals on time	_____ Work at my own pace
_____ Clear and concrete assignments	_____ Minimal supervision
_____ **Total** (from both charts above)	_____ **Total** (from both charts above)

Look at the charts above and notice whether you are more the judging type (orderly and organized) or the perceptive type (spontaneous and flexible). We need the qualities of both types to be successful and deal with the rapid changes in today's world. On the chart below, place an X on the line to indicate how much you prefer judging or perceiving.

Judging_____|_____Perceptive

Do you generally have judging or perceptive traits? In the box below, write **J** for judging or **P** for perceptive. If there is a tie between **J** and **P**, write **P**.

Journal Entry #4

Look at the results from Do What You Are and your own self-assessment above. Are you a judging, perceptive, or combination type? Can you give examples of how it affects your social life, school, or work? Write a paragraph about this preference.

"Knowing thyself is the height of wisdom."
Socrates

Exploring Your Personality and Major

ACTIVITY

Summarize Your Results

Look at your results above and summarize them on this composite chart. Notice that we are all unique, according to where the Xs fall on the scale.

Extravert (E) _____|_____ Introvert (I)

Sensing (S) _____|_____ Intuitive (N)

Thinking (T) _____|_____ Feeling (F)

Judging (J) _____|_____ Perceptive (P)

Write the letters representing each of your preferences.

The above letters represent your estimated personality type based on your understanding and knowledge of self. It is a good idea to confirm that this type is correct for you by completing the online personality assessment, Do What You Are.

© Gustavo Frazao/Shutterstock.com

QUIZ

Personality Types

Test what you have learned by selecting the correct answer to the following questions.

1. A person who is energized by social interaction is a/an:
   a. introvert
   b. extravert
   c. feeling type

2. A person who is quiet and reserved is a/an:
   a. introvert
   b. extravert
   c. perceptive type

3. A person who relies on experience and trusts information that is concrete and observable is a/an:
   a. judging type
   b. sensing type
   c. perceptive type

4. A person who focuses on "what could be" is a/an:
   a. perceptive type
   b. thinking type
   c. intuitive type

5. A person who makes decisions based on logic is a/an:
   a. thinker
   b. perceiver
   c. sensor

6. A person who makes decisions based on personal values is a/an:
   a. feeling type
   b. thinking type
   c. judging type

7. The perceptive type:
   a. has extrasensory perception
   b. likes to live life in a spontaneous and flexible way
   c. always considers feelings before making a decision

8. The judging type likes to:
   a. judge others
   b. use logic
   c. live in a structured and orderly way

9. Personality assessments are an exact predictor of your best major and career.
   a. true
   b. false

10. Some personality types are better than others.
    a. true
    b. false

How did you do on the quiz? Check your answers: 1. b, 2. a, 3. b, 4. c, 5. a, 6. a, 7. b, 8. c, 9. b, 10. b

Exploring Your Personality and Major

> "Choose a job you love, and you will never have to work a day in your life."
> — Confucius

Personality and Career Choice

While it is not possible to predict exactly your career and college major by knowing your personality type, it can help provide opportunities for exploration. The Do What You Are personality assessment links your personality type with suggested matching careers in the O*Net career database continually updated by the U.S. Department of Labor. You can find additional information at the College Success 1 website: http://www.collegesuccess1.com/careers.html. This page includes a description of each type, general occupations to consider, specific job titles, and suggested college majors.

© iQoncept/Shutterstock.com

Personality and Preferred Work Environment

Knowing your personality type will help you to understand your preferred work environment and provide some insights into selecting the major and career that you would enjoy. Selecting the work environment that matches your personal preferences helps you to be energized on the job and to minimize stress. Understanding other types will help you to work effectively with co-workers. As you read this section, think about your ideal work environment and how others are different.

Extraverts are career generalists who use their skills in a variety of ways. They like variety and action in a work environment that provides the opportunity for social interaction. Extraverts communicate well and meet people easily. They like to talk while working and are interested in other people and what they are doing. They enjoy variety on the job and like to perform their work in different settings. They learn new tasks by talking with others and trying out new ideas. Extraverts are energized by working as part of a team, leading others in achieving goals, and having opportunities to communicate with others.

Introverts are career specialists who develop in-depth skills. The introvert likes quiet for concentration and likes to focus on a work task until it is completed. They need time to think before taking action. This type often chooses to work alone or with one other person and prefers written communication such as emails to oral communication or presentations. They learn new tasks by reading and reflecting and using mental practice. Introverts are energized when they can work in a quiet environment with few interruptions. They are stressed when they have to work in a noisy environment and do not have time alone to concentrate on a project.

The **sensing** type is realistic and practical and likes to develop standard ways of doing the job and following a routine. They are observant and interested in facts and finding the truth. They keep accurate track of details, make lists, and are good at doing precise work. This type learns from personal experience and the experience of others. They use their experience to move up the job ladder. Sensing types are energized when they are doing practical work with tangible outcomes where they are required to organize facts and details, use common sense, and focus on one project at a time. They are stressed when they have to deal with frequent or unexpected change.

The **intuitive** type likes to work on challenging and complex problems where they can follow their inspirations to find creative solutions. They like change and finding new ways of doing work. This type focuses on the whole picture rather than the details. The intuitive type is an initiator, promoter, and inventor of ideas. They enjoy learning a new skill more than using it. They often change careers to follow their creative inspirations. Intuitive types are energized by working in an environment where they can use creative insight, imagination, originality, and individual initiative. They are stressed when they have to deal with too many details or have little opportunity for creativity.

The **thinking** type likes to use logical analysis in making decisions. They are objective and rational and treat others fairly. They want logical reasons before accepting any new ideas. They follow policy and are often firm-minded and critical, especially when dealing with illogic in others. They easily learn facts, theories, and principles. They are interested in careers with money, prestige, or influence. Thinking types are energized when they are respected for their expertise and recognized for a job well done. They enjoy working with others who are competent and efficient. They become stressed when they work with people they consider to be illogical, unfair, incompetent, or overly emotional.

© cristovao/Shutterstock.com

The **feeling** type likes harmony and the support of co-workers. They are personal, enjoy warm relationships, and relate well to most people. Feeling types know their personal values and apply them consistently. They enjoy doing work that provides a service to people and often do work that requires them to understand and analyze their own emotions and those of others. They prefer a friendly work environment and like to learn with others. They enjoy careers in which they can make a contribution to humanity. Feeling types are energized by working in a friendly, congenial, and supportive work environment. They are stressed when there is conflict in the work environment, especially when working with controlling or demanding people.

The **judging** type likes a work environment that is structured, settled, and organized. They prefer work assignments that are clear and definite. The judging type makes lists and plans to get the job done on time. They make quick decisions and like to have the work finished. They are good at doing purposeful and exacting work. They prefer to learn only the essentials that are necessary to do the job. This type carefully plans their career path. Judging types are energized by working in a predictable and orderly environment with clear responsibilities and deadlines. They become stressed when the work environment becomes disorganized or unpredictable.

> "True greatness is starting where you are, using what you have, and doing what you can."
>
> Arthur Ashe

The **perceptive** type likes to be spontaneous and go with the flow. They are comfortable in handling the unplanned or unexpected in the work environment. They prefer to be flexible in their work and feel restricted by structures and schedules. They are good at handling work which requires change and adaptation. They are tolerant and have a "live and let live" attitude toward others. Decisions are often postponed because this type wants to know all there is to know and explore all the options before making a decision. This type is often a career changer who takes advantage of new job openings and opportunities for change. Perceptive types are energized when the work environment is flexible and they can relax and control their own time. They are stressed when they have to meet deadlines or work under excessive rules and regulations.

More on Personality Type

Personality and Decision Making

Your personality type affects how you think and how you make decisions. Knowing your decision-making style will help you make good decisions about your career and personal life as well as work with others in creative problem solving. Each

© Stephen Coburn/Shutterstock.com

personality type views the decision-making process in a different way. Ideally, a variety of types would be involved in making a decision so that the strengths of each type could be utilized. As you read through the following descriptions, think about your personality type and how you make decisions as well as how others are different.

The **introvert** thinks up ideas and reflects on the problem before acting. The **extravert** acts as the communicator in the decision-making process. Once the decision is made, they take action and implement the decision. The **intuitive** type develops theories and uses intuition to come up with ingenious solutions to the problem. The **sensing** type applies personal experience to the decision-making process and focuses on solutions that are practical and realistic.

The thinking and feeling dimensions of personality are the most important factors in determining how a decision is made. Of course, people use both thinking and feeling in the decision-making process, but tend to prefer or trust either thinking or feeling. Those who prefer **thinking** use cause-and-effect reasoning and solve problems with logic. They use objective and impersonal criteria and include all the consequences of alternative solutions in the decision-making process. They are interested in finding out what is true and what is false. They use laws and principles to treat everyone fairly. Once a decision is made, they are firm-minded, since the decision was based on logic. This type is often critical of those who do not use logic in the decision-making process. The **feeling** type considers human values and motives in the decision-making process (whether they are logical or not) and values harmony and maintaining good relationships. They consider carefully how much they care about each of the alternatives and how they will affect other people. They are interested in making a decision that is agreeable to all parties. Feeling types are tactful and skillful in dealing with people.

It is often asked if thinking types have feelings. They do have feelings, but use them as a criterion to be factored into the decision-making process. Thinking types are more comfortable when feelings are controlled and often think that feeling types are too emotional. Thinking types may have difficulties when they apply logic in a situation where a feeling response is needed, such as in dealing with a spouse. Thinking types need to know that people are important in making decisions. Feeling types need to know that behavior will have logical consequences and that they may need to keep emotions more controlled to work effectively with thinking types.

Judging and **perceptive** types have opposite decision-making strategies. The judging type is very methodical and cautious in making decisions. Once they have gone through the decision-making steps, they like to make decisions quickly so that they can have closure and finish the project. The perceptive type is an adventurer who wants to look at all the possibilities before making a decision. They are open-minded and curious and often resist closure to look at more options.

If a combination of types collaborates on a decision, it is more likely that the decision will be a good one that takes into account creative possibilities, practicality, logical consequences, and human values.

Personality and Time Management

How we manage our time is not just a result of personal habits: it is also a reflection of our personality type. Probably the dimension of personality type most connected to time management is the judging or perceptive trait. **Judging** types like to have things under control and live in a planned and orderly manner. **Perceptive** types prefer more spontaneity and flexibility. Understanding the differences between these two types will help you to better understand yourself and others.

Judging types are naturally good at time management. They often use schedules as a tool for time management and organization. Judging types plan their time and work steadily to accomplish goals. They are good at meeting deadlines and often put off relaxation, recreation, and fun. They relax after projects are completed. If they have too many projects, they find it difficult to find time for recreation. Since judging types like to have projects under control, there is a danger that projects will be completed too quickly and that quality will suffer. Judging types may need to slow down and take the time to do quality work. They may also need to make relaxation and recreation a priority.

Perceptive types are more open-ended and prefer to be spontaneous. They take time to relax, have fun, and participate in recreation. In working on a project, perceptive types want to brainstorm all the possibilities and are not too concerned about finishing projects. This type procrastinates when the time comes to make a final decision and finish a project. There is always more information to gather and more possibilities to explore. Perceptive types are easily distracted and may move from project to project. They may have several jobs going at once. These types need to try to focus on a few projects at a time in order to complete them. Perceptive types need to work on becoming more organized so that projects can be completed on time.

Research has shown that students who are judging types are more likely to have a higher grade point average in the first semester.[1] It has also been found that the greater the preference for intuition, introversion, and judgment, the better the grade point average.[2] Why is this true? Many college professors are intuitive types that use intuition and creative ideas. The college environment requires quiet time for reading and studying, which is one of the preferences of introverts. Academic environments require structure, organization, and completion of assignments. To be successful in an academic environment requires adaptation by some personality types. Extroverts need to spend more quiet time reading and studying. Sensing types need to gain an understanding of intuitive types. Perceptive types need to use organization to complete assignments on time.

© STILLFX/Shutterstock.com

Personality and Money

Does your personality type affect how you deal with money? Otto Kroeger and Janet Thuesen make some interesting observations about how different personality types deal with money.

- **Judging types (orderly and organized).** These types excel at financial planning and money management. They file their tax forms early and pay their bills on time.
- **Perceptive types (spontaneous and flexible).** These types adapt to change and are more creative. Perceivers, especially intuitive perceivers, tend to freak out as the April 15 tax deadline approaches and as bills become due.
- **Feeling types (make decisions based on feelings).** These types are not very money-conscious. They believe that money should be used to serve humanity. They are often attracted to low-paying jobs that serve others.[3]

In studying stockbrokers, these same authors note that ISTJs (introvert, sensing, thinking, and judging types) are the most conservative investors, earning a small but reliable return on investments. The ESTPs (extravert, sensing, thinking, perceptive types) and ENTPs (extravert, intuitive, thinking, perceptive types) take the biggest risks and earn the greatest returns.[4]

Personality and Learning Strategies

Knowing about your personality type can help you to choose learning strategies that work for you.

© Monkey Business Images/Shutterstock.com

- **Extraverts** enjoy interactions with others and like to get to know other people. They learn best by discussing what they have learned with others. Form a study group. Be careful that excess socialization does not distract you from getting your studying done.
- **Introverts** are more quiet and reserved. They enjoy spending time alone to think about what they are studying. Study in the library. Be careful about missing out on the opportunities to share ideas with others.
- **Sensing** types focus on the senses (what they can see, hear, taste, touch, and smell.) These types are good at mastering the facts and details. Improve learning by first focusing on the big picture or broad outline and then the details will be easier to remember.
- **Intuitive** types focus on the big picture and may miss the details. Ask yourself, "What is the main point?" To improve learning, begin by looking at the big picture or broader outline and then organize the facts and details under the main ideas so you can recall them.
- **Thinking** types are good at logic. Make a personal connection with the material by asking yourself, "What do I think of these ideas?" Discuss or debate your ideas with others while remembering to respect their ideas.
- **Feeling** types are motivated by finding personal meaning in their studies. Ask yourself, "How is this material related to my life and what is important to me?" Look for a supportive environment or study group.
- **Judging** types are good at organizing the material to be learned and working steadily to accomplish their goals. Organize the material to be learned into manageable chunks to aid in recall.
- **Perceptive** types are spontaneous, flexible, adaptable, and open to new information. Pay attention to organizing your work and meeting deadlines to improve success in college and on the job. Be careful not to overextend yourself by working on too many projects at once.

Understanding Your Professor's Personality

© Alexander Raths/Shutterstock.com

Different personality types have different expectations of teachers.

- Extraverts want faculty who encourage class discussion.
- Introverts want faculty who give clear lectures.
- Sensing types want faculty who give clear and specific assignments.
- Intuitive types want faculty who encourage independent thinking.
- Thinking types want faculty who make logical presentations.
- Feeling types want faculty who establish personal rapport with students.
- Judging types want faculty to be organized.
- Perceptive types want faculty to be entertaining and inspiring.

College students and faculty often have different personality types. In summary,

College faculty tend to be	College students tend to be
Introverted	Extraverted
Intuitive	Sensing
Judging	Perceptive

Of course, the above is not always true, but there is a good probability that you will have college professors who are very different from you. What can you do if you and your professor have different personality types? First, try to understand the professor's personality. This has been called "psyching out the professor." You can usually tell the professor's personality type on the first day of class by examining class materials and observing his or her manner of presentation. If you understand the professor's personality type, you will know what to expect. Next, try to appreciate what the professor has to offer. You may need to adapt your expectations to be successful. For example, if you are an introvert, make an effort to participate in class discussions. If you are a perceptive type, be careful to meet the due dates of your assignments.

> **Journal Entry #5**
>
> Write a paragraph about how your personality type influences any of the following: preferred work environment, decision making, time management, money management, learning, and meeting the expectations of your professor.

Exploring Your Personal Strengths

Another way to explore your personal strengths is by understanding your multiple intelligences. **Multiple intelligences are defined as the human ability to solve problems or design or compose something valued in at least one culture**. A key idea in this theory is that most people can develop all of their intelligences and become relatively competent in each area. Another key idea is that these intelligences work together in complex ways to make us unique. Take the MI Advantage which is included in your online portfolio to see how your personal strengths can be connected to careers. Here is a summary of multiple intelligences:

- **Musical intelligence** involves hearing and remembering musical patterns and manipulating patterns in music. Related careers include musician, performer, composer, and music critic.
- **Interpersonal intelligence** is defined as understanding people. Related careers involve working with people and helping them, as in education or health care.
- **Logical-mathematical intelligence** involves understanding abstract principles and manipulating numbers, quantities, and operations. Related careers include mathematician, tax accountant, scientist, and computer programmer.
- **Spatial intelligence** involves the ability to manipulate objects in space. For example, a baseball player uses spatial intelligence to hit a ball. Related occupations include pilot, painter, sculptor, architect, inventor, and surgeon. This intelligence is often used in athletics, the arts, and the sciences.
- **Bodily-kinesthetic intelligence** is defined as being able to use your body to solve problems. People with this intelligence make or invent objects or perform. Related occupations include athlete, performer (dancer, actor), craftsperson, sculptor, mechanic, and surgeon.
- **Linguistic intelligence** describes people who are good with language and words. They have good reading, writing, and speaking skills. Linguistic intelligence is an asset in any occupation. Specific related careers include writing, education, and politics.
- **Intrapersonal intelligence** is the ability to understand yourself and how to best use your natural talents and abilities. Related careers include novelist, psychologist, or being self-employed.
- **Naturalist intelligence** includes people who are able to recognize, classify, and analyze plants, animals, and cultural artifacts. Related occupations include botanist, horticulturist, biologist, archeologist and environmental occupations.
- **Existential intelligence** is the capacity to ask profound questions about the meaning of life and death. This intelligence is the cornerstone of art, religion, and philosophy. Related occupations include philosopher, psychologist, and artist.

Other Factors in Choosing a Major

Once you have completed a thorough self-assessment, you may still have several majors to consider. At this point, it is important to do some research on the outlook for a selected career in the future and the pay you would receive. Sometimes students are disappointed after graduation when they find there are few job opportunities in their chosen career field. Sometimes students graduate and cannot find jobs with the salary they had hoped to earn. It is important to think about the opportunities you will have in the future. If you have several options for a career you would enjoy, you may want to consider seriously the career that has the best outlook and pay.

According to the Bureau of Labor Statistics, fields with the best outlook include health care, computers, and the new "green jobs" related to preserving the environment. The top-paying careers all require math skills and include the science, engineering, computer science, health care, and business fields. Only 4% of college graduates choose the engineering and computer science fields. Since there are fewer students in these majors, the salaries are higher. If you have a talent or interest in math, you can develop this skill and use it in high-paying careers.

> "Choose a job you love, and you will never have to work a day in your life."
> Confucius

© Maryna Pleshkun/Shutterstock.com

Majors with the Highest Earnings for Bachelor's Degrees 2015*[5]

College Major	Beginning Median Salary	Mid-Career Median Salary
Petroleum Engineering	103,000	160,000
Chemical Engineering	69,600	116,700
Nuclear Engineering	67,000	118,800
Computer Science	66,700	112,600
Electrical and Computer Engineering	66,500	113,000
Electrical Engineering	65,900	107,900
Materials Science and Engineering	64,000	99,700
Mechanical Engineering	62,100	101,600
Industrial Engineering	61,900	97,200
Software Engineering	1,700	99,800
Biomedical Engineering	9,600	92,200
Physics	57,200	105,100

(continued)

Exploring Your Personality and Major

Architectural Engineering	57,000	90,400
Business and Information Technology	56,900	99,100
Nursing	56,900	73,600
Civil Engineering	55,100	93,400
Statistics	54,900	103,100
Applied Mathematics	54,300	96,500
Construction Management	54,000	89,600
Information Security	53,400	85,800
Economics	51,400	97,700
Finance	50,900	89,300

*Includes bachelor's degrees only. Excludes medicine, law, and careers requiring advanced degrees.

Other Common Majors and Earnings for Bachelor's Degrees 2015*[6]

College Major	Beginning Median Salary	Mid-Career Median Salary
Marketing and Communications	41,000	81,100
Political Science	42,800	78,500
Architecture	42,600	77,000
Accounting	46,500	76,300
Business Administration	45,500	73,100
History	40,500	72,300
Biology	40,000	72,000
Health Sciences	38,300	71,200
Forestry	40,700	70,900
Journalism	39,000	71,300
Geography	41,500	70,200
Public Administration	40,000	68,500
English	39,300	64,600
Humanities	39,700	61,100
Psychology	37,300	61,800
Liberal Arts	37,000	59,400
Fashion Merchandising	40,000	60,100
Art History	39,100	64,800
Criminal Justice	35,900	58,800
Fine Arts	38,500	57,600
Education	38,100	54,600
Music	37,500	55,400
Hotel Management	42,500	73,200

*Includes bachelor's degrees only. Excludes medicine, law, and careers requiring advanced degrees.

© Anson0618/Shutterstock.com

Top Majors That Change the World*[7]

College Major	Beginning Median Salary	Mid-Career Median Salary
Pastoral Ministry	36,300	46,000
Nursing	56,900	73,600
Clinical Lab Science	48,000	59,900
Child Development	32,200	36,400
Athletic Training	35,000	45,900
Early Childhood Education	32,300	40,400
Sports Medicine	37,300	62,700
Medical Technology	47,800	60,200
Special Education	34,500	46,800
Therapeutic Recreation	34,500	46,900
Biblical Studies	34,900	48,500
Human Services	33,800	41,300
Social Work	38,600	60,300
Theology	36,800	51,600
Elementary Education	33,600	45,500
Child and Family Studies	31,200	38,600
Dietetics	44,000	59,100
Exercise Science	34,400	53,400

*Based on an extensive survey by Payscale.com asking college graduates with a bachelor's degree, "Does your work make the world a better place to live?"

"We act as though comfort and luxury were the chief requirements of life, when all that we need to make us really happy is something to be enthusiastic about."
Charles Kingsley

"Only passions, great passions, can elevate the soul to great things."
Denis Diderot

Every career counselor can tell stories about students who ask, "What is the career that makes the most money? That's the career I want!" However, if you choose a career based on money alone, you might find it difficult and uninteresting for a lifetime of work. You might even find yourself retraining later in life for a job that you really enjoy. Remember that the first step is to figure out who you are and what you like. Then look at career outlook and opportunity. If you find your passion in a career that is in demand and pays well, you will probably be very happy with your career choice. If you find your passion in a career that offers few jobs and does not pay well, you will have to use your ingenuity to find a job and make a living. Many students happily make this informed choice and find a way to make it work.

© iQoncept/Shutterstock.com

KEYS TO SUCCESS

© lculig/Shutterstock.com

Mark Twain said, "The secret of success is making your vocation your vacation." Find what you like to do. Better yet, find your passion. If you can find your passion, it is easy to invest the time and effort necessary to be successful.

How do you know when you have found your passion? You have found your passion when you are doing an activity and you do not notice that the time is passing. The great painter Picasso often talked about how quickly time passed while he was painting. He said, "When I work, I relax; doing nothing or entertaining visitors makes me tired." Whether you are an artist, an athlete, a scientist, or a business entrepreneur, passion provides the energy needed to be successful. It helps you to grow and create. When you are using your talents to grow and create, you can find meaning and happiness in your life.

Psychologist Martin Seligman has written a book entitled *Authentic Happiness,* in which he writes about three types of work orientation: a job, a career, and a calling.[8] A job is what you do for the paycheck at the end of the week. Many college students have jobs to earn money for college. A career has deeper personal meaning. It involves achievement, prestige, and power. A calling is defined as "a passionate commitment to work for its own sake."[9] When you have found your calling, the job itself is the reward. He notes that people who have found their calling are consistently happier than those who have a job or even a career. One of the ways that you know you have found your calling is when you are in the state of "flow." The state of "flow" is defined as "complete absorption in an activity whose challenges mesh perfectly with your abilities."[10] People who experience "flow" are happier and more productive. They do not spend their days looking forward to Friday. Understanding your personal strengths is the beginning step to finding your calling.

Seligman adds that any job can become a calling if you use your personal strengths to do the best possible job. He cited a study of hospital cleaners. Although some viewed their job as drudgery, others viewed the job as a calling. They believed that they helped patients get better by working efficiently and anticipating the needs of doctors and nurses. They rearranged furniture and decorated walls to help patients feel better. They found their calling by applying their personal talents to their jobs. As a result, their jobs became a calling.

Sometimes we wait around for passion to find us. That probably won't happen. The first step in finding your passion is to know yourself. Then find an occupation in which you can use your talents. You may be able to find your passion by looking at your present job and finding a creative way to do it based on your special talents. It has been said that there are no dead-end jobs, just people who cannot see the possibilities. Begin your search for passion by looking at your personal strengths and how you can apply them in the job market. If the job that you have now is not your passion, see what you can learn from it and then use your skills to find a career where you are more likely to find your passion.

> "Success is not the key to happiness; happiness is the key to success. If you love what you are doing, you will be successful."
> Anonymous

Appreciating Island Cultures: Tattoos

Tattooing is a traditional Pacific Island art form that is becoming increasingly popular throughout the world. The word "tattoo" comes from the Polynesian word "tatau." On Captain Cook's voyage to the Pacific Islands, his artist, John Webber sketched the tattoos of Indigenous people and introduced the art to Europe.

Tattoos are a way of wearing your life story on your skin. Tattoos could be used to denote occupational roles. For example, healers and Hula dancers have tattoos on their hands and wrists. Tattoos are an art form often connected to personal identity. They can be used for important milestones or to commemorate someone important to your life. Below is a Samoan story about the early origins of the tattoo:

Taema and Tilafaigā were Siamese twin sisters from Samoa who were joined together at the spine. One day, they decided to swim across the deep sea. Suddenly, a storm began. During the storm, a canoe mast struck them violently, separating them at the spine.

Aerial view of Fiji Islands. © Niko Nomad/Shutterstock.com

Pago, American Samoa. Camel Rock near the village of Lauli'i.
© Sorin Colac/Shutterstock.com

As they swam looking for help, they eventually found themselves in Fiji where they came across people who took them in and taught them the art of the tatau (tattoo). While they learned that art, they were even taught a song to chant or sing while they created tatau. The tatau were for women ONLY. For men to have a tatau at that time was not allowed. The chant said "Only women receive tattoos, not men."

The sisters begin their journey back to Samoa carrying their baskets filled with things to create their tatau and share this new-found art with their people. As they arrived at the coast of Falealupo, the sisters spotted a giant clam with magical powers. Putting them in a trance and confusing them as they swam, the chant was reversed saying "Only men receive tattoos, not women." As they swam home, this is what they chanted. After they left the clam, they were confused, forgetting which chant they learned in Fiji, so it became "Both men AND women receive tatau."

Today, the women of Samoa wear the "Malu tatau" and the men of Samoa wear the "Malofie tatau" better known today as the "Pe'a."

Questions

1. What was an obstacle that Taema and Tilafaigā faced?
2. How did they overcome that obstacle?
3. On their journey, they learned a new skill. What was that skill?
4. What are some skills that you have learned or improved on your educational, professional, or personal journey that have helped you get to where you are today?
5. What are the next steps you can take to improve your skills?
6. In this chapter, you learned about your personality, strengths, and talents. Could you write at least one sentence to describe your identity?

Tatau: tattoo
Malu: The type of tattoo Samoan women wear
Pe'a: The type of tattoo Samoan men wear

© Lyudmyla Kharlamova/Shutterstock.com

College Success 1

The College Success 1 website is continually updated with supplementary material for each chapter including Word documents of the journal entries, classroom activities, handouts, videos, links to related materials, and much more. See http://www.collegesuccess1.com/.

Notes

1. Judith Provost and Scott Anchors, eds., *Applications of the Myers-Briggs Type Indicator In Higher Education* (Palo Alto, CA: Consulting Psychologists Press, 1991), 51.
2. Ibid., 49.
3. Otto Kroeger and Janet Thuesen, *Type Talk: The 16 Personality Types That Determine How We Live, Love and Work* (New York: Dell, 1989), 204.
4. Ibid.
5. 2. Payscale, "2014–15 College Salary Report," from http://www.payscale.com/college-salary-report/majors-that-pay-you-back/bachelors, accessed July 2015.
6. Ibid.
7. Ibid.
8. Martin Seligman, Authentic Happiness (Free Press, 2002).
9. Martin Seligman, as reported by Geoffrey Cowley, "The Science of Happiness," *Newsweek*, September 16, 2002, 49.
10. Ibid.

Personality Preferences

Name _____ Date _____

Use the textbook and personality assessment to think about your personality type. Place an X on the scale to show your degree of preference for each dimension of personality.

Introvert _____|_____ Extravert

Sensing _____|_____ INtuitive

Thinking _____|_____ Feeling

Judging _____|_____ Perceptive

Write a key word or phrase to describe each preference.

Introvert

Extravert

Sensing

INtuitive

Thinking

Feeling

Judging

Perceptive

What careers are suggested by your personality assessment?

Was the personality assessment accurate and useful to you?

Talkers and Listeners

Name _____ Date _____

In the classroom, talkers (extroverts) volunteer to speak and do so frequently. Listeners (introverts) are people who prefer to stay quiet and rarely join in on the discussions. Even though you may prefer talking or listening, it is best to develop both of these skills. Decide whether you are generally a talker or a listener and answer the following questions. Your instructor may want to do this as a group activity in the classroom.

Talkers

1. What made me a talker?

2. How can I develop my listening skills?

3. How can I help listeners talk more?

Listeners

1. What made me a listener?

2. How can I develop my talking skills?

3. How can I help talkers listen more?

Exploring Your Personality and Major

Personality Scenarios

Name _____   Date _____

Read the chapter on personality before commenting on these scenarios. Keep in mind the theory that we are all born with certain personality types and there are no good or bad types. Each type has gifts and talents that can be used to be a successful and happy person. Relate your comments to the concepts in this chapter. Your instructor may have you do this exercise as a group activity in class.

Scenario 1 (Sensing vs. Intuitive): Julie is a preschool teacher. She assigns her class to draw a picture of a bicycle. Students share their pictures with the class. One of the students has drawn a bicycle with wings. Another student laughs at the drawing and says, "Bicycles don't have wings!" How should the teacher handle this situation?

Scenario 2 (Thinking vs. Feeling): John has the almost perfect girlfriend. She is beautiful, intelligent, and fun to be with. She only has one flaw: John thinks that she is too emotional and wishes she could be a little more rational. When his girlfriend tries to talk to him about emotional issues, he analyzes her problems and proposes a logical solution. His girlfriend doesn't like the solutions that John proposes. Should John find a new girlfriend?

Scenario 3 (Introvert vs. Extravert): Mary is the mother of two children, ages five (daughter) and eight (son). The five-year-old is very social and especially enjoys birthday parties. At the last party, she invited 24 girls and they all showed up at the party. Everyone had a great time. The eight-year-old is very quiet and spends his time reading, doing artwork, building models, and hanging out with his one best friend. Mary is concerned that her son does not have very many friends. She decides to have a birthday party for her son also. The only problem is that he cannot come up with a list of children to invite to the party. What should Mary do?

Scenario 4 (Judging vs. Perceptive): Jerry and Jennifer have just been married, and they love each other very much. Jennifer likes to keep the house neat and orderly and likes to plan out activities so that there are no surprises. Jerry likes creative disorder. He leaves his things all over the house. He often comes up with creative ideas for having fun. How can Jerry and Jennifer keep their good relationship going?

Multiple Intelligences Matching Quiz

Name _____   Date _____

Directions: Match the person with the intelligence at the right:

____Michael Jordan   A. Musical: hearing and remembering musical patterns

____Aristotle   B. Interpersonal: understanding other people

____Martin Luther King, Jr. C. Mathematical: working with numbers

____Sigmund Freud   D. Spatial: manipulating objects in space

____William Shakespeare   E. Bodily-Kinesthetic: using your body

____Albert Einstein   F. Linguistic: using language

____William James "will.i.am" G. Intrapersonal: understanding yourself

____Charles Darwin   H. Naturalist: understanding the environment

____George Lucas   I. Existential: pondering the meaning of life and our place in the universe

Work with other students in a group to give examples of other famous person's in these categories.

Musical

Interpersonal

Mathematical

Spatial

Bodily Kinesthetic

Linguistic

Intrapersonal

Naturalist

Existential

CHAPTER 4

Managing Time and Money

Learning Objectives

Read to answer these key questions:

- What are my lifetime goals?
- How can I manage my time to accomplish my goals?
- How much time do I need for study and work?
- How can I make an effective schedule?
- What are some time management tricks?
- How can I deal with procrastination?
- How can I manage my money to accomplish my financial goals?
- What are some ways to save money?
- How can I pay for my education?
- How can I use priorities to manage my time?

From *College & Career Success, Concise Version*, Seventh Edition, by Marsha Fralick. Copyright © 2016 by Kendall Hunt Publishing Company. Reprinted by permission.

Success in college requires that you manage both time and money. You will need time to study and money to pay for your education. The first step in managing time and money is to think about the goals that you wish to accomplish in your life. Having goals that are important to you provides a reason and motivation for managing time and money. This chapter provides some useful techniques for managing time and money so that you can accomplish the goals you have set for yourself.

What Are My Lifetime Goals?

Setting goals helps you to establish what is important and provides direction for your life. Goals help you to focus your energy on what you want to accomplish. Goals are a promise to yourself to improve your life. Setting goals can help you turn your dreams into reality. Steven Scott, in his book *A Millionaire's Notebook,* lays out five steps in this process:

1. Dream or visualize.
2. Convert the dream into goals.
3. Convert your goals into tasks.
4. Convert your task into steps.
5. Take your first step, and then the next.[1]

As you begin to think about your personal goals in life, make your goals specific and concrete. Rather than saying, "I want to be rich," make your goal something that you can break into specific steps. You might want to start learning about money management or begin a savings plan. Rather than setting a goal for happiness, think about what brings you happiness. If you want to live a long and healthy life, think about the health habits that will help you to accomplish your goal. You will need to break your goals down into specific tasks to be able to accomplish them.

© winui/Shutterstock.com

Here are some criteria for successful goal setting:

1. **Is it specific and measurable?** Can it be counted or observed? The most common goal mentioned by students is happiness in life. What is happiness, and how will you know when you have achieved it? Is happiness a career you enjoy, owning your own home, or a travel destination?

2. **Is it achievable?** Do you have the skills, abilities, and resources to accomplish this goal? If not, are you willing to spend the time to develop the skills, abilities, and resources needed to achieve this goal?
3. **Is it realistic?** Do you believe that you can achieve it? Are you positive and optimistic about this goal?
4. **Is it timely?** When will you finish this goal? Set a date to accomplish your goal.
5. **What steps do you need to take to begin?** Are you willing to take action to start working on it?
6. **Do you want to do it?** Is this a goal you are choosing because it provides personal satisfaction, rather than meeting a requirement or expectation of someone else?
7. **Are you motivated to achieve it?** What are your rewards for achieving it?
8. **Does the goal match your values?** Is it important to you?

> "A goal is a dream with a deadline."
> Napoleon Hill

Journal Entry #1

Write a paragraph about your lifetime goals. Use any of these questions to guide your thinking:

- What is your career goal? If you do not know what your career goal is, describe your preferred work environment. Would your ideal career require a college degree?
- What are your family goals? Are you interested in marriage and family? What would be your important family values?
- What are your social goals (friends, community, and recreation)?
- When you are older and look back on your life, what are the three most important life goals that you want to have accomplished?

A Goal or a Fantasy?

One of the best questions ever asked in my class was, "What is the difference between a goal and a fantasy?" As you look at your list of lifetime goals, are some of these items goals or fantasies? Think about this question as you read the following scenario:

When Linda was a college student, she was walking through the parking lot, noticed a beautiful red sports car, and decided that it would become a lifetime goal for her to own a similar car one day. However, with college expenses and her part-time job, it was not possible to buy the car. She would have to be content with the used car that her dad had given her so that she could drive to college. Years passed by, and Linda now has a good job, a home, and a family. She is reading a magazine and sees a picture of a similar red sports car. She cuts out this picture and tapes it to the refrigerator. After it has been on the refrigerator for several months, her children ask her why the picture is on the refrigerator. Linda replies, "I just like to dream about owning this car." One day, as Linda is driving past a car dealership, she sees the red sports car on display and stops in for a test drive. To her surprise, she decides that she does not like driving the car. It doesn't fit her lifestyle, either. She enjoys outdoor activities that would require a larger car. Buying a second car would be costly and reduce the amount of money that the family could spend on vacations. She decides that vacations are more important than owning the sports car. Linda goes home and removes the picture of the red sports car from the refrigerator.

© Natursports/Shutterstock.com

"Vision without action is a daydream. Action without vision is a nightmare."
Japanese Proverb

"In life, as in football, you won't go far unless you know where the goalposts are."
Arnold Glasgow

There are many differences between a goal and a fantasy. A fantasy is a dream that may or may not become a reality. A goal is something that we actually plan to achieve. Sometimes we begin with a fantasy and later it becomes a goal. A fantasy can become a goal if steps are taken to achieve it. In the preceding example, the sports car is a fantasy until Linda actually takes the car for a test drive. After driving the car, she decides that she really does not want it. The fantasy is sometimes better than the reality. Goals and fantasies change over a lifetime. We set goals, try them out, and change them as we grow and mature and find out what is most important in life. Knowing what we think is important, and what we value most, helps us make good decisions about lifetime goals.

What is the difference between a goal and a fantasy? **A goal is something that requires action.** Ask yourself if you are willing to take action on the goals you have set for yourself. Begin to take action by thinking about the steps needed to accomplish the goal. Then take the first step and continue. Change your goals if they are no longer important to you.

Journal Entry #2

Write a paragraph about how you will accomplish one of your important lifetime goals. Start your paragraph by stating an important goal from the previous journal entry. What is the first step in accomplishing this goal? Next, list some additional steps needed to accomplish it. How can you motivate yourself to begin taking these steps?

For example:

One of my important lifetime goals is _____. The first step in accomplishing this goal is . . . Some additional steps are . . . I can motivate myself to accomplish this goal by . . .

The ABCs of Time Management

Using the **ABCs of time management** is a way of thinking about priorities. Priorities are what you think is important. An **A priority** is a task that relates to your lifetime goal. For example, if my goal is to earn a college degree, studying becomes an A priority. This activity would become one of the most important tasks that I could accomplish today. If my goal is to be healthy, an A priority would be to exercise and plan a healthy diet. If my goal is to have a good family life, an A priority would be to spend time with family members. Knowing about your lifetime goals and spending time on those items that are most important to you will help you to accomplish the goals that you have set for yourself. If you do not spend time on your goals, you may want to look at them again and decide which ones are fantasies that you do not really value or want to accomplish.

A **B priority** is an activity that you have to do, but that is not directly related to your lifetime goal. Examples of B priorities might be getting out of bed, taking a shower, buying groceries, paying bills, or getting gas for the car. These activities are less important, but still are necessary for survival. If I do not put gas in the car, I cannot even get to school or work. If I do not pay the bills, I will soon have financial difficulties. While we often cannot postpone these activities in order to accomplish lifetime goals, we can learn efficient time management techniques to accomplish these tasks quickly.

A **C priority** is something that I can postpone until tomorrow with no harmful effect. For example, I could wait until tomorrow or another day to wash my car, do the laundry, buy groceries, or organize my desk. As these items are postponed, however, they can move up the list to a B priority. If I cannot see out of my car window or have no clean clothes to wear, it is time to move these tasks up on my list of priorities.

Have you ever been a victim of "**C fever**"? This is an illness in which we do the C activities first and do not get around to doing the A activities that are connected to lifetime goals. Tasks required to accomplish lifetime goals are often ones that are more difficult, challenge our abilities, and take some time to accomplish. These tasks are often more difficult than the B or C activities. The C activities can fill our time and exhaust the energy we need to accomplish the A activities. An example of C fever is the student who cleans the desk or organizes the DVD collection instead of studying. C fever is doing the endless tasks that keep us from accomplishing goals that are really important to us. Why do we fall victim to C fever? C activities are often easy to do and give us a sense of accomplishment. We can see immediate progress without too much effort. I can wash my car and get a sense of accomplishment and satisfaction in my shiny clean car. The task is easy and does not challenge my intellectual capabilities.

© iQoncept/Shutterstock.com

ACTIVITY

Setting Priorities

To see how the ABCs of time management work, read the profile of Justin, a typical college student, below.

Justin is a 19-year-old college student who plans to major in physical therapy. He is athletic and values his good health. He cares about people and likes helping others. He has a part-time job working as an assistant in the gym, where he monitors proper use of the weightlifting machines. Justin is also a member of the soccer team and practices with the team every afternoon.

Here is a list of activities that Justin would like to do today. Label each task as follows:

A if it relates to Justin's lifetime goals
B if it is something necessary to do
C if it is something that could be done tomorrow or later

_____ Get up, shower, get dressed

_____ Eat breakfast

_____ Go to work

_____ Go to class

_____ Visit with friends between classes

_____ Buy a new battery for his watch

_____ Go shopping for new gym shoes

_____ Attend soccer practice

_____ Do weightlifting exercises

_____ Study for biology test that is tomorrow

_____ Meet friends for pizza at lunch

_____ Call girlfriend

_____ Eat dinner

_____ Unpack gear from weekend camping trip

_____ Watch football game on TV

_____ Play video games

_____ Do math homework

While Justin is the only one who can decide how to spend his time, he can take some steps toward accomplishing his lifetime goal of being healthy by eating properly, exercising, and going to soccer practice. He can become a physical therapist by studying for the biology test and doing his math homework. He can gain valuable experience related to physical therapy by working in the gym. He cares about people and likes to maintain good relationships with others. Any tasks related to these goals are high-priority A activities.

What other activities are necessary B activities? He certainly needs to get up, shower, and get dressed. What are the C activities that could be postponed until tomorrow or later? Again, Justin needs to decide. Maybe he could postpone shopping for a new watch battery and gym shoes until the weekend. He would have to decide how much time to spend visiting with friends, watching TV, or playing video games. Since he likes these activities, he could use them as rewards for studying for the biology test and doing his math homework.

How to Estimate Study and Work Time

Students are often surprised at the amount of time necessary for study to be successful in college. A general rule is that you need to study two hours for every hour spent in a college class. A typical weekly schedule of a full-time student would look like this:

Typical College Schedule

> 15 hours of attending class
> +30 hours of reading, studying, and preparation
> 45 hours total

A full-time job involves working 40 hours a week. A full-time college student spends 45 hours or more attending classes and studying. Some students will need more than 45 hours a week if they are taking lab classes, need help with study and learning skills, or are taking a heavy course load.

Some students try to work full-time and go to school full-time. While some are successful, this schedule is extremely difficult.

The Nearly Impossible Schedule

> 15 hours attending class
> 30 hours studying
> +40 hours working
> 85 hours total

This schedule is the equivalent of having two full-time jobs! Working full-time makes it very difficult to find the time necessary to study for classes. Lack of study causes students to do poorly on exams and to doubt their abilities. Such a schedule causes stress and fatigue that make studying difficult. Increased stress can also lead to problems with personal relationships and emotional problems. These are all things that lead to dropping out of college.

Many students today work and go to college. Working during college can provide some valuable experience that will help you to find a job when you finish college. Working can teach you to manage your time efficiently and give you a feeling of independence and control over your own future. Many people need to work to pay for their education. A general guideline is to work no more than 20 hours a week if you plan to attend college full-time. Here is a workable schedule.

Part-Time Work Schedule

> 12 hours attending class
> 24 hours studying
> +20 hours working
> 56 hours total

A commitment of 56 hours a week is like having a full-time job and a part-time job. While this schedule takes extra energy and commitment, many students are successful with it. Notice that the course load is reduced to 12 hours. This schedule involves taking one less class per semester. The class missed can be made up in summer school, or the time needed to graduate can be extended. Many students take five years to earn the bachelor's degree because they work part-time. It is better to take longer to graduate than to give up because of frustration and drop out of college. If you must work full-time, consider reducing your course load to one or two courses. You will gradually reach your goal of a college degree.

> "The key is not to prioritize what's on the schedule, but to schedule your priorities."
> Stephen Covey
>
> "When you do the things you have to do when you have to do them, the day will come when you can do the things you want to do when you want to do them."
> Zig Ziglar

Part-Time Student Schedule

  6 hours attending class
 12 hours studying
 +40 hours working
 58 hours total

Add up the number of hours you are attending classes, double this figure for study time, and add to it your work time, as in the above examples. How many hours of commitment do you have? Can you be successful with your current level of commitment to school, work, and study?

To begin managing your schedule, use the weekly calendar located at the end of this chapter to write in your scheduled activities such as work, class times, and athletics.

> "The bad news is time flies. The good news is you're the pilot."
> Michael Althsuler

Schedule Your Success

What Is Your Chronotype?

It is interesting that scientists describe different time preferences or chronotypes as larks, owls, or hummingbirds.[2] Understanding your chronotype is important in scheduling your learning at a time when you can learn most efficiently and use the rest of the time for less important tasks.

- Larks like to get up and go to bed early. They are most alert during the day with productivity peaking about two hours before noon. If you are a lark or morning person, schedule your classes and study time for the morning.
- Owls prefer to get up and go to bed late. They are most productive around 6 pm. If you are an owl or evening person, schedule your classes and study time for later in the day or evening.
- Humming birds are combination types that tend to be more like larks or owls, or somewhere in between.

Another way to describe time of day preference is your prime time. Use your prime time for studying and you will accomplish more in less time.

Researchers have found that night owls often have lower GPAs because they are frequently sleep deprived. Did you know that sleep deprivation can reduce your intelligence, cause weight gain, and accelerate the aging process? Healthy 30-year-olds who slept for only four hours a night for six days had the body chemistry of a 60-year-old.[3] Loss of sleep interferes with attention, memory, mathematical skills, logical reasoning, and manual dexterity. If you are a night owl, consider changing your sleeping pattern to make sure you get enough sleep. This change will be helpful in your career after college. Here are some suggestions for getting more sleep:

Avoid

- Staying up all night or late in the night to study.
- Alcohol, nicotine, exercise, or food late in the evening. Note that alcohol initially makes you sleepy, but it interferes with sleep later in the night.

Do this

- Relax before bedtime by reading a good book or listening to soft music.
- Have a regular pattern of sleep. Go to bed at the same time each evening and get up at the same time each morning.
- Get some exercise every day so that you feel tired at night.

Using a Schedule

If you have not used a schedule in the past, consider trying a schedule for a couple of weeks to see if it is helpful in completing tasks and working toward your lifetime goals. There are several advantages to using a schedule:

- It gets you started on your work.
- It helps you avoid procrastination.
- It relieves pressure because you have things under control.
- It frees the mind of details.
- It helps you find time to study.
- It eliminates the panic caused by doing things at the last minute.
- It helps you find time for recreation and exercise.

Once you have made a master schedule that includes classes, work, and other activities, you will see that you have some blanks that provide opportunities for using your time productively. Here are some ideas for making the most of your schedule:

1. Fill in your study times. Use the time immediately before class for previewing and the time immediately after class for reviewing. Remember that you need to study two hours or more for each hour spent in a college class.

© Caroline Eibl/Shutterstock.com

2. Break large projects such as a term paper or studying for a test into small tasks and begin early. Double your time estimates for completion of the project. Larger projects often take longer than you think. If you finish early, use the extra time for something fun.

> "The only thing even in this world is the number of hours in a day. The difference in winning or losing is what you do with these hours."
> Woody Hayes

3. Set priorities. Make sure you include activities related to your lifetime goals.

4. Allow time for sleep and meals. It is easier to study if you are well rested and have good eating habits.

5. Schedule your time in manageable blocks of an hour or two. Having every moment scheduled leads to frustration when plans change.

6. Leave some time unscheduled to use as a shock absorber. You will need unscheduled time to relax and to deal with unexpected events.

7. Leave time for recreation, exercise, and fun.

See the weekly study schedule form at the end of this chapter.

If You Dislike Schedules

© iQoncept/Shutterstock.com

Some personality types like more freedom and do not like the structure that a schedule provides. There are alternatives for those who do not like to use a schedule. Here are some additional ideas.

1. A simple and fast way to organize your time is to use a to-do list. Take an index card or small piece of paper and simply write a list of what you need to do during the day. You can prioritize the list by putting an A or star by the most important items. Cross items off the list as you accomplish them. A list helps you focus on what is important and serves as a reminder not to forget certain tasks.

2. Another idea is to use monthly or yearly calendars to write down important events, tasks, and deadlines. Use these calendars to note the first day of school, when important assignments are due, vacations, and final exams. Place the calendars in a place where they are easily seen.

3. Use this simple question to keep you on track, "What is the best use of my time right now?"[4] This question works well if you keep in mind your goals and priorities.

4. Use reminders and sticky notes to keep on track and to remind yourself of what needs to be done each day. Place the notes in a place where you will see them, such as your computer, the bathroom mirror, or the dashboard of your car.

5. Some families use their refrigerators as time management devices. Use the refrigerator to post your calendars, reminders, goals, tasks, and to-do lists. You will see these reminders every time you open the refrigerator.

6. Invent your own unique ideas for managing time. Anything will work if it helps to accomplish your goals.

Manage Your Time with a Web Application

There are thousands of new web applications available to organize your life. You can use a web application on your phone, laptop, computer, or other mobile device to:

- Create a to-do list or schedule.
- Send reminders when assignments are due.
- Organize your calendar and plan your tasks.
- Organize your study time and plan assignments.
- Avoid procrastination.
- Create a virtual assistant to keep you organized.

QUIZ

Time Management, Part I

Test what you have learned by selecting the correct answers to the following questions.

1. The most important difference between a goal and a fantasy is
   a. imagination.
   b. procrastination.
   c. action.

2. An A priority is
   a. related to your lifetime goals.
   b. something important.
   c. something you have to do.

3. A general rule for college success is that you must spend ___ hours studying for every hour spent in a college class.
   a. one
   b. four
   c. two

4. For a workable study schedule,
   a. fill in all the blank time slots.
   b. leave some unscheduled time to deal with the unexpected.
   c. plan to study late at night.

5. To complete a large project such as a term paper,
   a. break the project into small tasks and begin early.
   b. schedule large blocks of time the day before the paper is due.
   c. leave time for exercise, recreation, and fun before beginning on the project.

How did you do on the quiz? Check your answers: 1. c, 2. a, 3. c, 4. b, 5. a

Time Management Tricks

Life is full of demands for work, study, family, friends, and recreation. Time management tricks can help you get started on the important tasks and make the most of your time. Try the following techniques when you are feeling frustrated and overwhelmed.

> **Time Management Tricks**
>
> - Divide and conquer
> - Do the first small step
> - 80/20 rule
> - Aim for excellence, not perfection
> - Make learning fun
> - Take a break
> - Study in the library
> - Learn to say no

Divide and Conquer

When large tasks seem overwhelming, think of the small tasks needed to complete the project and start on the first step. For example, suppose you have to write a term paper. You have to take out a paper and pencil, log onto your computer, brainstorm some ideas, go to the library to find information, think about your main ideas, and write the first sentence. Each of these steps is manageable. It's looking at the entire project that can be intimidating.

I once set out hiking on a mountain trail. When I got to the top of the mountain and looked down, I enjoyed a spectacular view and was amazed at how high I had climbed. If I had thought about how high the mountain was, I might not have attempted the hike. I climbed the mountain by taking it one step at a time. That's the secret to completing any large project: break it into small, manageable parts, then take the first step and keep going.

Learning a small part at a time is also easy and helps with motivation for learning. While in college, carry around some material that you need to study. Take advantage of five or ten minutes of time to study a small part of your material. In this way you make good use of your time and enhance memory by using distributed practice. Don't wait until you have large blocks of uninterrupted study time to begin your studies. You may not have the luxury of large blocks of time, or you may want to spend that time in other ways.

© iQoncept/Shutterstock.com

Do the First Small Step

The most difficult step in completing any project is the first step. If you have a challenging project to do, think of a small first step and complete that small step. Make the first step something that you can accomplish easily and in a short amount of time. Give yourself permission to stop after the first step. However, you may find that you are motivated to continue with the project. If you have a term paper to write, think about some small step you can take to get started. Log onto your computer and look at the blank screen. Start writing some ideas. Type the topic into a computer search engine and see what information is available. Go to the library and see what is available on your topic. If you can find some interesting ideas, you can motivate yourself to begin the project. Once you have started the project, it is easier to continue.

The 80/20 Rule

Alan Lakein is noted for many useful time management techniques. One that I have used over the years is the 80/20 rule. Lakein says, "If all items are arranged in order of value, 80 percent of the value would come from only 20 percent of the items, while the remaining 20 percent of the value would come from 80 percent of the items."[5] For example, if you have a list of ten items to do, two of the items on the list are more important than the others. If you were to do only the two most important items, you would have accomplished 80 percent of the value. If you are short on time, see if you can choose the 20 percent of the tasks that are the most valuable. Lakein noted that the 80/20 rule applies to many situations in life:

- 80 percent of file usage is in 20 percent of the files.
- 80 percent of dinners repeat 20 percent of the recipes.
- 80 percent of the washing is done on the 20 percent of the clothes worn most frequently.
- 80 percent of the dirt is on the 20 percent of the floor used most often.

Think about how the 80/20 rule applies in your life. It is another way of thinking about priorities and figuring out which of the tasks are C priorities. This prioritizing is especially important if you are short on time. The 80/20 rule helps you to focus on what is most important.

Aim for Excellence, Not Perfection

Are you satisfied with your work only if it is done perfectly? Do you put off a project because you cannot do it perfectly? Aiming for perfection in all tasks causes anxiety and procrastination. There are times when perfection is not necessary. Dave Ellis calls this time management technique "It Ain't No Piano."[6] If a construction worker bends a nail in the framing of a house, it does not matter. The construction worker simply puts in another nail. After all, "it ain't no piano." It is another matter if you are building a fine cabinet or finishing a piano. Perfection is more important in these circumstances. We need to ask: Is the task important enough to invest the time needed for perfection? A final term paper needs to be as perfect as we can make it. A rough draft is like the frame of a house that does not need to be perfect.

In aiming for excellence rather than perfection, challenge yourself to use perspective to see the big picture. How important is the project and how perfect does it need to be? Could your time be better invested accomplishing other tasks? This technique requires flexibility and the ability to change with different situations. Do not give up if you cannot complete a project perfectly. Do the best that you can in the time available. In some situations, if life is too hectic, you may need to settle for completing the project and getting it in on time rather than doing it perfectly. With this idea in mind, you may be able to relax and still achieve excellence.

Make Learning Fun by Finding a Reward

© carmen2011/Shutterstock.com

Time management is not about restriction, self-control, and deprivation. If it is done correctly, time can be managed to get more out of life and to have fun while doing it. Remember that behavior is likely to increase if followed by a reward. Think about activities that you find rewarding. In our time management example with Justin who wants to be a physical therapist, he could use many tasks as rewards for completing his studies. He could meet friends for pizza, call his girlfriend, play video games, or watch TV. The key idea is to do the studying first and then reward the behavior. Maybe Justin will not be able to do all of the activities we have mentioned as possible rewards, but he could choose what he enjoys most.

Studying first and then rewarding yourself leads to peace of mind and the ability to focus on tasks at hand. While Justin is out having pizza with his friends, he does not have to worry about work that he has not done. While Justin is studying, he does not have to feel that he is being deprived of having pizza with friends. In this way, he can focus on studying while he is studying and focus on having a good time while relaxing with his friends. It is not a good idea to think about having pizza with friends while studying or to think about studying while having pizza with friends. When you work, focus on your work and get it done. When you play, enjoy playing without having to think about work.

Take a Break

If you are overwhelmed with the task at hand, sometimes it is best to just take a break. If you're stuck on a computer program or a math problem, take a break and do

> "Don't say you don't have enough time. You have exactly the same number of hours per day that were given to Helen Keller, Pasteur, Michelangelo, Mother Teresa, Leonardo da Vinci, Thomas Jefferson, and Albert Einstein."
> H. Jackson Browne

© NorGal/Shutterstock.com

something else. As a general rule, take a break of 10 minutes for each hour of study. During the break, do something totally different. It is a good idea to get up and move around. Get up and pet your cat or dog, observe your goldfish, or shoot a few baskets. If time is really at a premium, use your break time to accomplish other important tasks. Put your clothes in the dryer, empty the dishwasher, or pay a bill.

Learn to Say No Sometimes

Learn to say no to tasks that you do not have time to do. Follow your statement with the reasons for saying no: you are going to college and need time to study. Most people will understand this answer and respect it. You may need to say no to yourself as well. Maybe you cannot go out on Wednesday night if you have a class early on Thursday morning. Maybe the best use of your time right now is to turn off the TV or get off the Internet and study for tomorrow's test. You are investing your time in your future.

Dealing with Time Bandits

Time bandits are the many things that keep us from spending time on the things we think are important. Another word for a time bandit is a time waster. In college, it is tempting to do many things other than studying. We are all victims of different kinds of bandits.

ACTIVITY

Put a checkmark next to the items that waste your time. Add your own personal time wasters at the end of the list.

_____ TV
_____ Other electronic devices
_____ Daydreaming
_____ Social networking
_____ Saying yes when you mean no
_____ Friends
_____ Internet
_____ Social time
_____ Family

_____ Phone
_____ Household chores
_____ Roommates
_____ Video games
_____ Partying
_____ Children
_____ iPod
_____ Waiting time
_____ Girlfriend, boyfriend, spouse

_____ Sleeping in
_____ Shopping
_____ Being easily distracted
_____ Studying at a bad time
_____ Reading magazines
_____ Studying in a distracting place
_____ Movies
_____ Commuting time (travel)

List some of your personal time bandits here.

_____

_____

Here are some ideas for keeping time bandits under control:

- **Schedule time for other people.** Friends and family are important, so we do not want to get rid of them! Discuss your goal of a college education with your friends and family. People who care about you will respect your goals. You may need to use a Do Not Disturb sign at times. If you are a parent, remember that you are a role model for your children. If they see you studying, they are more likely to value their own education. Plan to spend quality time with your children and the people who are important to you. Make sure they understand that you care about them.

- **Remember the rewards.** Many of the time bandits listed above make good rewards for completing your work. Put the time bandits to work for you by studying first and then enjoying a reward. Enjoy the TV, Internet, iPod, video games, or phone conversations after you have finished your studies. Aim for a balance of work, study, and leisure time.

- **Remind yourself about your priorities.** When time bandits attack, remind yourself of why you are in college. Think about your personal goals for the future. Remember that college is not forever. By doing well in college, you will finish in the shortest time possible.

- **Use a schedule.** Using a schedule or a to-do list is helpful in keeping you on track. Make sure you have some slack time in your schedule to handle unexpected phone calls and deal with the unplanned events that happen in life. If you cannot stick to your schedule, just get back on track as soon as you can.

Journal Entry #3

Write a paragraph about how you will manage your time to accomplish your goal of a college education. Use any of these questions to guide your thinking:

- What are your priorities?
- How will you balance school, work, and family/friends?
- What are some time management tools you plan to use?
- How can you deal with time bandits?

Dealing with Procrastination

Procrastination means putting off things until later. We all use delaying tactics at times. Procrastination that is habitual, however, can be self-destructive. Understanding some possible reasons for procrastination can help you use time more effectively and be more successful in accomplishing goals.

Why Do We Procrastinate?

There are many psychological reasons for procrastinating. Just becoming aware of these may help you deal with procrastination. If you have serious difficulty managing your time for psychological reasons, visit the counseling center at your college or university. Do you recognize any of these reasons for procrastination in yourself or others?

- **Fear of failure.** Sometimes we procrastinate because we are afraid of failing. We see our performance as related to how much ability we have and how worthwhile we are as human beings. We may procrastinate in our college studies because of doubts about our ability to do the work. Success, however, comes from trying and learning from mistakes. There is a popular saying: falling down is not failure, but failing to get up or not even trying is failure.

- **Fear of success.** Most students are surprised to find out that one of the reasons for procrastination is fear of success. Success in college means moving on with your life, getting a job, leaving a familiar situation, accepting increased responsibility, and sometimes leaving friends behind. None of these tasks is easy. An example of fear of success is not taking the last step required to be successful. Students sometimes do not take the last class needed to graduate. Some good students do not show up for the final exam or do not turn in a major project. If you ever find yourself procrastinating on an important last step, ask yourself if you are afraid of success and what lies ahead in your future.

© bloomua/ Shutterstock.com

- **Perfectionism.** Some people who procrastinate do not realize that they are perfectionists. Perfectionists expect more from themselves than is realistic and more than others expect of themselves. There is often no other choice than to procrastinate because perfectionism is usually unattainable. Perfectionism generates anxiety that further hinders performance. Perfectionists need to understand that perfection is seldom possible. They need to set time limits on projects and do their best within those time limits.

- **Need for excitement.** Some students can only be motivated by waiting until the last minute to begin a project. These students are excited and motivated by playing a game of "Beat the Clock." They like living on the edge and the adrenaline rush of responding to a crisis. Playing this game provides motivation, but it does not leave enough time to achieve the best results. Inevitably, things happen at the last minute to make the game even more exciting and dangerous: the printer breaks, the computer crashes, the student gets ill, the car breaks down, or the dog eats the homework. These students need to start projects earlier to improve their chances of success. It is best to seek excitement elsewhere, in sports or other competitive activities.

- **Excellence without effort.** In this scenario, students believe that they are truly outstanding and can achieve success without effort. These students think that they can go to college without attending classes or reading the text. They believe that they can pass the test without studying. They often do not succeed in college the first semester, which puts them at risk of dropping out of school. They often return to college later and improve their performance by putting in the effort required.

- **Loss of control.** Some students fear loss of control over their lives and procrastinate to gain control. An example is students who attend college because others (such as parents) want them to attend. Procrastination becomes a way of gaining control over the situation by saying, "You can't make me do this." They attend college but accomplish nothing. Parents can support and encourage education, but students need to choose their own goals in life and attend college because it is an important personal goal.

Tips for Dealing with Procrastination

When you find yourself procrastinating on a certain task, think about the consequences. Will the procrastination lead to failing an exam or getting a low grade? Think about the rewards of doing the task. If you do well, you can take pride in yourself and celebrate your success. How will you feel when the task is completed? Will you be able to enjoy your leisure time without guilt about not doing your work? How does the task help you to achieve your lifetime goals?

Maybe the procrastination is a warning sign that you need to reconsider lifetime goals and change them to better suit your needs.

Procrastination Scenario

George is a college student who is on academic probation for having low grades. He is required to make a plan for improving his grades in order to remain in college. George tells the counselor that he is making poor grades because of his procrastination. He is an accounting major and puts off doing homework because he dislikes it and does not find it interesting. The counselor asks George why he had chosen accounting as a major. He replies that accounting is a major that is in demand and has a good salary. The counselor suggests that George consider a major that he would enjoy more. After some consideration, George changes his major to psychology. He becomes more interested in college studies and is able to raise his grades to stay in college.

Most of the time, you will reap benefits by avoiding procrastination and completing the task at hand. Jane Burka and Lenora Yuen suggest the following steps to deal with procrastination:

1. Select a goal.
2. Visualize your progress.
3. Be careful not to sabotage yourself.
4. Stick to a time limit.
5. Don't wait until you feel like it.
6. Follow through. Watch out for excuses and focus on one step at a time.
7. Reward yourself after you have made some progress.
8. Be flexible about your goal.
9. Remember that it does not have to be perfect.[7]

© iQoncept/Shutterstock.com

Managing Time and Money

QUIZ

Time Management, Part II

Test what you have learned by selecting the correct answers to the following questions.

1. To get started on a challenging project,
   a. think of a small first step and complete it.
   b. wait until you have plenty of time to begin.
   c. wait until you are well rested and relaxed.

2. If you are completing a to-do list of 10 items, the 80/20 rule states that
   a. 80% of the value comes from completing most of the items on the list.
   b. 80% of the value comes from completing two of the most important items.
   c. 80% of the value comes from completing half of the items on the list.

3. It is suggested that students aim for
   a. perfection.
   b. excellence.
   c. passing.

4. Sometimes students procrastinate because of
   a. fear of failure.
   b. fear of success.
   c. all of the above.

5. Playing the game "Beat the Clock" when doing a term paper results in
   a. increased motivation and success.
   b. greater excitement and quality work.
   c. increased motivation and risk.

How did you do on the quiz? Check your answers: 1. a, 2. b, 3. b, 4. c, 5. c

Journal Entry #4

Write a paragraph about how you will avoid procrastination. Consider these ideas when thinking about procrastination: fear of failure, fear of success, perfectionism, need for excitement, excellence without effort, and loss of control. How will you complete your assignments on time?

Managing Your Money

To be successful in college and in life, you will need to manage not only time, but money. One of the top reasons that students drop out of college is that they cannot pay for their education or that they have to work so much that they do not have time for school. Take a look at your lifetime goals. Most students have a goal related to money, such as becoming financially secure or becoming wealthy. If financial security or wealth is one of your goals, you will need to begin to take some action to accomplish that goal. If you don't take action on a goal, it is merely a fantasy.

> "Education costs money, but then so does ignorance."
>
> Claus Moser

© ARENA Creative/Shutterstock.com

How to Become a Millionaire

Save regularly. Frances Leonard, author of *Time Is Money*, cites some statistics on how much money you need to save to become a millionaire.[8] You can retire with a million dollars by age 68 by saving the following amounts of money at various ages. These figures assume a 10 percent return on your investment.

At age 22, save $87 per month

At age 26, save $130 per month

At age 30, save $194 per month

At age 35, save $324 a month

Notice that the younger you start saving, the less money is required to reach the million-dollar goal. (And keep in mind that even a million dollars may not be enough money to save for retirement.) How can you start saving money when you are a student struggling to pay for college? The answer is to practice money management techniques and to begin a savings habit, even if the money you save is a small amount to buy your books for next semester. When you get that first good job, save 10 percent of the money. If you are serious about becoming financially secure, learn about investments such as real estate, stocks and bonds, and mutual funds. Learning how to save and invest your money can pay big dividends in the future.

Managing Your Money

- Monitor your spending
- Prepare a budget
- Beware of credit and interest
- Watch spending leaks

Budgeting: The Key to Money Management

Money management begins with looking at your attitude toward money. Pay attention to how you spend your money so that you can accomplish your financial goals such as getting a college education, buying a house or car, or saving for the future. One of the most important things that you can do to manage your money and begin saving is to use a budget. A budget helps you become aware of how you spend your money and will help your make a plan for the future. It is important to control your money, rather than letting your money control you.

Monitor how you spend your money. The first step in establishing a workable budget is to monitor how you are actually spending your money at the present time. For one month, keep a list of purchases with the date and amount of money spent for each. You can do this on a sheet of paper, on your calendar, on index cards, or on a money management application for your phone. If you write checks for items, include the checks written as part of your money monitor. At the end of the month, group your purchases in categories such as food, gas, entertainment, and credit card payments, and add them up. Doing this will yield some surprising results. For example, you may not be aware of just how much it costs to eat at a fast-food restaurant or to buy lunch or coffee every day.

© koya979/Shutterstock.com

Prepare a budget. One of the best tools for managing your money is a budget. At the end of this chapter, you will find a simple budget sheet that you can use as a college student. After you finish college, update your budget and continue to use it. Follow these three steps to make a budget:

1. Write down your income for the month.
2. List your expenses. Include tuition, books, supplies, rent, telephone, utilities (gas, electric, water, cable TV, internet), car payments, car insurance, car maintenance (oil, repairs), parking fees, food, personal grooming, clothes, entertainment, savings, credit card payments, loan payments, and other bills. Use your money monitor to discover how you are spending your money and include categories that are unique to you.
3. Subtract your total expenses from your total income. You cannot spend more than you have. Make adjustments as needed.

Beware of credit and interest. College students are often tempted to use credit cards to pay for college expenses. This type of borrowing is costly and difficult to repay. It is easy to pull out a plastic credit card and buy items that you need and want. Credit card companies earn a great deal of money from credit cards. Jane Bryant Quinn gives an example of the cost of credit cards.[9] She says that if you owe $3,000 at 18 percent interest and pay the minimum payment of $60 per month, it will take you 30 years and 10 months to get out of debt! Borrowing the $3,000 would cost about $22,320 over this time! If you use a credit card, make sure you can pay it off in one to three months. It is good to have a credit card in order to establish credit and to use in an emergency.

Watch those spending leaks. We all have spending problem areas. Often we spend small amounts of money each day that add up to large spending leaks over time. For example, if you spend $3 on coffee each weekday for a year, this adds up to $780 a year! If you eat lunch out each weekday and spend $8 for lunch, this adds up to $2,080 a year. Here are some common areas for spending leaks:

- Fast food and restaurants
- Entertainment and vacations
- Clothing
- Miscellaneous cash
- Gifts

© Andrey Armyagov/Shutterstock.com

Need More Money?

You may be tempted to work more hours to balance your budget. Remember that to be a full-time college student, it is recommended that you work no more than 20 hours per week. If you work more than 20 hours per week, you will probably need to decrease your course load. Before increasing your work hours, see if there is a way you can decrease your monthly expenses. Can you make your lunch instead of eating out? Can you get by without a car? Is the item you are purchasing a necessity, or do you just want to have it? These choices are yours.

1. **Check out financial aid.** All students can qualify for some type of financial aid. Visit the Financial Aid Office at your college for assistance. Depending on your income level, you may qualify for one or more of the following forms of aid.

    - **Loans.** A loan must be paid back. The interest rate and terms vary according to your financial need. With some loans, the federal government pays the interest while you are in school.

> "Money is, in some respects, like fire; it is a very excellent servant, but a terrible master."
> P. T. Barnum

> "Empty pockets never held anyone back. Only empty heads and empty hearts can do that."
> Norman Vincent Peale

- **Grants.** A grant does not need to be repaid. There are both state and federal grants based on need.
- **Work/study.** You may qualify for a federally subsidized job depending on your financial need. These jobs are often on campus and provide valuable work experience for the future.

The first step in applying for financial aid is to fill out the Free Application for Federal Student Aid (FAFSA). This form determines your eligibility for financial aid. You can obtain this form from your college's financial aid office or over the Internet at www.fafsa.ed.gov.

Here are some other financial aid resources that you can obtain from your financial aid office or over the Internet.

- **Federal Student Aid Resources.** This site provides resources on preparing for college, applying for aid, online tools, and other resources: https://studentaid.ed.gov/sa/resources.
- **How to apply for financial aid.** Learn how to apply for federal financial aid and scholarships at www.finaid.org.

2. **Apply for a scholarship.** Applying for a scholarship is like having a part-time job, only the pay is often better, the hours are flexible, and you can be your own boss. For this part-time job, you will need to research scholarship opportunities and fill out applications. There are multitudes of scholarships available, and sometimes no one even applies for them. Some students do not apply for scholarships because they think that high grades and financial need are required. While many scholarships are based on grades and financial need, many are not. Any person or organization can offer a scholarship for any reason they want. For example, scholarships can be based on hobbies, parent's occupation, religious background, military service, and personal interests, to name a few.

There are several ways to research a scholarship. As a first step, visit the financial aid office on your college campus. This office is staffed with persons knowledgeable about researching and applying for scholarships. Organizations or persons wishing to fund scholarships often contact this office to advertise opportunities.

You can also research scholarships through your public or college library. Ask the reference librarian for assistance. You can use the Internet to research scholarships as well. Use any search engine such as Google.com and simply type in the keyword scholarships. The following websites index thousands of scholarships:

- The Federal Student Aid Scholarship site is located at http://studentaid.ed.gov/types/grants-scholarships/finding-scholarships
- fastweb.com
- college-scholarships.com
- http://www.scholarships.com/
- collegenet.com/mach25
- studentscholarshipsearch.com
- collegeboard.com/paying

To apply for scholarships, start a file of useful material usually included in scholarship applications. You can use this same information to apply for many scholarships.

- Three current letters of recommendation
- A statement of your personal goals
- A statement of your financial need
- Copies of your transcripts
- Copies of any scholarship applications you have filled out

Be aware of scholarship scams. You do not need to pay money to apply for a scholarship. No one can guarantee that you will receive a scholarship. Use your college scholarship office and your own resources to research and apply for scholarships.

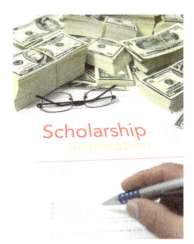
© mangostock/Shutterstock.com

The Best Ideas for Becoming Financially Secure

Financial planners provide the following ideas as the best ways to build wealth and independence.[10] If you have financial security as your goal, plan to do the following:

1. **Use a simple budget to track income and expenses.** Do not spend more than you earn.
2. **Have a financial plan.** Include goals such as saving for retirement, purchasing a home, paying for college, or taking vacations.
3. **Save 10 percent of your income.** As a college student, you may not be able to save this much, but plan to do it as soon as you get your first good-paying job. If you cannot save 10 percent, save something to get in the habit of saving. Save to pay for your tuition and books.
4. **Don't take on too much debt.** Be especially careful about credit cards and consumer debt. Credit card companies often visit college campuses and offer high-interest credit cards to students. It is important to have a credit card, but pay off the balance each month. Consider student loans instead of paying college fees by credit card.
5. **Don't procrastinate.** The earlier you take these steps toward financial security, the better.

Tips for Managing Your Money

Keeping these guidelines in mind can help you to manage your money.

- Don't let friends pressure you into spending too much money. If you can't afford something, learn to say no.
- Keep your checking account balanced or use online banking so you will know how much money you have.
- Don't lend money to friends. If your friends cannot manage their money, your loan will not help them.
- Use comparison shopping to find the best prices on the products that you buy.
- Get a part-time job while in college. You will earn money and gain valuable job experience.
- Don't use shopping as a recreational activity. When you visit the mall, you will find things you never knew you needed and will wind up spending more money than intended.
- Make a budget and follow it. This is the best way to achieve your financial goals.

KEYS TO SUCCESS

Do What Is Important First

The most important thing you can do to manage time and money is to spend it on what is most important. Manage time and money to help you live the life you want. How can you do this? Author Stephen Covey wrote a book titled *The Seven Habits of Highly Effective People.* One of the habits is "Put first things first." Covey suggests that in time management, the "challenge is not to manage our time but to manage ourselves."[11]

How can you manage yourself? Our first thoughts in answering this question often involve suggestions about willpower, restriction, and self-control. Schedules and budgets are seen as instruments for self-control. It seems that the human spirit resists attempts at control, even when we aim to control ourselves. Often the response to control is rebellion. With time and money management, we may not follow a schedule or budget. A better approach to begin managing yourself is to know your values. What is important in your life? Do you have a clear mental picture of what is important? Can you describe your values and make a list of what is important to you? With your values and goals in mind, you can begin to manage both your time and your money.

When you have given some thought to your values, you can begin to set goals. When you have established goals for your life, you can begin to think in terms of what is most important and establish your priorities. Knowing your values is essential in making decisions about how to invest your time and money. Schedules and budgets are merely tools for helping you accomplish what you have decided is important. Time and money management is not about restriction and control, but about making decisions regarding what is important in your life. If you know what is important, you can find the strength to say no to activities and expenditures that are less important.

As a counselor, I have the pleasure of working with many students who have recently explored and discovered their values and are highly motivated to succeed. They are willing to do what is important first. I recently worked with a young couple who came to enroll in college. They brought their young baby with them. The new father was interested in environmental engineering. He told me that in high school, he never saw a reason for school and did just the minimum needed to get by. He was working as a construction laborer and making a living, but did not see a future in the occupation. He had observed an environmental engineer who worked for the company and decided that was what he wanted for his future. As he looked at his new son, he told me that he needed to have a better future for himself and his family.

He and his wife decided to do what was important first. They were willing to make the sacrifice to attend school and invest the time needed to be successful. The father planned to work during the day and go to school at night. Later, he would go to school full-time and get a part-time job in the evening. His wife was willing to get a part-time job also, and they would share in taking care of the baby. They were willing to manage their money carefully to accomplish their goals. As they left, they added that their son would be going to college as well.

How do you get the energy to work all day, go to school at night, and raise a family? You can't do it by practicing self-control. You find the energy by having a clear idea of what you want in your life and focusing your time and resources on the goal. Finding what you want to do with your life is not easy either. Many times people find what they want to do when some significant event happens in their lives.

Begin to think about what you want out of life. Make a list of your important values and write down your lifetime goals. Don't forget about the people who are important to you, and include them in your priorities. Then you will be able to do what is important first.

> "Fathers send their sons to college either because they went to college or because they didn't."
>
> L. L. Henderson

> ### Journal Entry #5
>
> What is your plan for managing your money? Consider these ideas when thinking about your plan: monitoring how you spend your money, using a budget, applying for financial aid and scholarships, saving money, and spending money wisely.

Appreciating Island Cultures: The Sirena

In Guam, there once lived a playful young girl named Sirena. Sirena lived near the Hagatna River. She loved the water and would often steal moments away from her chores to go and play in the river.

One day Sirena's mother sent her to gather coconut shells to use for taking the wrinkles out of their clothes. While she was out gathering these coconut shells, she felt the water calling to her and she couldn't resist. She ran to the river, jumped in, and swam for a long time, not paying any attention to her responsibilities, or how quickly the day was moving. Meanwhile, Sirena's mother was calling and calling out to her, but she did not hear her. The more she called Sirena's name, the more impatient she grew.

During Sirena's time away, her godmother came by to visit with Sirena's mom and they waited together for her return. Her mother began to complain about her daughter, getting angrier and angrier with every moment that passed by. In her anger and frustration, she cursed her daughter Sirena. She said, "Since Sirena loves the water more than anything, let her become a fish!!"

Tropical Tumon Bay in the tropical Pacific Island of Guam, famous for its snorkeling.
© Michael Fitzsimmons/Shutterstock.com

Her godmother knew how powerful those words were. She also knew how much she might regret it and interjected, "Leave the part of her that belongs to me as human."

Sirena, still swimming in the river, began to feel her body changing. Quickly, the lower half of her body transformed into the tail of a fish! She was covered with scales and now had fins, too. Yet, from the waist up, she remained a girl. Sirena was transformed into a mermaid! Yet, as much as she loved being in the water, she knew she would never be able to go on land again.

Right after those words came out of her mother's mouth, she realized what had just happened to her daughter and immediately regretted what she had said. Unfortunately, she knew she was not able to take back the words that she had spoken and could never undo what Sirena had become. Sirena would be a mermaid forever.

Sirena did not want to be seen by anyone, and to assure this, she knew she would have to leave to live a life in the sea. But, before she left, she bid her final farewell to her mother. She said, "Do not worry for me, I am a mistress of the sea which I love. I wish you had punished me some other way, I wish to stay home with you. Take a look at me, for this will be the last time we see each other." Those were her final words before Sirena disappeared among the waves, never to come to shore again.

© Shafran/Shutterstock.com

Yet, it is said that many sailors have caught glimpses of Sirena at sea. Legend has it that Sirena will never appear willingly to people, and can be caught only by a net made from human hair.

Questions

1. Like Sirena loved the water and allowed it to distract her from the goal that was set before her, what are some obstacles that you may face that will keep you from achieving all you have set out to do?

2. What are some strategies that will help you accomplish all of your goals?

3. Sirena's mother spoke things that she would later regret because they kept her from her daughter. What power do words have on your ability to succeed or not?

4. What are some things that have been said directly to you that have helped you along your journey? Some that have hindered you?

5. What are some things that you wish you had done differently?

© Lyudmyla Kharlamova/Shutterstock.com

College Success 1

The College Success 1 website is continually updated with supplementary material for each chapter including Word documents of the journal entries, classroom activities, handouts, videos, links to related materials, and much more. See http://www.collegesuccess1.com/.

Notes

1. Steven K. Scott, *A Millionaire's Notebook,* quoted in Rob Gilbert, Editor, Bits & Pieces, November 4, 1999, 15.
2. John Medina, *Brain Rules,* (Seattle: Pear Press, 2008), 157.
3. Ibid, pp. 162–163.
4. Alan Lakein, *How to Get Control of Your Time and Your life* (New York: Peter H. Wyden, 1973).
5. Ibid., 70–71.
6. Dave Ellis, *Becoming a Master Student* (Boston: Houghton Mifflin, 1998).
7. Jane Burka and Lenora Yuen, *Procrastination* (Reading, MA: Addison-Wesley, 1983).
8. Francis Leonard, *Time is Money* (Addison-Wesley), cited in the San Diego Union Tribune, October 14, 1995.
9. Jane Bryant Quinn, "Money Watch," *Good Housekeeping*, November 1996, 80.
10. Robert Hanley, "Breaking Bad Habits," *San Diego Union Tribune*, September 7, 1992.
11. Stephen R. Covey, *The Seven Habits of Highly Effective People* (New York: Simon and Schuster, 1990), 150.

My Lifetime Goals: Brainstorming Activity

Name _____ Date _____

1. Think about the goals that you would like to accomplish in your life. At the end of your life, you do not want to say, "I wish I would have _____." Set a timer for five minutes and write whatever comes to mind about what you would like to do and accomplish over your lifetime. Include goals in these areas: career, personal relationships, travel, and financial security or any area that is important to you. Write down all your ideas. The goal is to generate as many ideas as possible in five minutes. You can reflect on which ones are most important later. You may want to do this as part of a group activity in your class.

Look over the ideas you wrote above and highlight or underline the goals that are most important to you.

2. Ask yourself what you would like to accomplish in the next five years. Think about where you want to be in college, what you want to do in your career, and what you want to do in your personal life. Set a timer and write whatever comes to mind in five minutes. The goal is to write down as many ideas as possible.

Again, look over the ideas you wrote and highlight or underline the ideas that are most important to you.

3. What goals would you like to accomplish in the next year? What are some steps that you can begin now to accomplish your lifetime goals? Consider work, study, leisure, and social goals. Set your timer for five minutes and write down your goals for the next year.

Review what you wrote and highlight or underline the ideas that are most important to you. When writing your goals, include fun activities as well as taking care of others.

Looking at the items that you have highlighted or underlined, make a list of your lifetime goals using the form that follows. Make sure your goals are specific enough so that you can break them into steps you can achieve.

My Lifetime Goals

Name _____ Date _____

Using the ideas that you brainstormed in the previous exercise, make a list of your lifetime goals. Make sure your goals are specific and concrete. Begin with goals that you would like to accomplish over a lifetime. In the second section, think about the goals you can accomplish over the next one to three years.

Long-Term Goals (lifetime goals)

Short-Term Goals (one to three years)

Managing Time and Money

What are some steps you can take now to accomplish intermediate and long-term goals?

Successful Goal Setting

Name _____ Date _____

Look at your list of lifetime goals. Which one is most important? Write the goal here:

Answer these questions about the goal you have listed above.

1. What skills, abilities, and resources do you have to achieve this goal? What skills, abilities, and resources will you need to develop to achieve this goal?

2. Do you believe you can achieve it? Write a brief positive statement about achieving this goal.

3. State your goal in specific terms that can be observed or counted. Rewrite your goal if necessary.

4. Write a brief statement about how this goal will give you personal satisfaction.

5. How will you motivate yourself to achieve this goal?

6. What are your personal values that match this goal?

7. List some steps that you will take to accomplish this goal.

8. When will you finish this goal?

9. What roadblocks will make this goal difficult to achieve?

10. How will you deal with these roadblocks?

Weekly College Schedule

Name _____   Date _____

Copy the following schedule to use in future weeks or design your own schedule. Fill in this schedule and try to follow it for at least one week. First, fill in scheduled commitments (classes, work, activities). Next, fill in the time you need for studying. Put in some tasks related to your lifetime goals. Leave some blank time as a shock absorber to handle unexpected activities.

Time	Monday	Tuesday	Wednesday	Thursday	Friday	Saturday	Sunday
7 A.M.							
8							
9							
10							
11							
Noon							
1 P.M.							
2							
3							
4							
5							
6							
7							
8							
9							
10							
11							

Managing Time and Money

Weekly To-Do Chart

Name _____   Date _____

Using a to-do list is an easy way to remind yourself of important priorities each day. This chart is divided into three areas representing types of tasks that college students need to balance: academic, personal, and social.

Weekly To-Do List

	Monday	Tuesday	Wednesday	Thursday	Friday
Academic					
Personal					
Social					

Study Schedule Analysis

Name _____ Date _____

Before completing this analysis, use the schedule form to create a master schedule. A master schedule blocks out class and work times as well as any regularly scheduled activities. Looking at the remaining time, write in your planned study times. It is recommended that you have two hours of study time for each hour in class. For example, a three-unit class would require six hours of study time. A student with 12 units would require 24 hours of study time. You may need more or fewer hours, depending on your study skills, reading skills, and difficulty of courses.

1. How many units are you enrolled in?

2. How many hours of planned study time do you have?

3. How many hours do you work each week?

4. How many hours do you spend in relaxation/social activities?

5. Do you have time planned for exercise?

6. Do you get enough sleep?

7. What are some of your time bandits (things that take up your time and make it difficult to accomplish your goals)?

Write a few discovery statements about how you use your time.

8. Are you spending enough time to earn the grades you want to achieve? Do you need to spend more time studying to become successful?

9. Does your work schedule allow you enough time to study?

10. How can you deal with your time bandits?

11. How can you use your time more effectively to achieve your goals?

Budgeting for College

Name _____   Date _____

Before you complete this budget, monitor your expenses for one month. Write down all expenditures and then divide them into categories that have meaning for you. Then complete the following budget and try to follow it for at least two months. Do this exercise on your own, since it is likely to contain private information.

College Student Monthly Budget

Monthly income for _____ (month)

Income from job _____

Money from home _____

Financial aid _____

Other _____

Total Income ☐

Budgeted Monthly Expenses:

Actual Monthly Expenses:

Total Budgeted ☐   Total Actual

Total Income ☐   Minus Total Budgeted ☐   Equals ☐

Managing Time and Money

CHAPTER 5

Using Brain Science to Improve Memory

Learning Objectives

Read to answer these key questions:

- How does the memory work?

- How can I improve my memory?

- Why do I forget?

- What are some practical memory techniques based on brain science?

- What are some memory tricks?

- How can I optimize my brain power?

- Why is positive thinking important for improving memory and studying?

From *College & Career Success, Concise Version*, Seventh Edition, by Marsha Fralick. Copyright © 2016 by Kendall Hunt Publishing Company. Reprinted by permission.

Learning how to improve your memory and remember what you are studying will be great assets in college, on the job, and in your personal life. This chapter translates the latest findings in brain science into some practical techniques for improving memory.

Improving Your Memory

Memory: Short Term versus Long Term

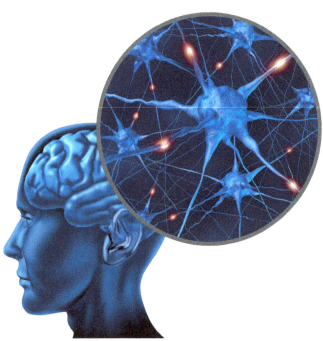

© Lightspring/Shutterstock.com

Effective studying in college involves transferring learning from short-term to long-term memory. Short-term memory is often called the working memory, which is a temporary space or desktop used to process information. The short-term memory has limited capacity and duration. If information is not transferred to long-term memory, it quickly disappears.

Through repetition or rehearsal, information is transferred to long-term memory, which has a higher capacity and duration. For example, if you just read your textbook, the information is stored in short-term memory and quickly disappears. Storing material in long-term memory is like making a trail through the jungle. The more the trail is used, the easier it is to follow and the more distinct it becomes. Learning requires effort; the more you practice or rehearse the more you learn.[1]

It is necessary to use some study strategies that involve repeating or reviewing the material to transfer the information to long-term memory available for passing tests and for later success in your career. To be most effective, this rehearsal or repetition must be done immediately and then at spaced intervals over time. Waiting to study just before a test by using intense marathon study sessions is not effective in transferring the material to long-term memory and is not very enjoyable either.

Forgetting

It was previously thought that once information was stored in long-term memory, it was there forever. However, scientists have found that our memories are often inaccurate and become distorted over time. Forgetting allows us to prioritize events. We forget items that are not important for our survival.

Examining the following lists of items frequently forgotten or remembered can give us insight into why forgetting occurs and how to minimize it.

We frequently forget these things:

- Names of people, places, or things
- Numbers and dates
- What we have barely learned
- Material we do not fully understand
- What we try to remember when embarrassed, frustrated, tired, or ill

- Material we have learned by cramming
- Ideas or theories that conflict with our beliefs

We tend to remember these things:

- Pleasant experiences
- Material that is important to us
- What we have put an effort into learning
- What we have reviewed or thought through often
- Material that is interesting to us
- Muscular skills such as riding a bike
- What we had an important reason to remember
- Items we discuss with others
- Material that we understand
- Frequently used information

© Edyta Pawlowska/Shutterstock.com

To improve memory, you must first fully understand the material. Then convince yourself that the material you are learning is important and find something interesting about it. If you approach your studies with a positive attitude, it is easier to recall what you are studying. It is helpful if you can think about the material and discuss it with others. The critical step is putting in the effort to review the material you have learned so that it is transferred to long-term memory.

Minimizing Forgetting

Herman Ebbinghaus (1850–1909), a German psychologist and pioneer in research on forgetting, described a curve of forgetting.[2] He invented nonsense syllables such as WUX, CAZ, BIJ, and ZOL. He chose these nonsense syllables so that there would be no meaning, associations, or organizations that could affect the memory of the words. He would learn these lists of words and measure forgetting over time. The following is a chart of time and forgetting of nonsense syllables.

> "Just as iron rusts from disuse, even so does inaction spoil the intellect."
> Leonardo da Vinci

Time	Percent Forgotten
After 20 minutes	47
After 1 day	62
After 2 days	69
After 15 days	75
After 31 days	78

We can draw three interesting conclusions from examining these figures. First, **most of the forgetting occurs within the first 20 minutes**. Immediate review, or at least review during the first 20 minutes, would prevent most of the forgetting. Second, forgetting slows down over time. The third conclusion is that forgetting is significant after 31 days. Fortunately, we do not need to memorize nonsense syllables. We can use meaning, associations, organization, and proper review to minimize forgetting.

Review is important in transferring information from short-term to long-term memory. You can also minimize forgetting over time through the proper use of review.[3] Let's assume that you spend 45 minutes studying and learning something new. The optimum schedule for review would look like this:

After 10 minutes	Review for 5 minutes
After 1 day	Review for 5 minutes
After 1 week	Review for 3 minutes
After 1 month	Review for 3 minutes
After 6 months	Review for 3 minutes

QUIZ

Improving Your Memory

Test what you have learned by circling the letters of the correct answers to the following questions:

1. Through _____, information is transferred to long-term memory.
   a. Reading
   b. Repetition
   c. Responding

2. To be most effective, rehearsal of information should be
   a. Within two weeks
   b. Immediately and at spaced intervals
   c. All at once

3. We are most likely to forget
   a. What we have thought about often
   b. What we have put in an effort to learn
   c. Material learned when we are embarrassed or frustrated

4. According to the experiments done by Ebbinghaus, 47% of the forgetting occurs after
   a. One day
   b. One week
   c. 20 minutes

5. Review is most efficient when done
   a. In short periods of time
   b. In long periods of time
   c. In long review sessions right before the test

How did you do on the quiz? Check your answers: 1. b, 2. b, 3. c, 4. c, 5. a

> **Journal Entry #1**
>
> Review the material on memory and forgetting. How can you use this information to improve your studying in college?

Practical Memory Techniques Based on Brain Science

Remember that recitation or rehearsal of information is crucial in transferring information to long-term memory. Based on current research on brain science and psychology, here are some additional practical suggestions for improving memory.[4]

Memorization Tips

- Meaningful organization
- Visualization
- Recitation
- Develop an interest
- See the big picture first
- Intend to remember
- Learn small amounts frequently
- Basic background
- Relax

Think Positively about Learning

Positive emotions such as interest, joy, amusement, contentment, and relaxation optimize learning and memory. These positive emotions increase openness to new information as well as improve attention, memory, and verbal fluency. For greater success and achievement, it is important to think positively about learning. Rather than viewing learning as stressful or an unpleasant obligation, view it as a new and interesting adventure, and it can be easier and more rewarding.

Develop an Interest

We tend to remember what interests us. People often have phenomenal memories when it comes to sports, automobiles, music, stamp collecting, or anything they consider fun or pursue as a hobby. Find something interesting in your college studies. If you are not interested in what you are studying, look for something interesting or even pretend that you are interested and then reward yourself by doing something enjoyable.

Motivation and attitude have a significant impact on memory. Being highly motivated and approaching your studies with a positive attitude will help you to find something interesting and make it easier to remember. In addition, the more you learn about a topic, the more interesting it becomes. Often we judge a subject as boring because we know nothing about it.

© Zurijeta/Shutterstock.com

Another way to make something interesting is to look for personal meaning. How can I use this information in my future career? Does the information relate to my personal experience in some way? How can I use this information? What is the importance of this information? And finally, is this information likely to be on the test?

See the Big Picture First

Imagine looking at a painting one inch at a time. It would be difficult to understand or appreciate a painting in this way. College students often approach reading a textbook in the same way. They focus on the small details without first understanding the main points. By focusing on the details without looking at the main points, it is easy to get lost. The first step in reading is to skim the chapter headings to form a mental outline of what you will be learning. Then read for detail.

Meaningful Organization

Another powerful memory technique is imposing your own form of personal organization on the material you are trying to remember. Psychologists have even suggested that your intelligence quotient (IQ) may be related to how well you have organized material you learned in the past. When learning new material, cluster facts and ideas into categories that are meaningful to you. Think of the mind as a file cabinet or a computer. Major topics are like folders in which we file detailed information. When we need to find the information, we think of the major topic and look in the folder to find the details. If we put all our papers into the file drawer without organization, it is difficult to find the information we need. Highlight or underline key ideas to focus on the main points and organize what you are learning.

The Magical Number 7 Theory

Grouping together or chunking bits of information together can make remembering easier. George Miller of the Harvard University found that the optimum number of chunks or bits of information that we can hold in short-term memory is five to nine.[5] It is much easier to remember material that is grouped in chunks of seven or less. You can find many examples of groups of seven used to enhance memory. There are seven digits in a phone number, seven days of the week, and seven numbers in your driver's license and license plate. There are also seven dwarfs, seven deadly sins, and Seven Wonders of the World!

Does this mean that we should try to remember only seven or less ideas in studying a textbook chapter? No, it is most efficient to identify seven or fewer key ideas and then cluster less important ideas under major headings. In this way, you can remember the key ideas in the chapter you are studying along with the details. The critical thinking required by this process also helps in remembering ideas and information.

ACTIVITY

Magical Number Seven

Remember George Miller's Magical Number Seven Theory? It is more efficient to limit the number of categories to seven or less, although you can have subcategories. Examine the following list of words.

goat	horse	cow
carrot	cat	lettuce
banana	tomato	pig
celery	orange	peas
cherry	apple	strawberry

Look at the list for one minute. Then look away from the list and write down all the words you can recall. Record the number of words you remembered: _____

Note that the following lists are divided into categories: animals, crops, and tropical fruits.

animals	crops	tropical fruits
lion	wheat	banana
giraffe	beans	kiwi
kangaroo	corn	mango
coyote	hay	guava
bear	oats	orange

Look at the above list for one minute. Then look away from the list and write down the words you recall. Record the number of words you remembered: _____

You probably remembered more from the second list because the list is organized into categories. Notice that there are only five words in each category. Remember that it is easier to remember lists with seven items or less. If these words have some meaning for you, it is easier to remember them. A farmer from the Midwest would probably have an easier time remembering the crops. A person from Hawaii would probably remember the list of tropical fruits. We also tend to remember unusual items and the first and last items on the list. If you need to memorize a list, pay more attention to the mundane items and the items in the middle of the list.

Visualization

One of the most powerful memory techniques is visualization. If you can read the words and accompany them with pictures, you are using your brain in the most efficient way. Advertisers use pictures as powerful influences to motivate you to purchase their products. You can use the same power of visualization to enhance your studying. While you are studying history, picture what life would be like in that time period. In engineering, make pictures in your mind or on paper to illustrate scientific principles. Challenge yourself to see the pictures along with the words. Add movement to your pictures, as in a video. During a test, relax and recall the pictures.

© scyther5/Shutterstock.com

> **To learn something new, it is helpful if you**
> - Are motivated.
> - Find it interesting.
> - Think it is valuable.
> - Pay attention to it.
> - Practice or repeat it.

Intend to Remember

Tell yourself that you are going to remember. If you think you won't remember, you won't remember. This step also relates to positive thinking and self-confidence and will take some practice to apply. Once you have told yourself to remember, apply some of the above techniques such as organizing, visualizing, and reciting. If you intend to remember, you will pay attention, make an effort to understand, and use memory techniques to strengthen your memory.

One practical technique that involves intent to remember is the memory jogger. This involves doing something unusual to jog or trigger your memory. If you want to be sure to remember your books, place your car keys on the books. Since you cannot go anywhere without your keys, you will find them and remember the books too. Another application is putting your watch on your right hand to remember to do something. When you look at your left hand and notice that the watch is not there, the surprise will jog your memory for the item you wish to recall. You can be creative with this technique and come up with your own memory joggers.

Elaboration

Just as decorations or stories can be made more elaborate, learning can be made more elaborate too. The more you add details, connect the information, or make it personally meaningful, the easier it is to learn. Here are some ways to elaborate:[6]

- Write it in your own words. Look for personal meaning.
- Make a silly song or rhyme with the material.
- Rewrite your notes.
- Use flash cards to quiz yourself.
- Make a mind map.
- Underline the important points in the text and make notes in the margin about important points.
- Discuss the information with others.
- Study with a scented candle.
- Use multisensory learning including audio (hearing), visual (seeing), tactile (touch), kinesthetic (movement) and olfactory (smell) strategies.
- Associate the material learned to something you already know. How does the information match your experiences?

Distribute the Practice

Learning small amounts of material and reviewing frequently are more effective than a marathon study session. One research study showed that a task that took 30 minutes to learn in one day could be learned in 22 minutes if spread over two days. This is almost a 30 percent increase in efficiency.[7]

If you have a list of vocabulary words or formulas to learn, break the material into small parts and frequently review each part for a short period of time. Consider putting these facts or figures on index cards to carry with you in your purse or pocket. Use small amounts of time to quickly review the cards. This technique works well because it prevents fatigue and helps to keep motivation high. One exception to the distributed practice rule is creative work such as writing a paper or doing an art project, where a longer time period is needed for creative inspiration and immediate follow-through.

A learning technique for distributed practice is summed up in the acronym **SAFMEDS**, which stands for Say All Fast for one Minute Each Day and Shuffle.[7] With this technique, you can easily and quickly learn 100 or more facts. To use this technique, prepare flash cards that contain the material to be learned (vocabulary, foreign language words, numbers, dates, places, names, formulas). For example, if you are learning Spanish, place the Spanish word on one side of the card and the English word on the other side. Just writing out the flash cards is an aid to learning and is often sufficient for learning the material. Once the cards are prepared, *say* the Spanish word and see if you can remember what it means in English. Look at the back of the card to see if your answer is correct. Do this with *all* of the cards as *fast* as you can for *one minute each day*. Then *shuffle* the cards and repeat the process the next day.

It is important that you do this activity quickly. Don't worry if you do not know the answer. Just flip each card over, quickly look at the answer, and put the cards that you missed into a separate pile. At the end of the minute, count the number of cards you answered correctly. You can learn even faster if you take the stack of cards you missed and practice them quickly one more time. Shuffling the cards helps you to remember the actual meanings of the words, instead of just the order in which they appear. In the case of the Spanish cards, turn the cards over and say each English word to see if you can remember the equivalent word in Spanish. Each day, the number of correct answers will increase, and you will have a concrete measure of your learning. Consider this activity as a fun and fast-moving game to challenge yourself.

Create a Basic Background

You remember information by connecting it to things you already know. The more you know, the easier it is to make connections that make remembering easier. You will even find that it is easier to remember material toward the end of a college class because you have established a basic background at the beginning of the semester. With this in mind, freshman-level courses will be the most difficult in college because they form the basic background for your college education. College does become easier as you establish this basic background and practice effective study techniques.

You can enhance your basic background by reading a variety of books. Making reading a habit also enhances vocabulary, writing, and spelling. College provides many opportunities for expanding your reading horizons and areas of basic knowledge.

Stress and Emotions

Memory and learning are affected by stress and emotions. Moderate stress can be turned into motivation. For example, if you are moderately stressed over an exam, you may be more motivated to study for it. However, severe or chronic stress, along with the feeling that you have no control over it, results in a reduced ability to learn. If you are overly stressed, both short- and long-term memories are decreased as well as your ability to process language and do math.

Fear and stress are closely related. Fear causes us to run away from threatening or dangerous situations or to avoid them. Fear is one of the most powerful causes of academic failure. If you are fearful or doubt your ability to succeed in college, seek help from your counselor or advisor and use services such as tutoring to increase your self-confidence and minimize fear.

Relax While Studying

The brain works much better when it is relaxed. As you become more confident in your study techniques, you can become more relaxed. Here are some suggestions to help you relax during study time.

- Use distributed practice to take away some of the pressure of learning; take breaks between periods of learning. Give yourself time to absorb the material.
- Plan ahead so that you do not have to cram. Waiting until the last minute to study produces anxiety that is counterproductive.
- If you are anxious, try a physical activity or relaxation exercise before study sessions. For example, imagine a warm, relaxing light beginning at the feet and moving slowly up the body to the top of the head. Feel each part of the body relax as the light makes contact with it. Take a few deep breaths and focus on your breathing.
- If you are feeling frustrated, it is often a good idea to stop and come back to your studies later. You may gain insight into your studies while you are more relaxed and doing something else. You can often benefit from a fresh perspective.

> ### Journal Entry #2
> Review the memory techniques explained in this chapter. List and briefly explain at least three techniques and give examples of how you can use them.

Using Mnemonics and Other Memory Tricks

© Lightspring/Shutterstock.com

Memory tricks can be used to enhance your memory. These memory tricks include acrostics, acronyms, peg systems, and loci systems. These systems are called *mnemonics*, from the Greek word *mneme* which means "to remember."

Mnemonic devices are very effective. A research study by Gerald R. Miller found that students who used mnemonic devices improved their test scores by up to 77 percent.[8] Mnemonics are effective because they help to organize material. They have been used throughout history, in part as a way to entertain people with amazing memory feats.

Mnemonics are best used for memorizing facts. They are not helpful for understanding or thinking critically about the information. Be sure to memorize your mnemonics carefully and review them right before exam time. Forgetting the mnemonic or a part of it can cause major problems.

Acrostics

Acrostics are creative rhymes, songs, poems, or sentences that help us to remember. Maybe you previously learned some of these in school.

- Continents: Eat an Aspirin after a Nighttime Snack (Europe, Antarctica, Asia, Africa, Australia, North America, South America)

- Directions of the compass: Never Eat Sour Watermelons (North, East, South, West)
- Geological ages: Practically Every Old Man Plays Poker Regularly (Paleocene, Eocene, Oligocene, Miocene, Pliocene, Pleistocene, Recent)
- Guitar Strings: Eat All Dead Gophers Before Easter (E, A, D, G, B, E)
- Oceans: I Am a Person (Indian, Arctic, Atlantic, Pacific)
- Metric system in order: King Henry Drinks Much Dark Chocolate Milk (Kilometer, hectometer, decameter, meter, decimeter, centimeter, millimeter
- Notes on the treble clef in music: Every Good Boy Does Fine (E, G, B, D, F)
- Classification in biology: Kings Play Cards on Fairly Good Soft Velvet (Kingdom, Phylum, Class, Order, Family, Genus, Species, Variety)
- Order of operations in algebra: Please Excuse My Dear Aunt Sally (Parenthesis, Exponents, Multiplication, Division, Addition, and Subtraction)

> **Memorization Tricks**
> - Acrostics
> - Acronyms
> - Peg systems
> - Loci systems
> - Visual clues
> - Say it aloud
> - Have a routine
> - Write it down

An effective way to invent your own acrostics is to first identify key ideas you need to remember, underline these key words or write them down as a list, and think of a word that starts with the first letter of each idea you want to remember. Rearrange the words if necessary to form a sentence. The more unusual the sentence, the easier it is to remember.

In addition to acrostics, there are many other creative memory aids:

- Days in each month: Thirty days hath September, April, June, and November. All the rest have 31, except February which has 28 until leap year gives it 29.
- Spelling rules: *i* before *e* except after *c*, or when sounding like *a* as in neighbor and weigh.
- Numbers: Can I remember the reciprocal? To remember the reciprocal of pi, count the letters in each word of the question above. The reciprocal of pi = .3 1 8 3 10

Mnemonics become more powerful when used with visualization. For example, if you are trying to remember the planets, use a mnemonic and then visualize Saturn as a hula-hoop dancer to remember that it has rings. Jupiter could be a king with a number of maids to represent its moons.

Acronyms

Acronyms are commonly used as shortcuts in our language. The military is especially fond of using acronyms. For example, NASA is the acronym for the National Aeronautics and Space Administration. You can invent your own acronyms as a memory trick. Here are some common ones that students have used:

- The colors of the spectrum: Roy G. Biv (red, orange, yellow, green, blue, indigo, violet)
- The Great Lakes: HOMES (Huron, Ontario, Michigan, Erie, Superior)
- The stages of cell division in biology: IPMAT (interphase, prophase, metaphase, and telophase)

To make your own acronym, list the items you wish to remember. Use the first letter of each word to make a new word. The word you make can be an actual word or an invented word.

Peg Systems

Peg systems start with numbers, typically 1 to 100. Each number is associated with an object. The object chosen to represent each number can be based on rhyme or on a logical association. The objects are memorized and used with a mental picture to recall a list.

There are entertainers who can have the audience call out a list of 100 objects and then repeat all of the objects through use of a peg system. Here is an example of a commonly used peg system based on rhyme:

One	Bun	Six	Sticks
Two	Shoe	Seven	Heaven
Three	Tree	Eight	Gate
Four	Door	Nine	Wine
Five	Hive	Ten	Hen

For example, if I want to remember a grocery list consisting of milk, eggs, carrots, and butter, I would make associations between the peg and the item I want to remember. The more unusual the association is, the better. I would start by making a visual connection between *bun*, my peg word, and *milk*, the first item on the list. I could picture dipping a bun into a glass of milk for a snack. Next I would make a connection between *shoe* and *eggs*. I could picture eggs being broken into my shoe as a joke. Next I would picture a *tree* with orange *carrots* hanging from it and then a *door* with *butter* dripping from the doorknob. The technique works because of the organization provided by the pegs and the power of visualization and association.

There are many variations of the peg system. One variation is using the letters of the alphabet instead of numbers. Another variation is to visualize objects and put them in a stack, one on top of the other, until you have a great tottering tower, like a totem pole telling a story. Still another variation is to use your body or your car as a peg system. Using our example of the grocery list above, visualize balancing the milk on your head, carrying eggs in your hands, having carrots tied around your waist and smearing butter on your feet. Remember that the more unusual the pictures, the easier they are to remember.

Loci Systems

Loci or location systems use a series of familiar places to aid the memory. The Roman orators often used this system to remember the outline of a speech. For example, the speaker might connect the entry of a house with the introduction, the living room with the first main point, and each part of the speech with a different room. Again, this technique works through organization and visualization.

Another example of using a loci system to remember a speech or dramatic production is to imagine a long hallway. Mentally draw a picture of each topic or section you need to remember, and then hang each picture on the wall. As you are giving your speech or acting out your part in the play, visualize walking down the hallway and looking at the pictures on the wall to remind yourself of the next topic. For multiple topics, you can place signs over several hallway entrances labeling the contents of each hallway.

Visual Clues

Visual clues are helpful memory devices. To remember your books, place them in front of the door so you will see them on your way to school. To remember to take your finished homework to school, put it in your car when you are done. To remember to fill a prescription, put the empty bottle on the front seat of your car. Tie a bright ribbon on your backpack to remind you to attend a meeting with your study group. When parking your car in the mall, look around and notice landmarks such as nearby stores or row numbers. When you enter a large department store, notice the items that are near the door you entered. Are you worried that you left the iron on? Tie a ribbon around the handle of the iron each time you turn it off or unplug it. To find out if you have all the items you need to go skiing, visualize yourself on the ski slope wearing all those items.

Say It Aloud

You can enhance memory by repeating aloud the items you are trying to remember. For example, if you want to remember where you hid your diamond ring, say it aloud a few times. Then reinforce the memory by making a visual picture of where you have hidden it. You can also make a rhyme or song to remember something. Commercials use this technique all the time to try to get you to remember a product and purchase it.

Have a Routine

Do you have a difficult time trying to remember where you left your keys, wallet, or purse? Having a routine can greatly simplify your life and help you to remember. As you enter your house, hang your keys on a hook each time. Decide where you will place your wallet or purse and put it in the same place each time. When I leave for work, I have a mental checklist with four items: keys, purse, glasses, and cell phone.

Write It Down

One of the easiest and most effective memory techniques is to simply write something down. Make a grocery list or to-do list, send yourself an email, or tape a note to your bathroom mirror or the dashboard of your car.

Remembering Names

Many people have difficulty remembering names of other people in social or business situations. The reason we have difficulty in remembering names is that we do not take the time to store the name properly in our memories. When we first meet someone, we are often distracted or thinking about ourselves. We are trying to remember our own names or wondering what impression we are making on the other person.

To remember a name, first make sure you have heard the name correctly. If you have not heard the name, there is no way you can remember it. Ask the person to repeat his or her name or check to see if you have heard it correctly. Immediately use the name. For example, say "It is nice to meet you, *Nancy*." If you can mentally repeat the name about five times, you have a good chance of remembering it. You can improve the chances of remembering the name if you can make an association. For example, you might think, "She looks like my daughter's friend Nancy." Some people remember names by making a rhyme such as "fancy Nancy."

Journal Entry #3

Review the material on using mnemonics and other memory tricks. List and explain at least three techniques that you find useful.

QUIZ

Memory Techniques

Test what you have learned by circling the letters of the correct answers to the following questions.

1. An effective memory technique is
    a. focusing on the details first.
    b. focusing on the main ideas first.
    c. realizing that learning in college is an unpleasant obligation.

2. Chunking information together can make learning easier. The optimum number of chunks which can be easily recalled is
    a. 10
    b. 20
    c. 7

3. To learn something new, it is helpful if you
    a. are interested in it.
    b. learn it right before the test.
    c. read it at least one time.

4. A mnemonic is
    a. a memory chip implanted in the brain to help you remember.
    b. a Greek word that means "repetition."
    c. an acrostic or acronym.

5. To remember names
    a. make sure you have heard the name correctly and repeat it.
    b. focus on the introduction and making a good impression.
    c. avoid saying the name aloud.

How did you do on the quiz? Check your answers: 1.b, 2.c, 3.a, 4.c, 5.a

© Hubis/Shutterstock.com

Optimize Your Brain Power

The health of the body is connected to the health of your brain and your ability to learn. Specifically, brain health and optimal learning are affected by exercise, sleep, nutrition, hydration, stress, caffeine, alcohol, and drugs.[10]

Do aerobic exercise. The brain needs oxygen to function and exercise improves the flow of oxygen to the brain. Researchers have found that the human brain can grow new nerve cells by putting subjects on a three-month aerobic workout regimen. It is interesting to note that these new nerve cells can be generated at any age and are important in reversing the aging process. Exercise lowers your chance of getting Alzheimer's disease by 60%.[11] Exercise produces chemicals in the brain that help you to be alert, motivated, and pay attention. It has a positive effect on long-term memory, reasoning, and problem solving. For optimum health and learning, it is important to exercise the body as well as the mind. How much is needed? It is recommended that you do 30 minutes of aerobic exercise four to five times a week.

Sleep to remember. During sleep, we organize and consolidate learning from the previous day. It is important for transferring the information from short-term to long-term memory. During sleep, memories are sorted and stored according to their importance to you. One powerful learning strategy is to review the material you want to remember just before going to sleep. If sleep does not occur or is interrupted, it is more difficult to remember what has been studied the previous day. Lack of sleep negatively affects attention, memory, logical reasoning, mathematical skills, and manual dexterity. Scientists have found that lack of sleep decreases mental abilities:[12]

- There is a 30% decline in mental abilities after missing one night of sleep.
- There is a 60% decline in mental abilities after missing two nights of sleep.
- When sleep is restricted to six hours or less for five nights, mental abilities also decline 60%.

How much sleep do you need for optimum memory? It is recommended that adults have between 7.5 and 9 hours of sleep each night. The last two hours between 5.5 hours and 7.5 hours are the most important since it is during this time that rapid eye movement (REM) sleep occurs that the memories from the day are reviewed and stored in long-term memory. During sleep, the short-term memory is cleared out leaving space for new learning to occur. After the proper amount of sleep, you are able to remember more accurately and with less stress and anxiety.

Good nutrition and water are important. The brain learns easier if it is well hydrated and has the energy from good nutrition including whole grains, fruits, and vegetables. Low-fat dits have been shown to improve mental performance.

Remember to relax. Chronic stress, which we do not feel we can control, interferes with both short- and long-term memory. Studies have shown that adults performed 50% worse on cognitive tests as compared to adults with low stress.[13]

Drink caffeine in moderation. Caffeine can make you feel stressed, making it difficult to think.

Don't smoke, abuse alcohol, or use drugs. Smoking blocks the carotid artery that supplies blood to the brain. Alcohol and drugs kill brain cells and change brain chemistry.

Use safety gear. Wear a seat belt when driving and a helmet when biking, boarding, or skating to reduce head injuries.

Keep active. Do puzzles, play a musical instrument, take something apart and fix it, draw or paint, dance, make friends with interesting people, read challenging books, or take a college course.

Journal Entry #4

What is your plan for keeping your brain healthy throughout life? Include some of these ideas: keeping mentally active, exercise, getting enough sleep, nutrition, drinking water, relaxation, avoiding addictions, and using safety gear.

KEYS TO SUCCESS

Positive Thinking

You can improve your memory as well as your life by using positive thinking. Positive thinking involves two aspects: thinking about yourself and thinking about the world around you. When you think positively about yourself, you develop confidence in your abilities and become more capable of whatever you are attempting to do. When you think positively about the world around you, you look for possibilities and find interest in what you are doing.

Golfer Arnold Palmer has won many trophies but places high value on a plaque on his wall with a poem by C.W. Longenecker:

> If you think you are beaten, you are.
> If you think you dare not, you don't.
> If you like to win but think you can't,
> It's almost certain that you won't.
> Life's battles don't always go
> To the stronger woman or man,
> But sooner or later, those who win
> Are those who think they can.[14]

Success in athletics, school, or any other endeavor begins with positive thinking. To remember anything, first, you have to believe that you can remember. Trust in your abilities. Then apply memory techniques to help you to remember. If you think that you cannot remember, you will not even try.

The second part of positive thinking involves thinking about the world around you. If you can convince yourself that the world and your college studies are full of interesting possibilities, you can start on a journey of adventure to discover new ideas. For example, it is easier to remember what you read if you find the subject interesting. If the topic is interesting, you will learn more about it. The more you learn about a topic, the more interesting it becomes, and you are well on your way in your journey of discovery. If you tell yourself that the task is boring, you will struggle and find the task difficult. You will also find it difficult to continue.

To find something interesting, look for personal meaning. How can I use this information? Does it relate to something I know? Will this information be useful in my future career? Why is this information important? Write down your personal goals and remind yourself of your purpose for attending college. You are not just completing an assignment: you are on a path to discovery.

To be successful in college, start with the belief that you can be successful. Anticipate that the journey will be interesting, challenging, and full of possibilities. Enjoy the journey!

© Anson0618/Shutterstock.com

> ## Journal Entry #5
>
> How can you use positive thinking to improve your memory and success in college? Use any of these questions to guide your thinking:
>
> - How can I think positively about myself?
> - How can I think positively about my college experience?
> - What is the connection between belief and success?
> - How can positive thinking make college more fun?

Appreciating Island Cultures: The Story of Haloa

Wakea, the man, the Father of the Hawaiian Islands, and Ho'ohokukalani, the woman, were Hapai, or carrying a child. This child would be the first, the oldest of the Hawaiian people. Ho'ohokukalani gave birth to a baby boy, premature and born without breath in his lungs. Sadly, he did not make it. Ho'ohokukalani chose to bury him on the east side of her house, where the sun rose each morning. A plant began to grow where the baby was buried. This plant was the first kalo, or taro plant. Ho'ohokukalani named him Haloanaka-laukapalili, meaning the long stalk whose leaves quiver in the wind. The kalo's leaves blow gently from side to side when the breeze hits.

In time, Wakea and Ho'ohokukalani were able to have another child. Ho'ohokukalani gave birth to a healthy baby boy with breath in his lungs. She named him Haloa after his older brother, Haloanakalaukapalili, the kalo planted on the east side of the house. Even though his body was no longer with them, Haloanakalaukapalili still took care of his 'ohana, or family, and gave much sustenance to his younger brother, Haloa. Haloa grew and more descendants came from him. Haloanakalaukapalili gave nutrients and life to his younger brother Haloa and his 'ohana and continues to give life to the Hawaiian people, and many others, even today, generations later.

Taro or kalo plants.
© Signature Message/Shutterstock.com

Questions

1. Like Haloanakalaukapalili, as part of the 'aina, or land, helps his brother grow, how does your environment play a role in who you are? Where do you see yourself?
2. Does your environment affect the way you learn?
3. How does knowing or not knowing your family lineage have an effect on the way you see yourself or your identity?
4. How important is the knowledge passed down from generation to generation to the goals that you make for your future?
5. Knowing the past and knowing what those that have come before you have done to benefit your people, their community, and their family, does that motivate you to do more for your people, community, and family?

- Haloanakalaukapalili: The long stalk whose leaves quiver in the wind. First ancestor of the Hawaiian people.
- Haloa: Long breath
- Hapai: With child
- Ho'okukalani: Mother of Haloanakalaukapalili
- Kalo: Taro
- 'Ohana: Family
- Wakea: Father of the Hawaiian Islands

College Success 1

The College Success 1 website is continually updated with supplementary material for each chapter including Word documents of the journal entries, classroom activities, handouts, videos, links to related materials, and much more. See http://www.collegesuccess1.com/.

Notes

1. Terry Doyle and Todd Zakrajsek, *The New Science of Learning, How to Learn in Harmony with Your Brain*, (Sterling, VA: Stylus, 2013), 6–7.
2. Colin Rose, *Accelerated Learning*, (New York: Dell Publishing, 1985), 33–36.
3. Ibid., 50–51.
4. Doyle and Zakrajsek, *The New Science of Learning, How to Learn in Harmony with Your Brain*, 77.
5. G.A. Miller, "The Magical Number Seven, Plus or Minus Two: Some Limits on Our Capacity for Processing Invformation," *Psychological Review* 63 (March 1956): 81–97.
6. Doyle and Zakrajsek, *The New Science of Learning, How to Learn in Harmony with Your Brain*, 49–50.
7. Adapted from Paul Chance, *Learning and Behavior* (Pacific Grove, CA: Brooks/Cole, 1979), 301.
8. Walter Pauk, *How to Study in College* (Boston: Houghton Mifflin, 1989), 108.
9. Colin Rose, *Accelerated Learning* (New York: Dell Publishing, 1985), 33–36.
10. John Medina, *Brain Rules: 12 Principles for Surviving and Thriving at Work, Home, and School*, (Seattle, WA: Pear Press, 2008).
11. Ibid., p. 16.
12. Ibid., p. 162.
13. Ibid., p. 178.
14. Rob Gilbert, ed., *Bits and Pieces* (Fairfield, NJ: The Economics Press, 1998), Vol. R, No. 40, p. 12.

Scenarios

Name _____ Date _____

Review the main ideas on improving memory and reading. Based on these ideas, how would you be successful in the following situations? You may want to do this as a group activity in your class.

1. You just read the assigned chapter in economics and cannot remember what you read. It went in one ear and out the other.

2. In your anatomy and physiology class, you are required to remember the scientific names for 100 different muscles in the body.

3. You signed up for a philosophy class because it meets general education requirements. You are not interested in the class at all.

4. You have a midterm in your literature class and have to read 400 pages in one month.

5. You must take American history to graduate from college. You think that history is boring.

6. You have been introduced to an important business contact and would like to remember his/her name.

7. You are enrolled in an algebra class. You continually remind yourself that you have never been good at math. You don't think that you will pass this class.

8. You have noticed that your grandmother is becoming very forgetful. You want to do whatever is possible to keep your mind healthy as you age.

Memory Test

Name _____ Date _____

Part 1. Your professor will read a list of 15 items. Do not write them down. After listening to this list, see how many you can remember and write them here.

1.	6.	11.
2.	7.	12.
3.	8.	13.
4.	9.	14.
5.	10.	15.

After your professor has given you the answers, write the number of words you remembered: _____

Part 2. Your professor will discuss memory techniques that you can use to improve your test scores and then will read another list. Again, do not write the words down, but try to apply the recommended techniques. Write as many words as you can remember.

1.	6.	11.
2.	7.	12.
3.	8.	13.
4.	9.	14.
5.	10.	15.

How many words did you remember this time? _____

Practice with Mnemonics

Name _____ Date _____

Join with a group of students in your class to invent some acrostics and acronyms.

Acrostics

Acrostics are creative rhymes, songs, poems, or sentences that help us to remember. To write an acrostic, think of a word that starts with the same letter as each idea you want to remember. Sometimes you can rearrange the words if necessary to form a sentence. At other times, it is necessary to keep the words in order. The more unusual the sentence, the easier it is to remember.

Example: Classification in biology: Kings Play Cards on Fairly Good Soft Velvet (Kingdom, Phylum, Class, Order, Family, Genus, Species, Variety)

Create an acrostic for the planets in the solar system. Keep the words in the same order as the planets from closest to the sun to farthest from the sun.

Mercury, Venus, Earth, Mars, Jupiter, Saturn, Uranus, Neptune, Pluto (now a dwarf planet)

_____

_____

_____

Acronyms

To make your own acronym, list the items you wish to remember. Use the first letter of each word to make a new word. The new word you invented can be an actual word or an invented word.

Example: The Great Lakes: HOMES (Huron, Ontario, Michigan, Erie, and Superior)

The following are the excretory organs of the body. Make an acronym to remember them. Rearrange the words if necessary.

intestines, liver, lungs, kidneys, skin

_____

_____

_____

Write down any acrostics or acronyms that you know. Share them with your group.

CHAPTER 6

Using Brain Science to Improve Study Skills

Learning Objectives

Read to answer these key questions:

- What are some learning strategies based on brain science?

- How can I apply memory techniques to reading?

- What is a reading system for college texts?

- What are some reading strategies for different subjects?

- What are some e-learning strategies?

- What are the best ways to study math?

- How can I create my success in college, careers, and life?

From *College & Career Success, Concise Version*, Seventh Edition, by Marsha Fralick. Copyright © 2016 by Kendall Hunt Publishing Company. Reprinted by permission.

© VLADGRIN/Shutterstock.com

"The minute you are not learning I believe you're dead!"
Jack Nicholson

Learning how to learn is not only important in college but also in your future career. The world is in a constant state of change requiring continued learning on the job. Learning strategies based on current research in neuroscience, psychology, and education can make studying easier, more effective, and more productive. This chapter explores some key ideas that can make you an efficient lifelong learner. Apply these memory strategies to improve study skills, make reading more effective, and increase your success in math.

Neuroscience and Practical Learning Strategies

Recent discoveries in neuroscience can be translated into practical and efficient learning strategies for students. Neuroscientists have shown that learning can be increased by **using and integrating all the senses**, not just the preferred ones. This process is called **multi-sensory integration**.

Learning is optimized when more senses are used when trying to remember what we are studying. Researchers note that "it is likely that the human brain has evolved to develop, learn, and operate optimally in multi-sensory environments."[1]

The senses work together as a team to optimize learning by encoding the information into the brain in the form of long-term memories. Sensory inputs include

- **Visual:** learning through reading, observing, or seeing things.
- **Auditory:** learning through listening and talking.
- **Tactile:** learning through touching the material or using a "hands-on approach."
- **Kinesthetic:** learning through movement as in learning to ride a bicycle.
- **Olfactory:** learning by smell.
- **Gustatory:** learning through taste.

Use all of your senses to help you to remember. For example, when studying Spanish, motivate yourself to learn by watching videos of Spanish speaking countries, listen to the words and say them out loud, use flash cards you can touch to practice the vocabulary, imagine the smell of Mexican food, eat some salsa and chips, and if possible, travel to a Spanish speaking country where you can practice the language.

Are there differences between the left brain and right brain that affect how we learn? Educators have often taught students that there is a difference between the right brain and left brain, with one side being more creative and the other more analytical. This idea is not supported by current brain research that shows that **both sides of the brain work together**. New findings show that the right side of the brain tends to remember the main ideas and the left side remembers the details, but every brain is unique.[2] It is suggested that to improve memory, it is important to begin with the main idea (right brain) and then remember the details (left brain).

Visual Learning Strategies

Some scientists have found that vision is the best tool for learning anything. The more visual the input, the more likely it is to be remembered. It was found that 72 hours after learning something, people recalled only 10% of material presented orally versus 65% recollection when a picture was added.[3] When we animate the pictures, learning is further improved. It is important to use visualization as an aid to studying and remembering. Make a visual picture of what you need to remember. If you can make a mental video, recall is further enhanced.

Here are some visual learning strategies. Highlight or place a checkmark in front of the learning strategies that you can use:

____Make a visual image of what you are learning. For example, while reading history, picture in your mind's eye what it would be like to live in that historical period. Even better, make a video.

____If you are having difficulties understanding a concept, find an online video that explains it.

____Use color to highlight the important points in the text while reading. Review the important points by looking at the highlighted passages again.

____Take notes and use underlining and highlighting in different colors to highlight the important points. Include flow charts, graphs, and pictures in your notes.

____Make summary sheets or mind maps to summarize and review your notes.

____Use pictures, diagrams, flow charts, maps, graphs, time lines, videos, and multimedia to aid in learning and preparing for exams.

____Use flash cards to remember the details.

____Sit in front of the class so you can carefully observe the professor. Copy what is written on the board or use your cell phone to photograph it.

____Create visual reminders to keep on track. Make lists on note pads or use sticky notes as reminders.

____Before answering an essay question, picture the answer in your mind and then make an outline or mind map.

____Use mind maps and outlines to review for exams.

____When learning new material, begin with visual learning strategies and then reinforce them with audio, kinesthetic, tactile, or olfactory strategies.

Audio Learning Strategies

Audio learning strategies involve using the sense of hearing to learn new information. Use these techniques to reinforce visual learning. Highlight or place a checkmark next to the strategies you can use.

____As you are reading, ask questions or say out loud what you think will be important to remember.

____Make it a priority to attend lectures and participate in classroom discussions.

____To prepare for exams, rehearse or say the information verbally. For example, while studying math, say the equations out loud.

____Discuss what you are learning with other students or friends. Form a study group.

____Use memory devices, rhymes, poems, rhythms, or music to remember what you are studying. For example, turn facts into a rap song or musical jingle to aid in recall.

____Memorize key concepts by repeating them aloud.

____If you are having problems reading your textbook or understanding the directions, read them out loud.

____Some students can study better with music. However, if your attention shifts to the music, you are multi-tasking and it will take longer to complete your work. On the other hand, some students use music for relaxation, which can be beneficial to studying. Experiment to see if you can be more efficient with the music on or off.

Tactile Learning Techniques

You can increase your learning by using your sense of touch to learn new information. Here are some tactile learning strategies: highlight or place a checkmark next to the ones you can use:

____Writing is one of the best tactile learning strategies. Take notes, write a journal, list key ideas, make an outline, or create a mind map.

____Use real objects to help you learn. For example, in a physics course, if you are studying levers, make a simple lever and observe how it works. If you are studying geography, use a globe or map to aid in studying.

____Use flash cards to review the key ideas as well as the details.

Kinesthetic Learning Strategies

These strategies involve moving around while studying. Highlight or place a checkmark in front of the strategies that you can use.

____Move while studying. For example, review material while on your exercise bike or stair stepper.

____Participate in kinesthetic learning experiences such as drama, building, designing, visiting, interviewing, and going on field trips.

____Take frequent breaks and study in different locations.

____Use a study group to teach the material to someone else.

Olfactory Learning Strategies

Olfactory refers to our sense of smell and is strongly associated with learning and memory. Marketing companies are using this sense to increase sales. For example, bakeries often distribute the smells from baking outside as a way of drawing in customers. Perfumes and body sprays are often advertised as a way to attract the opposite sex. Researchers had two groups watch a movie and tested them for recall. One group was tested without smell, and one was tested with the smell of popcorn in the room. The group with the popcorn smell had significantly increased recall.[4] Smells are powerful because they are often connected to emotions. In our previous example, movies and popcorn are positive experiences. Can you think of creative ways to use smell to increase memory? When creating that visual picture or video to enhance memory, include the sense of smell. Make it a four-dimensional movie (visual, audio, kinesthetic and olfactory!). You can use smells to create a positive learning environment.

Gustatory Learning Strategies

Gustatory refers to our sense of taste and can be used to enhance recall. You can eat your favorite piece of candy or chewing gum when trying to remember something that is difficult or seems uninteresting to you. Your sense of taste can be used to stimulate the reward center of the brain which regulates motivation, learning, memory, and goal-directed behavior. A caution on this technique is to avoid overeating and the resultant weight gain. One piece of candy or sugarless gum will do!

> ### Journal Entry #1
>
> Neuroscientists have discovered that learning is increased by using and integrating all the senses. How would you study a chapter in history, biology, or one of your current courses by using all your senses?

Applying Memory Strategies to Reading

You can apply memory strategies to store information from reading in your long-term memory.

A Study System for Reading a College Textbook: SQ4R

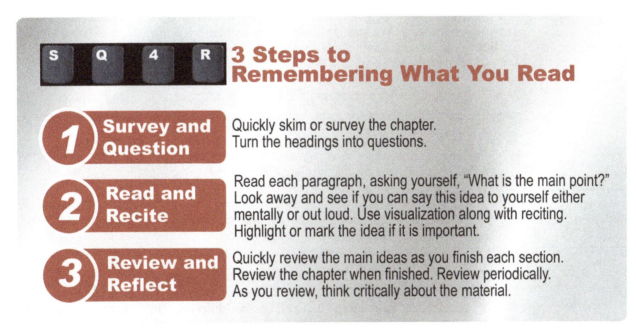

Figure 5.1 The SQ4R System for reading a college textbook.

Many students spend time reading their college textbooks with little benefit. Often students say that they cannot remember the material they have just read. The reason for this problem is not lack of intelligence, but rather a simple lack of rehearsal. If you are just reading the material, you are placing it in short-term memory, which quickly disappears. Effective study systems for reading a college textbook include techniques for storing information in long-term memory including recognizing major points, organizing the material to be learned, reviewing, intending to remember, and critical thinking about reading. It helps to think positively about the material and look for something interesting or meaningful in it. The essential point is that you must repeat or rehearse the material to transfer it to long-term memory. The **SQ4R system** (**Survey**, **Question**, **Read**, **Recite**, **Review**, and **Reflect**) is a simple and effective way to store information in long-term memory. This system can be broken down into three steps.

Step 1: Survey and Question. Finding the important points and understanding the organization of the reading is essential for learning and recall. The typical pattern of a college text is title, subtitle, paragraph, and topic sentence. Learn to focus on the pattern and major points and then add the details. This is accomplished by surveying and questioning the chapter before you begin reading it in detail. Read the title and first paragraph or introduction to the chapter and then look quickly through the chapter, letting your eyes glide across bold headings, diagrams, illustrations, and photos. Read the last paragraph or summary of the chapter. This process should take five minutes or less for a typical chapter in a college textbook. It is time well spent for transferring the information to your long-term memory.

While you are surveying the chapter, ask yourself questions. Take each major heading in the chapter and turn it into a question. For example, in this section of the book you might ask: What is a system for reading a college text? Why do I need a system? What is SQ4R? What is the first step of SQ4R? You can also ask some general questions as you survey the chapter: What is the main point? What will I learn? Do I know something about this? Can I find something that interests me? How can I use this? Does this relate to something said in class? What does this mean? Is this a possible test question? Asking questions will help you to become an active reader and to find some personal meaning in the content that will help you remember it. If you at least survey and question the relevant textbook material before you go to class, you will have the advantage of being familiar with some of the key ideas to be discussed.

There are several benefits to taking this first step:

- This is the first step in rehearsal for storage of information into long-term memory.
- The quick survey is a warmup for the brain, similar to an athlete's warmup before exercise.
- A survey step is also good practice for improving your reading speed.
- Reading to answer questions increases comprehension, sparks interest, and has the added bonus of keeping you awake while reading.

> "The important thing is to not stop questioning."
> Albert Einstein

If you want to be able to read faster, improve your reading comprehension, and increase retention of your reading material, practice the survey and question step before you begin your detailed reading.

Step 2: Read and recite. The second step in reading a text is to read and recite. Read each paragraph and look for the most important point or topic sentence. If the point is important, highlight or underline it. You might use different colors to organize the ideas. You can also make a notation or outline in the margin of the text if the point is especially significant, meaningful, useful, or likely to appear on an exam. A picture, diagram, or chart drawn in the margin is a great way to use visualization to improve retention of the material. If you are reading online, take notes on the important points or use cut and paste to collect the main ideas in a separate document.

Next, look away and see if you can say the main point to yourself either silently or out loud. Reciting is even more powerful if you combine it with visualization. Make a video in your head to illustrate what you are learning. Include color, movement, and sound if possible. Reciting is crucial to long-term memory storage. It will also keep you awake. Beginning college students will find this step a challenge, but practice makes it a habit that becomes easier and easier.

© George Dolgikh/Shutterstock.com

If you read a paragraph or section and do not understand the main point, try these techniques:

1. **Notice any vocabulary or technical terms that are unfamiliar.** Look up these words in a dictionary or in the glossary at the back of the book. Use index cards; write the words on one side and the definition on the other side. Use the SAFMEDS technique (Say All Fast in one Minute Each Day Shuffle) discussed earlier in this textbook. You are likely to see these vocabulary words on quizzes and exams.

2. **Read the paragraph again.** Until you get into the habit of searching for the main point, you may need to reread a paragraph until you understand. If this does not work, reread the paragraphs before and after the one you do not understand.

3. **Write a question in the margin and ask your instructor or tutor to explain.** College instructors have office hours set aside to assist students with questions, and faculty are generally favorably impressed with students who care enough to ask questions. Most colleges offer tutoring free of charge.

4. **If you are really frustrated, put your reading away and come back to it later.** You may be able to relax and gain some insight about the material.

5. **Make sure you have the proper background for the course.** Take the introductory course first.

6. **Assess your reading skills.** Colleges offer reading assessments, and counselors can help you understand your skill level and suggest appropriate courses. Most colleges offer reading courses that can help you to be successful in college.

7. **If you have always had a problem with reading, you may have a learning disability.** A person with a learning disability is of average or higher-than-average intelligence, but has a problem that interferes with learning. Most colleges offer assessment that can help you understand your learning disability and tutoring that is designed to help you to compensate for the disability.

Step 3: Review and reflect. The last step in reading is to review and reflect. After each section, quickly review what you have highlighted or underlined. Again, ask questions. How can I use this information? How does it relate to what I already know? What is most important? What is likely to be on the exam? Is it true? Learn to think critically about the material you have learned.

When you finish the chapter, quickly (in a couple of minutes) look over the highlights again. This last step, review and reflect, is another opportunity for rehearsal. At this point, you have stored the information in long-term memory and want to make sure that you can access the information again in the future. Think of this last step as a creative step in which you put the pieces together, gain an understanding, and begin to think of how you can apply your new knowledge to your personal life. This is the true reward of studying.

Review is faster, easier, and more effective if done immediately. As discussed previously, most forgetting occurs in the first 20 minutes after exposure to new information. If you wait 24 hours to review, you will probably have forgotten 80 percent of the material and will have to spend a longer time in review. Review periodically to make sure that you can access the material easily in the future, and review again right before the test.

As you read about the above steps, you may think that this process takes a lot of time. Remember that it is not how much you read, but how you read that is important. In reality, the SQ4R technique is a time-saver in that you do not have to reread all the material before the test. You just need to quickly review information that is stored in long-term memory. Rereading can be purely mechanical and consume your time with little payoff. Rather than rereading, spend your time reciting the important points. With proper review, you can remember 80 to 90 percent of the material.

Research has shown that you can retain 88% of the material you study using the following review schedule.[5] The rate of retention using this schedule is four times better.

1. Review immediately within 30 seconds.
2. Review after a few minutes.
3. Review after one hour.
4. Review a day later after an overnight rest.
5. Review after a week.
6. Review after one month.

Suggestions for review schedules vary, but the key point is that review is most effective when it is done in short sessions spaced out over time.

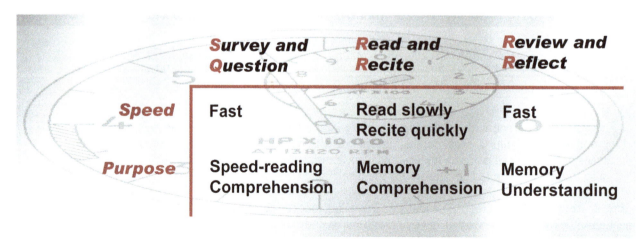

Figure 5.2 This chart summarizes the speed and purpose of each SQ4R step.

What to Do If Your Reading Goes in One Ear and Out the Other

1. **Silence your inner critic.**
   If you have always told yourself that you are a poor reader or hate reading, these thoughts make it difficult to read. Think positively and tell yourself that with some effort, you can read and understand. Focus on what you can do, rather than what you can't do.

2. Look for the key ideas and underline them.

3. **Try visualization.**
   Make a mental picture or video with the material you are reading.

4. **Look for personal meaning.**
   Can you relate the material to your life in any way?

5. Do a quick scan of the material to find some major points and then reread the material closely.

6. Try talking to the text as you read it. Ask questions. Why is this important? Do you know anything about this? Do you agree or disagree? Do you think it is a good or bad idea? Can you use this information in the future? Can you find something interesting in the text? Challenge the material and think critically about it. Make humorous remarks. Imagine yourself in the situation. What would it be like and what would you do? You can write your comments in the text or do this silently in your head.

© wavebreakmedia/Shutterstock.com

Reading Strategies for Different Subjects
Math

1. Skimming the textbook can help you to decide if you are enrolled in the correct course. While skimming a math book, keep in mind that many of the topics will be unfamiliar to you. You should be able to understand the first few pages and build your knowledge from there. If you do not understand these first few pages, you may need to go back and take a review math course, especially if there has been a gap in studying math. If all the concepts are familiar to you, you may be taking a class that you do not need.

2. It is helpful to read your math textbook before you go to class so you can begin to understand key concepts and vocabulary. Make note of areas that need special attention to increase your understanding. Pre-reading or at least skimming the text will help you to understand the lecture better.

3. As you are reading, make flash cards to review important formulas, vocabulary, and definitions.

4. It is not enough to read and understand mathematical concepts. Make sure that you add practice to your study system. Practice builds self-confidence needed for success on math exams.

5. Focus on understanding math concepts rather than on memorizing problems.

Science

1. In science classes, the scientific method is used to describe the world. The scientific method relies on questioning, observing, hypothesizing, researching, and analyzing. You will learn about theories and scientific principles. Highlight or mark theories, names of scientists, definitions, concepts, and procedures.

2. Understand the scientific principles and use flash cards to remember details and formulas.

3. Study the charts, diagrams, tables, and graphs. Draw your own pictures and graphs to get a visual picture of the material.

4. Use lab time as an opportunity to practice the theories and principles that you have learned.

Social and Behavioral Sciences

1. Social and behavioral scientists focus on principles of behavior, theories, and research. Notice that there are different theories that explain the same phenomena. Highlight, underline, and summarize these theories in your own words.

2. When looking at the research, ask yourself what the point of the research was, who conducted the research, when the research was completed, what data was collected, and what conclusions were drawn.

3. Think of practical applications of theories.

4. Use flash cards to remember details.

Literature Courses

When taking a course in literature, you will be asked to understand, appreciate, interpret, evaluate, and write about the literature.

1. Underline the names of characters and write plot summaries.

2. Write notes about your evaluation of literary works.

3. Make flash cards to remember literary terms.

4. Write down important quotes or note page numbers on a separate piece of paper so that you don't have to go back and find them later when you are writing about a work.

Foreign Language Courses

Foreign language courses require memorization and practice.

1. Distribute the practice. Practice a small amount each day. It is not possible to learn everything at once.

2. Complete the exercises as a way to practice and remember.

3. Study out loud.

4. Practice speaking the language with others.

5. Use flash cards to remember vocabulary.

6. Make charts to practice verb conjugations.

7. Ask for help if you do not understand.

8. Learn to think in the foreign language. Translating from English causes confusion because the structures of languages are different.

> "Whatever the mind of man can conceive and believe, it can achieve."
> Napoleon Hill

Improving Reading Concentration

Hank Aaron said that what separates the superstar from the average ballplayer is that the superstar concentrates just a little longer. Athletes are very aware of the power of concentration in improving athletic performance. Coaches remind athletes to focus on the ball and to develop good powers of concentration and visualization. Being able to concentrate on your reading helps you to study more efficiently.

Here are some ideas for dealing with internal mental distractions while reading.

1. **Become an active reader.** Read to answer questions. Search for the main idea. Recite or re-say the main idea in your mind. Reflect and think critically about the material you are reading. Mark or highlight the text. Visualize what you are reading.

2. **Remind yourself of your purpose for reading.** Think of your future college and career goals.

3. **Give yourself permission to daydream.** Use daydreaming as a break from your studies. Come back to your studies with a relaxed attitude.

4. **Break the task into small parts.** If the task seems overwhelming, break it into small parts and do the first part. If you have 400 pages to read in 10 days, read 40 pages each day. Make a schedule that allows time to read each day until you have accomplished your goal. Use distributed practice in your studies. Study for a short time each day rather than holding a marathon study session before the test.

© Diego Cervo/Shutterstock.com

> **Improving Reading Concentration**
> 1. Become an active reader
> 2. Remember your purpose
> 3. Use daydreaming to relax
> 5. Plan to deal with worry
> 6. Break tasks into small parts

E-Learning Strategies

Reading and studying online require some different strategies. Here are some online reading strategies and tips for succeeding in online courses.

Online Reading Strategies

The amount of online reading we do is increasing, so it is important to have some online reading strategies. First, determine your purpose for reading. If you are reading for entertainment, to interact with others, or to find needed information, quickly scan the material to see if it meets your needs. Look for bulleted lists, menu bars, highlighted words, and headers. Read only what suits your purpose. Avoid getting lost on your search by using browser tools such as favorites, bookmarks, or the history menu, which is a list of the pages you have visited before. Use multiple browser windows to compare and synthesize information. To avoid eyestrain while reading online, be sure to take breaks and look away from the screen. It is important to get up and stretch periodically.

If you are studying for an online course, first scan the material for key words. Then carefully read each section and summarize what you have learned. If you cannot summarize the material, then read it

© Naypong/Shutterstock.com

again, searching for the main ideas. Take notes or highlight the important points. You can save time by opening a separate document in a new window and cutting and pasting the important points into your notes. Be sure to include the source of the material, so that you can find it again and use it in writing papers. As in reading print material, use some techniques to assure good comprehension: as you read each section, visualize what you are reading, ask questions, and think critically about the material. As in reading print materials, you will need to practice, rehearse, or repeat the material to store it in your long-term memory.

Tips for Online Learning

There are many opportunities for learning online, including online courses, professional development, or learning for your personal life. Students who are independent learners or introverts who enjoy individual learning in a quiet place may prefer online learning. Students who prefer having a professor to guide learning with immediate feedback and extraverts who are energized by social interaction may prefer traditional classroom education. Because of work, family, and time constraints, online learning might be a convenient way to complete your courses.

If you have never taken an online course, be aware of some of the myths of online learning. One of the most popular myths is that online courses are easier than traditional courses. Online courses typically involve more writing, cover the same content, and are just as rigorous as traditional face-to-face courses. However, you will save time in commuting to class and have the added convenience of working on your class at any time or place where you can access the Internet.

Here are some suggestions for a successful e-learning experience.

- The most important key to success in online learning is to **log in regularly** and complete the work in a systematic way, rather than waiting to complete assignments just before the deadline. Set goals for what you need to accomplish each week and do the work a step at a time. Get in the habit of regularly doing your online study, just as you would do in a traditional course each week.
- It is important to **carefully read the instructions** for the assignments and **ask for help** if you need it. Your online professor will not know when you need help.
- Begin your online work by getting familiar with the requirements and components of the course. Generally, online courses have reading material, quizzes, discussion boards, chat rooms, assignments, and multimedia presentations. Make sure that you **understand all the resources**, **components**, and **requirements** of the course.
- **Have a backup plan** if your computer crashes or your Internet connection is interrupted. Colleges generally have computer labs where you can do your work if you have technical problems at home.
- Remember to **participate** in the online discussions or chats. It is usually part of your grade and a good way to learn from other students and apply what you have learned. The advantage of online communication is that you have time to think about your responses.
- **Check your grades** online to make sure you are completing all the requirements. Celebrate your success as you complete each component of your online course. Online learning becomes easier with experience.

Guidelines for Marking Your Textbook

Marking your textbook can help you pick out what is important, save time, and review the material. It is a great way to reinforce your memory. In high school, you were given the command, "Thou shalt not mark in thy book!" College is different. You have paid for

> "The illiterate of the 21st Century will not be those who cannot read or write, but those who cannot learn, unlearn, and relearn."
>
> Alvin Toffler

the book and need to use it as a tool. Even if you plan to sell your book, you can still mark it up. Here are some guidelines for marking your book:

- Underline or mark only the key ideas in your text. You don't have to underline complete sentences; just underline enough to make sense when you review your markings. If reading online, use the highlighter tool to mark the main points and then cut and paste the main points into a separate document.
- Aim for marking or highlighting about 20 percent of the most important material. If you mark too much of your reading, it will be difficult to review the main points.
- Read each paragraph first. Ask yourself, "What is the main point?" Highlight or mark the main point if it is important. Not every paragraph has a main point that needs to be marked.
- Use other marks to help you organize what you have read. Write in numbers or letters and use different colors to help you organize ideas.
- Most college texts have wide margins. Use these margins to write down questions, outlines, or key points to remember.
- Learn to be brief, fast, and neat in your marking or highlighting.
- If you are tempted to mark too much, use the double system of first underlining with a pencil as much as you want and then using a highlighter to pick out the most important 20 percent of the material in the chapter.

© SnowWhiteimages/
Shutterstock.com

QUIZ

Learning Strategies and Reading

Test what you have learned by selecting the correct answers to the following questions.

1. For optimal learning, brain scientist believe that it is best to use
   a. your left brain.
   b. your right brain.
   c. multisensory input.

2. Brain scientists have recently found that you learn best by using
   a. your preferred learning style.
   b. all of your senses to remember.
   c. auditory techniques.

3. Most scientists believe that the most powerful strategy for learning anything is
   a. visual.
   b. auditory.
   c. kinesthetic.

4. If you have read the chapter and can't remember what you have read,
   a. read the chapter again.
   b. remember to select important points and review them.
   c. the material is stored in long-term memory.

5. When you start reading a new textbook,
   a. begin with chapter one.
   b. focus on the details you will need to remember.
   c. skim over the text to get a general idea of what you will be reading.

How did you do on the quiz? Check your answers: 1. c, 2. b, 3. a, 4. b, 5. c

> **Journal Entry #2**
>
> You have just read a chapter in your economics textbook and can't remember what you have just read. How can you apply the ideas in this chapter to improve your reading comprehension?

How to Be Successful in Your Math Courses

To improve math study, it is helpful to begin by realizing the importance of math. The careers with the highest salaries require math and it is a requirement for graduation from college. However, students often have math phobia and postpone taking math courses until the end of their college studies. This can result in limited choice of a college major, dropping out of college, or a delay in graduation. It is important to take math early in your college studies and to enroll in math courses each semester until your math requirement is complete.

Researchers have studied the variables contributing to success in math.[6] About 50% of math success depends on your previous knowledge of math skills and how fast you can learn math. For this reason, it is important to take a math placement test and start at the level that is right for you. If you have had a gap in your math studies, you may need to go back and enroll in math review courses. About 25% of success in math depends on the quality of instruction in math. You may need to find the math instructor who matches how you learn best. The remaining 25% of success depends on math study skills and personal characteristics related to success in math. Successful students:

- Think positively about their ability to succeed in math. If you have had difficulties with math in the past and believe that you may not be successful in your college math courses, you will not take the steps needed to be successful in math. If you have self-statements such as "I hate math" or "I'm not good at math," change your statement to "I can learn to be successful in math."
- Use an internal locus of control, which means taking responsibility for your own success. Rather than blaming a teacher or past bad experiences, take the steps necessary to be successful.
- Use the motivation techniques from the first chapter to increase success.
- Prepare adequately for math courses to minimize test anxiety. This topic is covered more in depth in the test-taking chapter.
- Make it a goal to earn an A or a B in their math courses. Lower grades will make it difficult to succeed in the next level.
Here are some tips for improving your math success:

It is estimated that you will need to spend at least 10 hours a week studying math to be successful in a college math course. College math courses go four times faster than high-school math courses and require more work outside of class.[7] Make a study schedule and plan the time needed for reading your math text, reviewing your notes, doing your homework, and practicing math problems. Invest the time and effort needed to be successful.

Make studying math a priority. Study math first and then study subjects that are easier for you. Make use of your prime time when you are most alert to study math.

Math involves practice. Unlike other courses that rely on critical thinking, memorization, and recall, math also requires the application of math concepts to solving problems. To be successful on math exams, practice solving problems until you feel comfortable with them. Make practice tests to prepare for exams. It is important to apply the concept of distributed practice to study math. Study frequently over a period of time and review what you have learned in the past. Massed study will not work in a math course. Math can be compared to success in sports or music in that they all require practice to be successful. Rehearsal and practice are needed to store math concepts in long-term memory.

Use effective review techniques. It is important to review what is learned in your math classes as soon as practical after class. Remember that most of the forgetting occurs immediately after learning something new. Review your notes right after class, review what you have read in your math text at the end of your reading session, and use small amounts of time to quickly review important concepts on flash cards. Immediate review is a powerful memory technique.

Realize that math is sequential. You must understand the first step before you can go on to the next. For this reason, start at your level, attend every class, and make it your goal to earn an A or a B on your first test. If you miss any step, see a tutor early in the semester or use online resources to fill in the gap.

Math is like a foreign language. Math uses specialized vocabulary that you must understand in order to do your math problems. Make sure to write down the definitions of math terms in your notes and review these terms. Use flash cards to review the vocabulary.

Use a study group. Choose two to six students who are serious about math success. Have each group member bring note cards with sample questions for the group to practice. Create practice tests and practice taking the tests. Sometimes it is easier learning from your peers and you may be more comfortable asking questions.

Use additional resources. Find out about tutoring in your college and use these services early in your math course. If you are stuck on a problem, use Google or You Tube to find out how to solve the problems.

Ask questions in class. As soon as you don't understand something in class, ask questions. Other students probably have the same question and may be thankful that you asked it. Faculty generally appreciate questions because it shows you are paying attention and interested in the course. Student questions help faculty to make sure students understand what they are teaching.

Use multisensory techniques to study math. Remember that learning is easier if you use all of your senses. Highlight or place a checkmark in front of the study techniques that you can use:

    ____ Read important math concepts out loud.

    ____ Use flash cards make from note cards or virtual flashcards from Study Stacks: http://www.studystack.com/.

____Watch YouTube videos on math concepts and solving problems.

____Use different colors of ink to take notes on math.

____Take pictures of the board with your cell phone.

____Say important concepts, formulas, or definitions out loud.

____Record important concepts and listen to them in your car.

____Teach group members how to solve problems.

____Use math manipulatives to understand problems. Math manipulatives are letters, numbers, magnetic boards, and other pieces that help to understand math concepts. They are available at learning stores. There are also virtual manipulative sites such as the Computing Technology for Math Excellence site at: http://www.ct4me.net/math_manipulatives_2.htm.

____Use Facebook to post pictures of your math homework and discuss it with friends.

____Move around while studying.

____Rewrite or highlight your math notes.

____Use a math app to learn how to solve problems.

Some Useful Math Apps

Search for math apps on any search engine such as Google. Here are some useful ones:

MyScript Calculator allows you to write problems on your tablet screen and the built in calculator solves the problem.

Algebra Tutor includes many different apps to solve algebra problems.

Algeo is an online graphing calculator.

Photomath allows you to take a photo of a problem and solve it with the app.

Wolfram Alpa is a collection of data and algorithms used to solve problems. It is used in Siri to calculate the answers to problems.

QUIZ

Math Success

1. About 50% of your success in math depends on
   a. placement in the proper level of math.
   b. your attitude toward math.
   c. your math study skills.

2. The estimated time needed per week to study for a college math course is
   a. 3 hours.
   b. 10 hours.
   c. 6 hours.

3. Preparation for exams in math is different from other subjects. To be successful on math exams, the most important strategy is
   a. memorization.
   b. recall.
   c. practice.

4. The best time to review in your math class is
   a. a marathon study session just before the test.
   b. as soon as possible after learning new material.
   c. on weekends when you are relaxed.

5. Learning in math is sequential which means
   a. it is OK to miss your math class once in awhile.
   b. it is not too important to do the math homework if it is not collected.
   c. you must understand the first step before you can understand the next step.

How did you do on the quiz? Check your answers: 1. a, 2. b, 3. c, 4. b, 5. c

Journal Entry #3

How studying math is different from studying other subjects in college?

Journal Entry #4

During the first week of your math class, one of your friends in the class tells you that he/she has never been good at math and is afraid of dropping the class. This student needs math to graduate from college. What advice would you give?

Using Brain Science to Improve Study Skills

KEYS TO SUCCESS

Create Your Success

We are responsible for our success in college as well as what happens in our lives. We make decisions and choices that create the future. Our behavior leads to success or failure. Too often we believe that we are victims of circumstance. When looking at our lives, we often look for others to blame for how our lives are going.

- I failed math. I had a bad math teacher.
- My grandparents did it to me. I inherited these genes.
- My parents did it to me. My childhood experiences shaped who I am.
- It was my teacher's fault. He gave me a bad grade.
- My boss did it to me. She gave me a poor evaluation.
- The government did it to me. All my money goes to taxes.
- Society did it to me. I have no opportunity.

These factors are all powerful influences in our lives, but we are still left with choices. You can study independently and be successful in math in spite of your math teacher. You can ask yourself how you created your failing grade and how you can improve in the future. You can use your job evaluation as a way to improve your job performance. You can create your own opportunity.

Concentration camp survivor Viktor Frankl wrote a book, Man's Search for Meaning, in which he describes his experiences and how he survived his ordeal in a concentration camp. His parents, brother, and wife died in the camps. He suffered starvation and torture. Through all of his sufferings and imprisonment, he still maintained that he was a free man because he could make choices.

We who lived in concentration camps can remember the men who walked through the huts comforting others, giving away their last piece of bread. They may have been few in number, but they offer sufficient proof that everything can be taken from a man but one thing: the last of the human freedoms—to choose one's attitude in any given set of circumstances, to choose one's own way. . . . Fundamentally, therefore, any man can, even under such circumstances, decide what shall become of him—mentally and spiritually. He may retain his human dignity even in a concentration camp.[7]

Viktor Frankl could not choose his circumstance at that time, but he did choose his attitude. He decided how he would respond to the situation. He realized that he still had the freedom to make choices. He used his memory and imagination to exercise his freedom. When times were the most difficult, he would imagine that he was in the classroom lecturing to his students about psychology. He eventually did get out of the concentration camp and became a famous psychiatrist.

Hopefully, none of you will ever have to experience the circumstances faced by Viktor Frankl, but we all face challenging situations. It is empowering to think that our behavior is more a function of our decisions than of our circumstances. It is not productive to look around and find someone to blame for your problems. Psychologist Abraham Maslow says that instead of blaming, we should see how we can make the best of the situation.

One can spend a lifetime assigning blame, finding a cause, "out there" for all the troubles that exist. Contrast this with the responsible attitude of confronting the situation, bad or good, and instead of asking, "What caused the trouble? Who was to blame?" asking, "How can I handle the present situation to make the best of it?"[9]

Author Stephen Covey suggests that we look at the word responsibility as "response-ability."[10] It is the ability to choose responses and make decisions about the future. When you are dealing with a problem, it is useful to ask yourself what decisions you made that led to the problem. How did you create the situation? If you created the problems, you can create a solution.

At times, you may ask, "How did I create this?" and find that the answer is that you did not create the situation. We certainly do not create earthquakes or hurricanes, for example. But we do create or at least contribute to many of the things that happen to us. Even if you did not create your circumstances, you can create your reaction to the situation. In the case of an earthquake, you can decide to panic or find the best course of action at the moment.

Author Steven Covey relates this concept to careers:

> But the people who end up with the good jobs are the proactive ones who are solutions to problems, not problems themselves, who seize the initiative to do whatever is necessary, consistent with correct principles, to get the job done.[11]

Use your resourcefulness and initiative to create the future that you want.

© Anson0618/Shutterstock.com

Journal Entry #5

Give your thoughts on the following:

Each of us is responsible for what happens in our life. We make decisions and choices that create the future. We create our own success.

Appreciating Island Cultures: Tiare Apetahi

Tiare Apetahi is a white flower with five petals shaped like an open hand. It is a beautiful flower with a lovely smell that only grows on the slopes of Mount Temehani and cannot be cultivated anywhere else in the world. There is a legend accompanying the flower.

Long ago there was a beautiful young girl named Tiaitau who lived in the valley of Araau in Raiatea. She was more beautiful than any other. One day her parents decided to go and live in Opoa because in that district a missionary had come who was teaching the alphabet and basic writing. They wanted Tiaitau to learn.

As Tiaitau grew into a beautiful woman, she met King Tamatoa and they fell in love. After a time, King Tamatoa had to leave Raiatea to join King Pomare of Tahiti in a battle. He was accompanied by his warriors. He was set to leave his island and Tiaitau, the woman he loved. Before he left, he asked her to wait for him at home. She spoke to him of her fears and told him it felt as

Beautiful landscape of Raiatea island, French Polynesia.
© Styve Reineck/Shutterstock.com

if this would be the last time she would see him. King Tamatoa spoke words of reassurance, telling her he was accompanied by his best and strongest warriors. Tiaitau, grabbing a coconut, told him she would climb the sacred mountain, Temehani, and watch over the sea until his return. She told him she would put the coconut in the deep, dark hole of Apo'oHihiUra and it would journey through the earth, drifting from island to island to follow Tamatoa. When he was thirsty, he would be able to put a hole in the coconut and drink the sweet water inside it, drawing the coconut to his mouth, reminiscing of their kisses.

King Tamatoa finally departed and Tiaitau started on her journey to Mount Temehani. On her way there, she stopped at the Torea cave to rest and fell asleep. The next day she continued, finally arriving at Apo'oHihiUra, the deep, dark hole on Mount Temehani. Putting the coconut in the hole, Tiaitau turned in the direction of Taputaputea, and saw the canoe that had carried King Tamatoa. "Oh my love, your oar is shining in the sun and your canoe is bobbing up and down in the waves and it is empty. My heart hurts so badly! I must plant my arm in the ground of this mountain and it will flower. The flower will resemble my open hand, the hand that will be a sign of my love. If you ever return to me, you will smell this flower and know it is me."

Tiaitau planted her arm there and placed herself into the deep, dark hole of Apo'oHihiUra, never to be seen again.

The flower that grew there would never leave that sacred mountain and would never grow anywhere else, just as Tiaitau never left and her love never grew for anyone else.

Questions

1. Tiaitau's parents sent her to the missionaries to learn. How important is education to your culture?
2. What is the definition of legacy?
3. How did Tiaitau leave a legacy?
4. What part of your legacy will live and why?
5. How do you want to be remembered by those who are important to you? Why?
6. How far are you willing to go to leave that legacy?

© Lyudmyla Kharlamova/Shutterstock.com

College Success 1

The College Success 1 website is continually updated with supplementary material for each chapter including Word documents of the journal entries, classroom activities, handouts, videos, links to related materials, and much more. See http://www.collegesuccess1.com/.

Notes

1. Terry Doyle and Todd Zakrajsek, *The New Science of Learning, How to Learn in Harmony with Your Brain*, (Sterling, Virginia: Stylus), 45.
2. John Medina, *Brain Rules*, (Seattle: Pear Press, 2008), 250.
3. Ibid., 233–234.
4. Ibid., 212.
5. Colin Rose, *Accelerated Learning,* (New York: Dell Publishing, 1985), 51.
6. Paul Nolting, *Winning at Math*, (Bradenton, FL: Academic Success Press, 2014), 37.
7. Ibid., 19.
8. Viktor Frankl, *Man's Search for Meaning* (New York: Pocket Books, 1963), 104–105.
9. Quoted in Rob Gilbert, ed., *Bits and Pieces*, November 4, 1999.
10. Stephen Covey, *The Seven Habits of Highly Effective People* (New York: Simon and Schuster, 1989), 71.
11. Ibid., 75

Check Your Textbook Reading Skills

Name _____ Date _____

As you read each of the following statements, mark your response using this key:

1 I seldom or never do this.

2 I occasionally do this, depending on the class.

3 I almost always or always do this.

_____ 1. Before I read the chapter, I quickly skim through it to get main ideas.

_____ 2. As I skim through the chapter, I form questions based on the bold printed section headings.

_____ 3. I read with a positive attitude and look for something interesting.

_____ 4. I read the introductory and summary paragraphs in the chapter before I begin reading.

_____ 5. As I read each paragraph, I look for the main idea.

_____ 6. I recite the main idea so I can remember it.

_____ 7. I underline, highlight, or take notes on the main ideas.

_____ 8. I write notes or outlines in the margin of the text.

_____ 9. After reading each section, I do a quick review.

_____ 10. I quickly review the chapter immediately after reading it.

_____ 11. During or after reading, I reflect on how the material is useful or meaningful to me.

_____ 12. I read or at least skim the assigned chapter before I come to class.

_____ 13. I have planned reading time in my weekly schedule.

_____ 14. I generally think positively about my reading assignments.

_____ **Total points**

Check your score.
42–36   You have excellent college reading skills.
35–30   You have good skills, but can improve.
29–24   Some changes are needed.
23–14   Major changes are needed.

Becoming an Efficient College Reader

Name _____ Date _____

1. Based on your responses to the reading skills checklist on the previous page, list some of your good reading habits.

2. Based on this same checklist, what are some areas you need to improve?

3. Review the material on SQ4R and reading for speed and comprehension. Write five intention statements about how you plan to improve your reading. I intend to . . .

4. Review the material on how to concentrate while reading. List some ideas that you can use.

Surveying and Questioning a Chapter

Name _____   Date _____

Using the *next chapter* assigned in this class or any other class, answer these questions. Again, challenge yourself to do this activity quickly. Can you finish the exercise in five to seven minutes? Notice your beginning and end times.

1. What is the title of the chapter? For example, the title of this chapter is "Using Brain Science to Improve Study Skills." A good question would be, "How can I use brain science to improve my study skills?"

2. Briefly list one key idea mentioned in the introduction or first paragraph.

3. Write five questions you asked yourself while surveying this chapter. Read the bold section headings in the chapter and turn them into questions. For example, one heading in this chapter is "Neuroscience and Practical Learning Strategies." This heading might prompt you to ask, "What are some new findings in neuroscience? How can this help me to improve study skills?"

4. List three topics that interest you.

5. Briefly write one key idea from the last paragraph or chapter summary.

6. How long did it take you to do this exercise? Write your time here.

7. What did you think of this exercise on surveying and questioning a chapter?

CHAPTER 7

Taking Notes, Writing, and Speaking

Learning Objectives

Read to answer these key questions:

- Why is it important to take notes?

- What are some good listening techniques?

- What are some tips for taking good lecture notes?

- What are some note-taking systems?

- What is the best way to take notes in math?

- What is the best way to review my notes for the test?

- What is power writing?

- How can I make a good speech?

From *College & Career Success, Concise Version*, Seventh Edition, by Marsha Fralick. Copyright © 2016 by Kendall Hunt Publishing Company. Reprinted by permission.

Knowing how to listen and take good notes can make your college life easier and may help you in your future career as well. Professionals in many occupations take notes as a way of recording key ideas for later use. Whether you become a journalist, attorney, architect, engineer, or other professional, listening and taking good notes can help you to get ahead in your career.

Good writing and speaking skills are important to your success in college and in your career. In college, you will be asked to write term papers and complete other writing assignments. The writing skills you learn in college will be used later in jobs involving high responsibility and good pay; on the job, you will write reports, memos, and proposals. In college, you will probably take a speech class and give oral reports in other classes; on the job, you will present your ideas orally to your colleagues and business associates.

Why Take Notes?

The most important reason for taking notes is to remember important material for tests or for future use in your career. If you just attend class without taking notes, you will forget most of the material by the next day.

How does taking notes enhance memory?

- In college, the lecture is a way of supplementing the written material in the textbook. Without good notes, an important part of the course is missing. Note taking provides material to rehearse or recite, so that it can be stored in long-term memory.
- When you take notes and impose your own organization on them, the notes become more personally meaningful. If they are meaningful, they are easier to remember.
- Taking notes helps you to make new connections. New material is remembered by connecting it to what you already know.
- The physical act of writing the material is helpful in learning and remembering it.
- Notes provide a visual map of the material to be learned.
- Taking notes is a way to listen carefully and record information to be stored in the memory.
- Note taking helps students to concentrate, maintain focus, and stay awake.
- Attending the lectures and taking notes helps you to understand what the professor thinks is important and to know what to study for the exam.

© Monkey Business Images/Shutterstock.com

The College Lecture

You will experience many different types of lectures while in college. At larger universities, many of the beginning-level courses are taught in large lecture halls with 300 people or more. More advanced courses tend to have fewer students. In large lecture situations, it is not always possible or appropriate to ask questions. Under these circumstances, the large lecture is often supplemented by smaller discussion sessions where you can ask questions and review the lecture material. Although attendance may not be checked, it is important to attend both the lectures and the discussion sessions.

A formal college lecture is divided into four parts. Understanding these parts will help you to be a good listener and take good notes.

> "Education is not a problem. It is an opportunity."
> Lyndon B. Johnson

1. **Introduction.** The professor uses the introduction to set the stage and to introduce the topic of the lecture. Often an overview or outline of the lecture is presented. Use the introduction as a way to begin thinking about the organization of your notes and the key ideas you will need to write down.

2. **Thesis.** The thesis is the key idea in the lecture. In a one-hour lecture, there is usually one thesis statement. Listen carefully for the thesis statement and write it down in your notes. Review the thesis statement and related ideas for the exam.

3. **Body.** The body of the lecture usually consists of five or six main ideas with discussion and clarification of each idea. As a note taker, your job is to identify the main ideas, write them in your notes, and put in enough of the explanation or examples to understand the key ideas.

4. **Conclusion.** In the conclusion, the professor summarizes the key points of the lecture and sometimes asks for questions. Use the conclusion as an opportunity to check your understanding of the lecture and to ask questions to clarify the key points.

How to Be a Good Listener

Effective note taking begins with good listening. What is good listening? Sometimes students confuse listening with hearing. Hearing is done with the ears. Listening is a more active process done with the ears and the brain engaged. Good listening requires attention and concentration. Practice these ideas for good listening:

- **Be physically ready.** It is difficult to listen to a lecture if you are tired, hungry, or ill. Get enough sleep so that you can stay awake. Eat a balanced diet without too much caffeine or sugar. Take care of your health and participate in an exercise program so that you feel your best.

- **Prepare a mental framework.** Look at the course syllabus to become familiar with the topic of the lecture. Use your textbook to read, or at least survey, the material to be covered in the lecture. If you are familiar with the key concepts from the textbook, you will be able to understand the lecture and know what to write down in your notes. If the material is in your book, there is no need to write it down in your notes.

  The more complex the topic, the more important it is for you to read the text first. If you go to the lecture and have no idea what is being discussed, you may be overwhelmed and find it difficult to take notes on material that is totally new to you. Remember that it is easier to remember material if you can connect it to material you already know.

- **Find a good place to sit.** Arrive early to get a good seat. The best seats in the classroom are in the front and center of the room. If you were buying concert tickets, these would be the best and most expensive seats. Find a seat that will help you to hear and focus on the speaker. You may need to find a seat away from your friends to avoid distractions.

- **Have a positive mental attitude.** Convince yourself that the speaker has something important to say and be open to new ideas. This may require you to focus on your goals and to look past some distractions. Maybe the lecturer doesn't have the best speaking voice or you don't like his or her appearance. Focus on what you can learn from the professor rather than outward appearances.
- **Listen actively to identify the main points.** As you are listening to the lecture, ask yourself, "What is the main idea?" In your own words, write the main points down in your notes. Do not try to write down everything the professor says. This will be impossible and unnecessary. Imagine that your mind is a filter and you are actively sorting through the material to find the key ideas and write them down in your notes. Try to identify the key points that will be on the test and write them in your notes.
- **Stay awake and engaged in learning.** The best way to stay awake and focused is to listen actively and take notes. Have a mental debate with the professor. Listen for the main points and the logical connection between ideas. The physical act of writing the notes will help to keep you awake.

Tips for Good Note Taking

Here are some suggestions for taking good notes:

1. Attend all of the lectures. Because many professors do not take attendance, students are often tempted to miss class. If you do not attend the lectures, however, you will not know what the professor thinks is important and what to study for the test. There will be important points covered in the lectures that are not in the book.

2. Have the proper materials. A three-ring notebook and notebook paper are recommended. Organize notes chronologically and include any handouts given in class. You can have a small notebook for each class or a single large notebook with dividers for each class. Just take the notebook paper to class and later file it in your notebook at home. Use your laptop as an alternative to a paper notebook.

3. Begin your notes by writing the date of the lecture, so you can keep your notes in order.

4. Write notes on the front side only of each piece of paper. This will allow you to spread the pages out and see the big picture or pattern in the lectures when you are reviewing.

© Monkey Business Images/Shutterstock.com

5. Write notes neatly and legibly so you can read and review them easily.

6. Do not waste time recopying or typing your notes. Your time would be better spent reviewing your notes.

7. As a general rule, do not rely on a tape recorder for taking notes. With a tape recorder, you will have to listen to the lecture again on tape. For a semester course, this would be about 45 hours of tape! It is much faster to review carefully written notes.

8. Copy down everything written on the board and the main points from PowerPoint or other visual presentations. If it is important enough for the professor to write on the board, it is important enough to be on the test.

9. Use key words and phrases in your notes. Leave out unimportant words and don't worry about grammar.

10. Use abbreviations as long as you can read them. Entire sentences or paragraphs are not necessary and you may not have time to write them.

11. Don't loan your whole notebook to someone else because you may not get it back. If you want to share your notes, make copies.

12. If the professor talks too fast, listen carefully for the key ideas and write them down. Leave spaces in your notes to fill in later. You may be able to find the information in the text or get the information from another student.

13. Explore new uses of technology for note taking. Students are taking notes and sharing them on Facebook and GradeGuru, for example.

Journal Entry #1

Write one paragraph giving advice to a new student about taking notes in college. Use any of these questions to guide your thinking:

- Why is note taking necessary in college?
- How can you be a good listener?
- What are some tips for taking good notes?
- What are some ideas that don't work?

Note-Taking Systems

We remember by finding patterns in new information including similarities, differences, hierarchy, and relationships among items. Recognizing patterns is useful in taking good notes. There are several systems for taking notes, depending on the patterns and organization that make sense to you. The most familiar pattern is using your own words to record the important points.

Note-Taking Systems
- Cornell format
- Outline method
- Mind map

The Cornell Format

The Cornell format is an efficient method of taking notes and reviewing them. It appeals to students who are logical, orderly, and organized and have lectures that fit into this pattern. The Cornell format is especially helpful for thinking about key points as you review your notes.

Step 1: Prepare. To use the Cornell format, you will need a three-ring notebook with looseleaf paper. Draw or fold a vertical line 2½ inches from the left side of the paper.

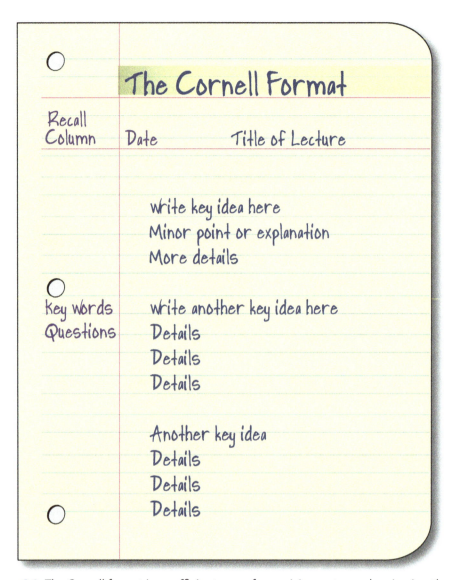

Figure 6.1 The Cornell format is an efficient way of organizing notes and reviewing them.

This is the recall column that can be used to write key ideas when reviewing. Use the remaining section of the paper for your notes. Write the date and title of the lecture at the top of the page.

Step 2: Take notes. Use the large area to the right of the recall column to take notes. Listen for key ideas and write them just to the right of the recall column line, as in the diagram above. Indent your notes for minor points and illustrative details. Then skip a space and write the next key idea. Don't worry about using numbers or letters as in an outline format. Just use the indentations and spacing to highlight and separate key ideas. Use short phrases, key words, and abbreviations. Complete sentences are not necessary, but write legibly so you can read your notes later.

Step 3: Use the recall column for review. Read over your notes and write down key words or ideas from the lecture in the recall column. Ask yourself, "What is this about?" Cover up the notes on the right-hand side and recite the key ideas of the lecture. Another variation is to write questions in the margin. Find the key ideas and then write possible exam questions in the recall column. Cover your notes and see if you can answer the questions.

The Outline Method

If the lecture is well organized, some students just take notes in outline format. Sometimes lecturers will show their outline as they speak.

- Use Roman numerals to label main topics. Then use capital letters for main ideas and Arabic numerals for related details or examples.
- You can make a free-form outline using just indentation to separate main ideas and supporting details.
- Leave spaces to fill in material later.
- Use a highlighter to review your notes as soon as possible after the lecture.

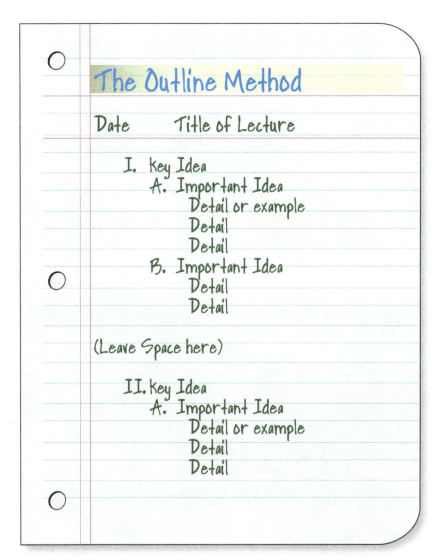

Figure 6.2 If a lecture is well organized, the outline format of taking notes works well.

The Mind Map

A mind map shows the relationship between ideas in a visual way. It is much easier to remember items that are organized and linked together in a personally meaningful way. As a result, recall and review is quicker and more effective. Mind maps can be used show the contents of a lecture in a visual way and appeal to those who do not want to be limited to a set structure, as in the outline formats. They can also be used for lectures that are not highly structured. Here are some suggestions for using the mind-mapping technique:

- Turn your paper sideways to give you more space. Use standard-size notebook paper or consider larger sheets if possible.
- Write the main idea in the center of the page and circle it.
- Arrange ideas so that more important ideas are closer to the center and less important ideas are farther out.
- Show the relationship of the minor points to the main ideas using lines, circles, boxes, charts, and other visual devices. Here is where you can use your creativity and imagination to make a visual picture of the key ideas in the lecture.

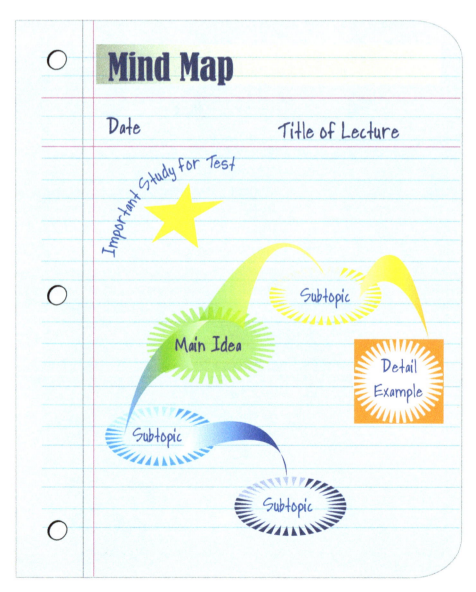

Figure 6.3 The mind map format of taking notes shows the relationship between ideas in a visual way.

- Use symbols and drawings.
- Use different colors to separate main ideas.
- When the lecturer moves to another main idea, start a new mind map.
- When you are done with the lecture, quickly review your mind maps. Add any written material that will be helpful in understanding the map later.
- A mind map can also be used as:
  - a review tool for remembering and relating the key ideas in the textbook;
  - a preparation tool for essay exams in which remembering main ideas and relationships is important; and
  - the first step in organizing ideas for a term paper.

Taking Notes in Math

Prepare for note-taking in math by prereading the chapter. This will help you to understand key ideas and areas where you need help. As you are reading, note some areas for asking questions in class. It is also a good idea to review the notes from the previous

Modified Three Column Note-Taking Method

Key words/ Rules	Examples	Explanations
Solve a linear equation	$5(x + 4) + 3(x - 4) = 2(x - 2)$	Have to get x on one side of the = and numbers on the other side of the =.
Distributive Property	$5x + 20 + 3x - 12 = 2x - 4$	Multiply numbers to the left of the () by each variable and number in the ().
Commutative Property	$5x + 3x + 20 - 12 = 2x - 4$	Regroup numbers and variables
Combine Like Terms	$8x + 8 = 2x - 4$	Add x's together and numbers together.

Adapted from *Winning at Math* by Paul Nolting. Illustrated by Charlotte Moore.
© Charlotte Moore.

lecture so you can build on previous knowledge. Make sure to copy down anything written on the board or use your cell phone to photograph the board and write notes later. The Modified Three Column Note-Taking Method is recommended for taking notes in a math class.[1] Once you are used to using this system, you may no longer need to label the columns.

There are three steps to using this format. Begin with writing the example in the middle of the page. Next write the explanation, and lastly, write down the key words to the left. To review the notes, cover up the examples and explanations and say the meaning of the key word or term. Then place a checkmark next to the terms you don't know so you can review them again. Make note cards or use the StudyStack website (http://www.studystack.com/ to create flashcards for review.

Improving Note-Taking Efficiency

Improve note-taking efficiency by listening for key words that signal the main ideas and supporting details. Learn to write faster by using telegraphic sentences, abbreviations, and symbols.

Telegraphic Sentences

Telegraphic sentences are short, abbreviated sentences used in note taking. They are very similar to the text messages sent on a cell phone. There are four rules for telegraphic sentences:

1. Write key words only.
2. Omit unnecessary words (*a, an, the*).
3. Ignore rules of grammar.
4. Use abbreviations and symbols.

Here is an example of a small part of a lecture followed by a student's telegraphic notes:

Heavy drinking of alcoholic beverages causes students to miss class and to fall behind in schoolwork. College students who are considered binge drinkers are at risk for many alcohol-related problems. Binge drinking is simply drinking too much alcohol at one time. Binge drinking is defined by researchers as drinking five or more drinks in a row for men or four or more drinks in a row for women. Researchers estimate that two out of five college students (40 percent) are binge drinkers.

Binge drinking—too much alcohol at one time
Men = 5 in row
Women = 4
2 out of 5 (40%) college students binge

Signal Words

Signal words are clues to the patterns, structure, and content of a lecture. Recognizing signal words can help you to identify key ideas and organize them in your notes. The table on the following page lists some common signal words and their meaning.

© Lightspring/Shutterstock.com

Signal Words

Type	Examples	Meaning
Main idea words	And most important A major development The basic concept is Remember that The main idea is We will focus on The key is	Introduce the key points that need to be written in your notes.
Example words	To illustrate For example For instance	Clarify and illustrate the main ideas in the lecture. Write these examples in your notes after the main idea. If multiple examples are given, write down the ones you have time for or the ones that you understand the best.
Addition words	In addition Also Furthermore	Add more important information. Write these points down in your notes.
Enumeration words	The five steps First, second, third Next	Signal a list. Write down the list in your notes and number the items.
Time words	Before, after Formerly Subsequently Prior Meanwhile	Signal the order of events. Write down the events in the correct order in your notes.
Cause and effect words	Therefore As a result If . . ., then	Signal important concepts that might be on the exam. When you hear these words, label them "cause" and "effect" in your notes and review these ideas for the exam.
Definition words	In other words It simply means That is In essence	Provide the meanings of words or simplify complex ideas. Write these definitions or clarifications in your notes.
Swivel words	However Nevertheless Yes, but Still	Provide exceptions, qualifications, or further clarification. Write down qualifying comments in your notes.
Compare and contrast words	Similarly Likewise In contrast	Present similarities or differences. Write these similarities and differences in your notes and label them.
Summary words	In conclusion To sum up In a nutshell	Restate the important ideas of the lecture. Write the summaries in your notes.
Test words	This is important. Remember this. You'll see this again. You might want to study this for the test.	Provide a clue that the material will be on the test. Write these down in your notes and mark them in a way that stands out. Put a star or asterisk next to these items or highlight them. Each professor has his or her own test clue words.

How to Review Your Notes

Immediate review. Review your notes as soon as possible after the lecture. The most effective review is done immediately or at least within 20 minutes. If you wait until the next day to review, you may already have forgotten much of the information. During the immediate review, fill in any missing or incomplete information. Say the important points to yourself. This begins the process of rehearsal for storing the information in long-term memory.

There are various methods for review depending on your note-taking system:

- For the Cornell format, use the recall column to write in key words or questions. Cover your notes and see if you can recall the main ideas. Place checkmarks by the items you have mastered. Don't worry about mastering all the key points from the beginning. With each review, it will be easier to remember the information.
- For the outline format, use a highlighter to mark the key ideas as you repeat them silently to yourself.
- For mind maps, look over the information and think about the key ideas and their relationships. Fill in additional information or clarification. Highlight important points or relationships with color.
- For your math notes, cover up the examples and explanations and see if you can remember the key word or rule. Make flash cards to review key concepts.

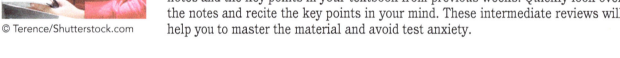
© Terence/Shutterstock.com

Intermediate review. Set up some time each week for short reviews of your notes and the key points in your textbook from previous weeks. Quickly look over the notes and recite the key points in your mind. These intermediate reviews will help you to master the material and avoid test anxiety.

Test review. Complete a major review as part of your test preparation strategy. As you look through your notes, turn the key ideas into possible test questions and answer them.

"You have to get your education. Then nobody can control your destiny."
Charles Barkley

Final review. The final review occurs after you have received the results of your test. Ask yourself these questions:

- What percentage of the test questions came from the lecture notes?
- Were you prepared for the exam? If so, congratulate yourself on a job well done. If not, how can you improve next time?
- Were your notes adequate? If not, what needs to be added or changed?

QUIZ

Listening and Note Taking

Test what you have learned by selecting the correct answer to the following questions.

1. When taking notes on a college lecture, it is most important to
   a. write down everything you hear.
   b. write down the main ideas and enough explanation to understand them.
   c. write down names, dates, places, and numbers.

2. To be a good listener,
   a. read or skim over the material before you attend the lecture.
   b. attend the lecture first and then read the text.
   c. remember that listening is more important than note taking.

3. To stay awake during the lecture,
   a. drink lots of coffee.
   b. sit near your friends so you can make some comments on the lecture.
   c. listen actively by taking notes.

4. Since attendance is not always checked in college classes,
   a. it is not necessary to attend class if you read the textbook.
   b. it is acceptable to miss lectures as long as you show up for the exams.
   c. it is up to you to attend every class.

5. The best time to review your notes is
   a. as soon as possible after the lecture.
   b. within 24 hours.
   c. within one week.

How did you do on the quiz? Check your answers: 1. b, 2. a, 3. c, 4. c, 5. a

---

Journal Entry #2

Write five intention statements about improving your note-taking skills. Consider your note-taking system, how to take notes more efficiently, and the best way to review your notes. I intend to . . .

> "The highest reward for a person's toil is not what they get for it, but what they become by it."
> — John Ruskin

Power Writing

Effective writing will help you in school, on the job, and in your personal life. Good writing will help you to create quality term papers. The writing skills that you learn in college will be used later in jobs involving high responsibility and good pay. You can become an excellent writer by learning about the steps in POWER writing: prepare, organize, write, edit, and revise.

Power Writing
- Prepare
- Organize
- Write
- Edit
- Revise

Prepare

Plan your time. The first step in writing is to plan your time so that the project can be completed by the due date. Picture this scene: It is the day that the term paper is due. A few students proudly hand in their term papers and are ready to celebrate their accomplishments. Many of the students in the class are absent, and some will never return to the class. Some of the students look as though they haven't slept the night before. They look stressed and weary. At the front of the class is a line of students wanting to talk with the instructor. The instructor has heard it all before:

- I had my paper all completed and my printer jammed.
- My hard drive crashed and I lost my paper.
- I was driving to school and my paper flew off my motorcycle.
- I had the flu.
- My children were sick.
- I had to take my dog to the vet.
- My dog ate my paper.
- My car broke down and I could not get to the library.
- My grandmother died and I had to go to the funeral.
- My roommate accidentally took my backpack to school.
- I spilled salad dressing on my paper, so I put it in the microwave to dry it out and the writing disappeared!

> "The most valuable of all education is the ability to make yourself do the thing you have to do, when it has to be done, whether you like it or not."
>
> Aldous Huxley

© Benjamin Howell/Shutterstock.com

To avoid being in this uncomfortable and stressful situation, plan ahead. Plan to complete your project at least one week ahead of time so that you can deal with life's emergencies. Life does not always go as planned. You or your children may get sick, or your dog may do strange things to your homework. Your computer may malfunction, leading you to believe it senses stress and malfunctions just to frustrate you even more.

To avoid stress and do your best work, start with the date that the project is due and then think about the steps needed to finish. Write these dates on your calendar or on your list of things to do. Consider all these components:

Prepare
- Plan your time
- Find space and time
- Choose general topic
- Gather information
- Write thesis statement

Project due date:

To do	By when?
1. Brainstorm ideas.	_____
2. Choose a topic.	_____
3. Gather information.	_____
4. Write a thesis statement.	_____
5. Write an outline.	_____
6. Write the introduction.	_____
7. Write the first draft.	_____
8. Prepare the bibliography.	_____
9. Edit.	_____
10. Revise.	_____
11. Print and assemble.	_____

You can also try an assignment calculator app that helps you to develop a timeline such as the one created at the University of Minnesota at https://www.lib.umn.edu/apps/ac/

Find a space and time. Find a space where you can work. Gather the materials that you will need to write. Generally, writing is best done in longer blocks of time. Determine when you will work on your paper and write the time on your schedule. Start right away to avoid panic later.

Choose a general topic. This task will be easy if your topic is already clearly defined by your instructor or your boss at work. Make sure that you have a clear idea of what is required, such as length, format, purpose, and method of citing references and topic. Many times the choice of a topic is left to you. Begin by doing some brainstorming. Think about topics that interest you. Write them down. You may want to focus your attention on brainstorming ideas for five or 10 minutes, and then put the project aside and come back to it later. Once you have started the process of thinking about the ideas, your mind will continue to work and you may have some creative inspiration. If inspiration does not come, repeat the brainstorming process.

Gather information. Go to your college library and use the Internet to gather your information. As you begin, you can see what is available, what is interesting to you, and what the current thinking is on your topic. Note the major topics of interest that might be useful to you. Once you have found some interesting material, you will feel motivated to continue your project. As you find information relevant to your topic, make sure to write down the sources of your information to use in your bibliography. The bibliography contains information about where you found your material. Write down the author, the title of the publication, the publisher, and the place and date of publication. For Internet resources, list the address of the website and the date accessed.

Write the thesis statement. The thesis statement is the key idea in your paper. It provides a direction for you to follow. It is the first step in organizing your work. To write a thesis statement, review the material you have gathered and then ask these questions:

- What is the most important idea?
- What question would I like to ask about it?
- What is my answer?

© Elena Elisseeva/Shutterstock.com

For example, if I decide to write a paper for my health class on the harmful effects of smoking, I would look at current references on the topic. I might become interested in how the tobacco companies misled the public on the dangers of smoking. I would think about my thesis statement and answer the questions stated above.

- **What is the most important idea?** Smoking is harmful to your health.
- **What question would I like to ask about it?** Did the tobacco companies mislead the public about the health hazards of smoking?
- **What is my answer?** The tobacco companies misled the public about the hazards of smoking in order to protect their business interests.
- **My thesis statement:** Tobacco companies knew that smoking was hazardous to health, but to protect their business interests, they deliberately misled the public.

The thesis statement helps to narrow the topic and provide direction for the paper. I can now focus on reference material related to my topic: research on health effects of smoking, congressional testimony relating to regulation of the tobacco industry, and how advertising influences people to smoke.

Organize

At this point you have many ideas about what to include in your paper, and you have a central focus, your thesis statement. Start to organize your paper by listing the topics that are related to your thesis statement. Here is a list of topics related to my thesis statement about smoking:

- Tobacco companies' awareness that nicotine is addictive
- Minimizing health hazards in tobacco advertisements
- How advertisements encourage people to smoke
- Money earned by the tobacco industry
- Health problems caused by smoking
- Statistics on numbers of people who have health problems or die from smoking
- Regulation of the tobacco industry
- Advertisements aimed at children

Think about the topics and arrange them in logical order. Use an outline, a mind map, a flowchart, or a drawing to think about how you will organize the important topics. Keep in mind that you will need an introduction, a body, and a conclusion.

Organize
- List related topics
- Arrange in logical order
- Have an organizational structure

Having an organizational structure will make it easier for you to write because you will not need to wonder what comes next.

Write

Write the First Sentence
Begin with the main idea.

Write the Introduction
This is the road map for the rest of the paper. The introduction includes your thesis statement and establishes the foundation of the paper. It introduces topics that will be discussed in the body of the paper. The introduction should include some interesting points that provide a "hook" to motivate the audience to read your paper. For example, for a paper on the hazards of smoking, you might begin with statistics on how many people suffer from smoking-related illnesses and premature death. Note the large profits earned by the tobacco industry. Then introduce other topics: deception, advertisements, and regulation. The introduction provides a guide or outline of what will follow in the paper.

> **Write**
> - First sentence
> - Introduction
> - Body
> - Conclusion
> - References

Write the Body of the Paper
The body of the paper is divided into paragraphs that discuss the topics that you have introduced. As you write each paragraph, include the main idea and then explain it and give examples. Here are some good tips for writing:

1. **Good writing reflects clear thinking.** Think about what you want to say and write about it so the reader can understand your point of view.

2. **Use clear and concise language.** Avoid using too many words or scholarly-sounding words that might get in the way of understanding.

3. **Don't assume that the audience knows what you are writing about.** Provide complete information.

4. **Provide examples, stories, and quotes to support your main points.** Include your own ideas and experiences.

5. **Beware of plagiarism.** Plagiarism is copying the work of others without giving them credit. It is illegal and can cause you to receive a failing grade on your project or even get you into legal trouble. Faculty regularly uses software programs that identify plagiarized material in student papers. You can avoid plagiarism by using quotation marks around an author's words and providing a reference indicating where you found the material. Another way to avoid plagiarism is by carefully reading your source material while using critical thinking to evaluate it. Then look away from the source and write about the ideas in your own words, including your critical thinking about the subject. Don't forget to include a reference for the source material in your bibliography.

Write the Conclusion
The conclusion summarizes the topics in the paper and presents your point of view. It makes reference to the introduction and answers the question posed in your thesis statement. It often makes the reader think about the significance of your point and the implications for the future. Make your conclusion interesting and powerful.

Include References
No college paper is complete without references. References may be given in footnotes, endnotes, a list of works cited, or a bibliography. You can use your computer to insert these references. There are various styles for citing references depending on your subject area.

There are computer programs that put your information into the correct style. Ask your instructor which style to use for your particular class or project. Three frequently used styles for citing references are APA, Chicago, and MLA.

1. The American Psychological Association (APA) style is used in psychology and other behavioral sciences. Consult the *Publication Manual of the American Psychological Association*, 6th ed. (Washington, DC: American Psychological Association, 2010). You can find this source online at www.apastyle.org.

2. Chicago style is used by many professional writers in a variety of fields. Consult the *Chicago Manual of Style*, 16th ed. (Chicago: University of Chicago Press, 2010). You can find this source online at www.chicagomanualofstyle.org/home.html.

3. The Modern Language Association (MLA) style is used in English, classical languages, and the humanities. Consult the *MLA Handbook for Writers of Research Papers*, 7th ed. (New York: Modern Language Association, 2009). This source is available online at www.mla.org/style.

Each of these styles uses a different format for listing sources, but all include the same information. Make sure you write down this information as you collect your reference material. If you forget this step, it is very time-consuming and difficult to find later.

- Author's name
- Title of the book or article
- Journal name
- Publisher
- City where book was published
- Publication date
- Page number (and volume and issue numbers, if available)

Save Your Work

As soon as you have written the first paragraph, save it on your computer. If your computer is not backed up by a remote server such as iCloud or Carbonite, save another copy on a flash drive. When you are finished, print your work and save a paper copy. Then, if your hard drive crashes, you will still have your work at another location. If your file becomes corrupted, you will still have the paper copy. Following these procedures can save you a lot of headaches. Any writer can tell you stories of lost work because of computer problems, lightning storms, power outages, and other unpredictable events.

> "All things are difficult before they are easy."
> John Norley

Put It Away for a While

The last step in writing the first draft is to take a break. Put it away for a while and come back to it later. In this way, you can relax and gain some perspective on your work. You will be able to take a more objective look at your work to begin the process of editing and revising.

Writer's Block

Many people who are anxious about writing experience "writer's block." You have writer's block if you find yourself staring at that blank piece of paper or computer screen not knowing how to begin or what to write. Here are some tips for avoiding writer's block.

- **Write freely.** Just write anything about your topic that comes to mind. Don't worry about organization or perfection at this point. Don't censure your ideas. You can

© Creativa/Shutterstock.com

always go back to organize and edit later. Free-writing helps you to overcome one of the main causes of writer's block: you think it has to be perfect from the beginning. This expectation of perfection causes anxiety. You freeze up and become unable to write. Perhaps you have past memories of writing where the teacher made many corrections on your paper. Maybe you lack confidence in your writing skills. The only way you will become a better writer is to keep writing and perfecting your writing skills. Don't worry how great it is. You can fix it later. Just begin.

- **Use brainstorming if you get stuck.** For five minutes, focus your attention on the topic and write whatever comes to mind. You don't even need to write full sentences; just jot down ideas. If you are really stuck, try working on a different topic or take a break and come back to it later.
- **Realize that it is only the first draft.** It is not the finished product and it does not have to be perfect. Just write some ideas on paper; you can revise them later.
- **Read through your reference materials.** The ideas you find can get your mind working. Also, reading can make you a better writer.
- **Break the assignment up into small parts.** If you find writing difficult, write for five minutes at a time. Do this consistently and you can get used to writing and can complete your paper.
- **Find a good place for writing.** If you are an introvert, look for a quiet place for concentration. If you are an extrovert, go to a restaurant or coffee shop and start your writing.
- **Beware of procrastination.** The more you put off writing, the more anxious you will become and the more difficult the task will be. Make a schedule and stick to it.

> **Tips to Overcome Writer's Block**
>
> 1. Write freely
> 2. Use brainstorming
> 3. Realize it's a first draft
> 4. Read reference materials
> 5. Break up assignment
> 6. Find a good place to write
> 7. Beware of procrastination

Edit and Revise

The editing and revising stage allows you to take a critical look at what you have written. It takes some courage to do this step. Once people see their ideas in writing, they become attached to them. With careful editing and revising, you can turn in your best work and be proud of your accomplishments. Here are some tips for editing and revising:

1. **Read your paper as if you were the audience.** Pretend that you are the instructor or another person reading your paper. Does every sentence make sense? Did you say what you meant to say? Read what you have written, and the result will be a more effective paper.

© Madhourses/Shutterstock.com

2. **Read paragraph by paragraph.** Does each paragraph have a main idea and supporting details? Do the paragraphs fit logically together? Use the cut-and-paste feature on your computer to move sentences and paragraphs around if needed.

3. **Check your grammar and spelling.** Use the spell check and grammar check on your computer. These tools are helpful, but they are not thorough enough. The spell check will pick up only misspelled words. It will skip words that are spelled correctly but not the intended word—for example, if you use "of" instead of "on" or "their" instead of "there." To find such errors, you need to read your paper after doing a spell check.

4. **Check for language that is biased in terms of gender, disability, or ethnic group.** Use words that are gender neutral. If a book or paper uses only the pronoun "he" or "she," half of the population is left out. You can often avoid sexist language by using the plural forms of nouns:

   (singular) The successful student knows *his* values and sets goals for the future.

   (plural)   Successful students know *their* values and set goals for the future.

After all, we are trying to make the world a better place, with opportunity for all. Here are some examples of biased language and better alternatives.

Biased Language	*Better Alternatives*
policeman	police officer
chairman	chair
fireman	firefighter
postman	mail carrier
mankind	humanity
manmade	handcrafted
housewife	homemaker

5. **Have someone else read your paper.** Ask your reader to check for clarity and meaning. After you have read your paper many times, you do not really see it anymore. If you need assistance in writing, colleges offer tutoring or writing labs where you can get help with editing and revising.

6. **Review your introduction and conclusion.** They should be clear, interesting, and concise. The introduction and conclusion are the most powerful parts of your paper.

Tips for Editing and Revising

1. Read your paper objectively
2. Read paragraph by paragraph
3. Check grammar and spelling
4. Check for biased language
5. Have someone else read your paper
6. Review the introduction and conclusion
7. Prepare final copy
8. Prepare title page

7. **Prepare the final copy.** Check your instructor's instructions on the format required. If there are no instructions, use the following format:
   - Use double-spacing.
   - Use 10- or 12-point font.
   - Use one-inch margins on all sides.
   - Use a three-inch top margin on the first page.
   - Single-space footnotes and endnotes.
   - Number your pages.

8. **Prepare the title page.** Center the title of your paper and place it one third of the page from the top. On the bottom third of the page, center your name, the professor's name, the name of the class, and the date.

Final Steps

Make sure you follow instructions about using a folder or cover for your paper. Generally professors dislike bulky folders or notebooks because they are difficult to carry. Imagine your professor trying to carry 50 notebooks to his or her office! Unless asked to do so, do not use plastic page protectors. Professors like to write comments on papers, and it is extremely difficult to write on papers with page protectors.

If you are submitting your paper online, check to make sure you have submitted the correct document and that is was successfully uploaded.

Turning your paper in on time is very important. Some professors do not accept late papers. Others subtract points if your paper is late. Put your paper in the car or someplace where you will have to see it before you go to class. **Then reward yourself for a job well done!**

> ### Journal Entry #3
> Write five intention statements about improving your writing. While thinking about your statements, consider the steps of POWER writing: prepare, organize, write, edit, and revise. Do you need to work on problems such as writer's block or getting your writing done on time? I intend to . . .

Effective Public Speaking

You may need to take a speech class in order to graduate from college, and many of your classes will require oral presentations. Being a good speaker can contribute to your success on the job as well. A study done at Stanford University showed that one of the top predictors of success in professional positions was the ability to be a good public speaker.[2] You will need to present information to your boss, your colleagues, and your customers or clients.

> "Let us think of education as the means of developing our greatest abilities, because in each of us there is a private hope and dream which, fulfilled, can be translated into greater benefit for everyone and greater strength for our nation."
>
> John F. Kennedy

© Sanjay Deva/Shutterstock.com

Learn to Relax

Students often panic when they find out that they have to make a speech. Good preparation can help you to feel confident about your oral presentation. Professional speaker Lilly Walters believes that you can deal with 75 percent of your anxiety by being well prepared.[3] You can deal with the remaining 25 percent by using some relaxation techniques.

- If you are anxious, admit to yourself that you are anxious. If it is appropriate, as in a beginning speech class, you can even admit to the audience that you are anxious. Once you have admitted that you are anxious, visualize yourself confidently making the speech.
- You do not have to be perfect; it is okay to make mistakes. Making mistakes just shows you are human like the rest of us.
- If you are anxious before your speech, take three to five deep breaths. Breathe in slowly and hold your breath for five seconds, and then breathe out slowly. Focus your mind on your breathing rather than your speech.
- Use positive self-talk to help you to relax. Instead of saying to yourself, "I will look like a fool up there giving the speech," tell yourself, "I can do this" or "It will be okay."
- Once you start speaking, anxiety will generally decline.
- With experience, you will gain confidence in your speaking ability and will be able to relax more easily.

Preparing and Delivering Your Speech

Write the Beginning of the Speech

The beginning includes a statement of your objective and what your speech will be about. It should prepare the audience for what comes next. You can begin your speech with a personal experience, a quote, a news article, or a joke. Jokes can be effective, but they are risky. Try out your joke with your friends to make sure that it is funny. Do not tell jokes that put down other people or groups.

Write the Main Body of the Speech

The main body of the speech consists of four or five main points. Just as in your term paper, state your main points and then provide details, examples, or stories that illustrate them. As you present the main points of your speech, consider your audience. Your speech will be different depending on whether it is made to a group of high school students, your college classmates, or a group of professionals. You can add interest to your speech by using props, pictures, charts, PowerPoint, music, or video clips. College students today are increasingly using PowerPoint software to make classroom presentations. If you are planning to enter a professional career, learning how to make PowerPoint presentations will be an asset.

Write the Conclusion

In your conclusion, summarize and review the key points of your speech. The conclusion is like the icing on a cake. It should be strong, persuasive, and interesting. Invest some time in your ending statement. It can be a call to action, a recommendation for the future, a quote, or a story.

Practice Your Speech

Practice your speech until you feel comfortable with it. Prepare a memory system or notes to help you deliver your speech. You will want to make eye contact with your audience, which is difficult if you are trying to read your speech. A memory system useful for delivering speeches is the loci system. Visualize a house, for example: the entryway is the introduction, and each room represents a main point in the speech. Visualize walking into each room and what you will say in each room. Each room can have items that remind you of what you are going to say. At the conclusion, you say good-bye at the door. Another technique is to prepare brief notes or outlines on index cards or sheets of paper. When you are practicing your speech, time it to see how long it is. Keep your speech within the time allowed. Most people tend to speak longer than necessary.

Review the Setup

If you are using props, make sure that you have them ready. If you are using equipment, make sure it is available and in working condition. Make arrangements in advance for the equipment you need and, if possible, check to see that it is running properly right before your presentation.

Deliver the Speech

Wear clothes that make you feel comfortable, but not out of place. Remember to smile and make eye contact with members of the audience. Take a few deep breaths if you are nervous. You will probably be less nervous once you begin. If you make a mistake, keep your sense of humor. I recall the famous chef Julia Child doing a live television production on how to cook a turkey. As she took the turkey out of the oven, it slipped and landed on the floor right in front of the television cameras. She calmly picked it up and said, "And remember that you are the only one that really knows what goes on in the kitchen." It was one of the shows that made her famous.

QUIZ

Writing and Speaking

Test what you have learned by selecting the correct answers to the following questions.

1. To make sure to get your paper done on time,
   a. have someone remind you of the deadline.
   b. write the due date on your calendar and the date for completion of each step.
   c. write your paper just before the due date to increase motivation.

2. The thesis statement is the
   a. most important sentence in each paragraph.
   b. key idea in the paper.
   c. summary of the paper.

3. If you have writer's block, it is helpful to
   a. delay writing your paper until you feel relaxed.
   b. make sure that your writing is perfect from the beginning.
   c. begin with brainstorming or free writing.

4. No college paper is complete without
   a. the references.
   b. a professional-looking cover.
   c. printing on quality paper.

5. You can deal with most of your anxiety about public speaking by
   a. striving for perfection.
   b. visualizing your anxiety.
   c. being well prepared.

How did you do on the quiz? Check your answers: 1. b, 2. b, 3. c, 4. a, 5. c

Journal Entry #4

Write one paragraph giving advice to a new college student on how to make a speech. Use any of these questions to guide your thinking:

- What are some ways to deal with anxiety about public speaking?
- How can you make your speech interesting?
- What are some steps in preparing a speech?
- What are some ideas that don't work?

© iQoncept/Shutterstock.com

KEYS TO SUCCESS

Be Selective

Psychologist and philosopher William James said, "The essence of genius is knowing what to overlook."[4] This saying has a variety of meanings. In reading, note taking, marking a college textbook, and writing, it is important to be able to pick out the main points first and then identify the supporting details. Imagine you are trying to put together a jigsaw puzzle. You bought the puzzle at a garage sale and all the pieces are there, but the lid to the box with the picture of the puzzle is missing. It will be very difficult, if not impossible, to put this puzzle together. Reading, note taking, marking, and writing are very much like putting a puzzle together. First you will need an understanding of the main ideas (the big picture) and then you can focus on the details.

How can you get the overall picture? When reading, you can get the overall picture by skimming the text. As you skim the text, you get a general outline of what the chapter contains and what you will learn. In note taking, actively listen for the main ideas and write them down in your notes. In marking your text, try to pick out about 20 percent of the most important material and underline or highlight it. In writing, think about what is most important, write your thesis statement, and then provide the supporting details. To select what is most important, be courageous, think, and analyze.

Does this mean that you should forget about the details? No, you will need to know some details too. The supporting details help you to understand and assess the value of the main idea. They help you to understand the relationship between ideas. Being selective means getting the general idea first, and then the details will make sense to you and you will be able to remember them. The main ideas are like scaffolding or a net that holds the details in some kind of framework so you can remember them. If you focus on the details first, you will have no framework or point of reference for remembering them.

Experiment with the idea of being selective in your personal life. If your schedule is impossibly busy, be selective and choose to do the most important or most valuable activities. This takes some thinking and courage too. If your desk drawer is stuffed with odds and ends and you can never find what you are looking for, take everything out and only put back what you need. Recycle, give away, or throw away surplus items around the house. You can take steps toward being a genius by being selective and taking steps to simplify and organize your life and your work.

> ### Journal Entry #5
>
> How can being selective help you achieve success in college and in life? Use any of these questions to guide your thinking:
>
> - How can being selective help you to be a better note taker, writer, or speaker?
> - How can being selective help you to manage your time and your life?
> - What is the meaning of this quote by William James: "The essence of genius is knowing what to overlook?"

Appreciating Island Cultures: How the 'Ulu Tree Came to Hawai'i

I Ka Wa Kahiko, in Hawai'i of old, there was a man named Ku who had a wife and two keiki, or children. They had a keikikane, a son, and a kaikamahine, a daughter. He loved them very much. In those days they had the ahupua'a (land division), that divided each moku, or district. These ahupua'a stretched from mauka (toward the mountains), to Makai (toward the ocean), and everyone within it had a kuleana, or responsibility. Because everyone considered each other 'ohana (family), they each worked together to share their strengths with one another. One day a drought hit Hawai'i. Month after month went by, and the people began to grow hungry because there was an increasing lack of food. Ku watched his children and watched the rest of his kaiaulu, or community, suffer.

One day, they finally ran out of everything. The keiki were crying because they were pololi (hungry). That night when Ku's keiki went to sleep, he and his wife had a discussion. There were options that were considered, but Ku knew that he had to do something that was best for everyone, not just what was best for him. The next morning, he woke up and sat down in the middle of his yard. His keiki and his wife finally came out to sit with him and he explained what he was going to do to save them and their kaiaulu. Ku told them that he was going to dig a hole in the middle of the yard and set himself in it. From that hole, there would be a tree that would grow forth called the 'Ulu tree, or breadfruit tree. This tree would feed his family and the rest of their kaiaulu. As much as he didn't want to, he knew this was the only way everyone else would survive. He said his last goodbyes to his family, hugged them, and began to dig his hole in the ground. As he began digging, the hole began to close up until you could no longer see him. The tears of his little 'ohana fell on the ground and soon, the 'ulu tree began to grow. It grew so big that it produced much fruit for everyone to eat. They could feed their families throughout the drought and for generations to come. Soon, everyone would have a piece of the tree for their own 'ohana to have a plant in their yard.

So every time the tree was seen, you would be able to remember Ku's sacrifice for his family and his community, and later, for Hawai'i's generations.

Breadfruit Tree © LilyTiger/Shutterstock.com

Questions

1. What did Ku do and why?
2. Did he do this to benefit himself or the future of his family, community, and generations to come?
3. How will what you are doing benefit the future generations of your family?
4. What are the things that you are struggling with?
5. What are the things that you can do better so that the effects will be felt for generations?

- Ahupua'a: Land division from mountain to the sea
- Moku: District
- I KaWaKahiko: In Hawai'i of old
- Kaiaulu: Community
- Kaikamahine: Girl or daughter
- Keiki: Child
- Keikikane: Boy or son
- Ku: One of the four major gods
- Kuleana: Responsibility
- Ma Kai: Toward the sea
- Mauka: Toward mountain
- 'Ohana: Family
- Pololi: Hungry
- 'Ulu: Breadfruit

Slices of Uncooked Breadfruit © Jfanchin/Shutterstock.com

© Lyudmyla Kharlamova/Shutterstock.com

College Success 1

The College Success 1 website is continually updated with supplementary material for each chapter including Word documents of the journal entries, classroom activities, handouts, videos, links to related materials, and much more. See http://www.collegesuccess1.com/.

Notes

1. Paul Nolting, *Winning at Math*, (Bradenton, FL: Academic Success Press, 2014), 139.
2. T. Allesandra and P. Hunsaker, *Communicating at Work* (New York: Fireside, 1993), 169.
3. Lilly Walters, *Secrets of Successful Speakers: How You Can Motivate, Captivate, and Persuade* (New York: McGraw-Hill, 1993), 203.
4. Quoted in Rob Gilbert, ed., *Bits and Pieces,* August 12, 1999, 15.

Note-Taking Checklist

Name _____ Date _____

Place a checkmark next to the note-taking skills you have now.

_____ I attend every (or almost every) lecture in all my classes.

_____ I check the syllabus to find out what is being covered before I go to class.

_____ I read or at least skim through the reading assignment before attending the lecture.

_____ I attend lectures with a positive attitude about learning as much as possible.

_____ I am well rested so that I can focus on the lecture.

_____ I eat a light, nutritious meal before going to class.

_____ I sit in a location where I can see and hear easily.

_____ I have a laptop or a three-ring binder, looseleaf paper, and a pen for taking notes.

_____ I avoid external distractions (friends, sitting by the door).

_____ I am alert and able to concentrate on the lecture.

_____ I have a system for taking notes that works for me.

_____ I am able to determine the key ideas of the lecture and write them down in my notes.

_____ I can identify signal words that help to understand key points and organize my notes.

_____ I can write quickly using telegraphic sentences, abbreviations, and symbols.

_____ If I don't understand something in the lecture, I ask a question and get help.

_____ I write down everything written on the board or on visual materials used in the class.

_____ I review my notes immediately after class.

_____ I have intermediate review sessions to review previous notes.

_____ I use my notes to predict questions for the exam.

_____ I have clear and complete notes that help me to prepare adequately for exams.

Evaluate Your Note-Taking Skills

Name _____ Date _____

Use the note-taking checklist on the previous page to answer these questions.

1. Look at the items that you checked. What are your strengths in note taking?

2. What are some areas that you need to improve?

3. Write at least three intention statements about improving your listening and note-taking skills.

Assess Your College Writing Skills

Name _____   Date _____

Read the following statements and rate how true they are for you at the present time. Use the following scale:

5 Definitely true
4 Mostly true
3 Somewhat true
2 Seldom true
1 Never true

_____ I am generally confident in my writing skills.

_____ I have a system for reminding myself of due dates for writing projects.

_____ I start writing projects early so that I am not stressed by finishing them at the last minute.

_____ I have the proper materials and a space to write comfortably.

_____ I know how to use the library and the Internet to gather information for a term paper.

_____ I can write a thesis statement for a term paper.

_____ I know how to organize a term paper.

_____ I know how to write the introduction, body, and conclusion of a paper.

_____ I can cite references in the appropriate style for my subject.

_____ I know where to find information about citing material in APA, MLA, or Chicago style.

_____ I know what plagiarism is and know how to avoid it.

_____ I can deal with "writer's block" and get started on my writing project.

_____ I know how to edit and revise a paper.

_____ I know where I can get help with my writing.

_____ **Total**

60–70   You have excellent writing skills, but can always learn new ideas.
50–59   You have good writing skills, but there is room for improvement.
Below 50 You need to improve writing skills. The skills presented in this chapter will help. Consider taking a writing class early in your college studies.

Thinking about Writing

Name _____   Date _____

List 10 suggestions from this chapter that could help you improve your writing skills.

1.

2.

3.

4.

5.

6.

7.

8.

9.

10.

Taking Notes, Writing, and Speaking

CHAPTER 8

Test Taking

Learning Objectives

Read to answer these key questions:

- What are some test preparation techniques?

- How should I review the material?

- How can I predict the test questions?

- What are some emergency test preparation techniques?

- How can I deal with test anxiety?

- How can I overcome math anxiety and be successful on math tests?

- What are some tips for taking math tests?

- What are some tips for taking objective tests?

- How can I write a good essay?

From *College & Career Success, Concise Version*, Seventh Edition, by Marsha Fralick. Copyright © 2016 by Kendall Hunt Publishing Company. Reprinted by permission.

An important skill for survival in college is the ability to take tests. Passing tests is also important in careers that require licenses, certificates, or continuing education. Knowing how to prepare for and take tests with confidence will help you to accomplish your educational and career goals while maintaining your good mental health. Once you have learned some basic test-taking and relaxation techniques, you can turn your test anxiety into motivation and good test results.

Preparing for Tests

Attend Every Class

> "Eighty percent of success is showing up"
> Woody Allen

The most significant factor in poor performance in college is lack of attendance. Students who attend the lectures and complete their assignments have the best chance for success in college. Attending the lectures helps you to be involved in learning and to know what to expect on the test. College professors know that students who miss three classes in a row are not likely to return, and some professors drop students after three absences. After three absences, students can fall behind in their schoolwork and become overwhelmed with makeup work.

Photo courtesy of Lilieni Tuitupou, Salt Lake Community College.

Distribute the Practice

The key to successful test preparation is to begin early and do a little at a time. Test preparation begins the first day of class. During the first class, the professor gives an overview of the course content, requirements, tests, and grading. These items are described in writing in the class calendar and syllabus. It is very important to attend the first class to obtain this essential information. If you have to miss the first class, make sure to ask the professor for the syllabus and calendar and read it carefully.

Early test preparation helps you to take advantage of the powerful memory technique called distributed practice. In distributed practice, the material learned is broken up into small parts and reviewed frequently. Using this method can enable you to learn a large quantity of material without becoming overwhelmed. Here are some examples of using distributed practice:

- If you have a test on 50 Spanish vocabulary words in two weeks, don't wait until the day before the test to try to learn all 50 words. Waiting until the day before the test will result in difficulty remembering the words, test anxiety, and a dislike of studying

Spanish. If you have 50 Spanish vocabulary words to learn in two weeks, learn five words each day and quickly review the words you learned previously. For example, on Monday you would learn five words, and on Tuesday, you would learn five new words and review the ones learned on Monday. Give yourself the weekends off as a reward for planning ahead.

- If you have to read a history book with 400 pages, divide that number by the number of days in the semester or quarter. If there are 80 days in the semester, you will only have to read five pages per day or 10 pages every other day. This is a much easier and more efficient way to master a long assignment.
- Don't wait until the last minute to study for a midterm or final exam. Keep up with the class each week. As you read each chapter, quickly review a previous chapter. In this way you can comfortably master the material. Just before a major test, you can review the material that you already know and feel confident about your ability to get a good grade on the test.

Schedule a Time and a Place for Studying

To take advantage of distributed practice, you will need to develop a study schedule. Write down your work time and school time and other scheduled activities. Identify times that can be used for studying each day. Get in the habit of using these available times for studying each week. As a general rule, you need two hours of study time for each hour spent in a college classroom. If you cannot find enough time for studying, consider either reducing your course load or reducing work hours.

Use your study schedule or calendar to note the due dates of major projects and all test dates. Schedule enough time to complete projects and to finish major reviews for exams. Look at each due date and write in reminders to begin work or review well in advance of the due date. Give yourself plenty of time to meet the deadlines. It seems that around exam time, students are often ill or have problems that prevent them from being successful. Having some extra time scheduled will help you to cope with the many unexpected events that happen in everyday life.

Find a place to study. This can be an area of your home where you have a desk, computer, and all the necessary supplies for studying. As a general rule, do not study at the kitchen table, in front of the television, or in your bed. These places provide powerful cues for eating, watching television, or sleeping instead of studying. If you cannot find an appropriate place at home, use the college library as a place to study. The library is usually quiet and others are studying, so there are not too many distractions. Studying in different places can aid in recall.

© Alexander Raths/Shutterstock.com

> **Review Tools**
> - Flash cards
> - Summary sheets
> - Mind maps
> - Study groups

Test Review Tools

There are a variety of tools you can use to review for tests. Choose the tools according to personal preference and the type of test for which you are preparing.

- **Flash cards.** Flash cards are an effective way to learn facts and details for objective tests such as true-false, multiple-choice, matching, and fill-in-the-blank. For example, if you have 100 vocabulary words to learn in biology, put each word on one side of a card and the definition on the other side. First, look at each definition and see if you can recall the word. It is helpful to visualize the word and even say it out loud. Carry the cards with you and briefly look at them as you are going about your daily activities. Make a game of studying by sorting the cards into stacks of information you know and those you still have to practice. Work with the flash cards frequently and review them quickly. Don't worry about learning all the items at once. Each day that you practice, you will recall the items more easily. You can also use online tools such as Quizlet (https://quizlet.com/) for making flashcards.

- **Summary sheets.** Summary sheets are used to record the key ideas from your lecture notes or textbook. It is important to be selective; write only the most important ideas on the summary sheets. At the end of the semester, you might have approximately 10 pages of summary sheets from the text and 10 pages from your notes.

- **Mind maps.** A mind map is a visual picture of the items you wish to remember. Start in the center of the page with a key idea and then surround it with related topics. You can use drawings, lines, circles, or colors to link and group the ideas. A mind map will help you to learn material in an organized way that will be useful when writing essay exams.

- **Study groups.** A study group is helpful in motivating yourself to learn through discussions of the material with other people. For the study group, select three to seven people who are motivated to be successful in class and can coordinate schedules. Study groups are often used in math and science classes. Groups of students work problems together and help each other understand the material. The study group is also useful in studying for exams. Give each member a part of the material to be studied. Have each person predict test questions and quiz the study group. Teaching the material to the study group can be the best way to learn it.

> "I can accept failure. Everyone fails at something. But I can't accept not trying."
> Michael Jordan

Reviewing Effectively

Begin your review early and break it into small parts. Remember that repetition is one of the effective ways to store information in long-term memory. Here are some types of review that help you to store information in long-term memory:

- **Immediate review.** This type of review is fast and powerful and helps to minimize forgetting. It is the first step in storing information in long-term memory. Begin the process by turning each bold-faced heading in the text into a question. Read each section to answer the question you have asked. Read your college texts with a highlighter in hand so that you can mark the key ideas for review. Some students use a variety of colors to distinguish main ideas, supporting points, and key examples, for instance. When you are finished using the highlighter, quickly review the items you have marked. As you complete each section, quickly review the main points. When you finish the chapter, immediately review the key points in the entire chapter again. As soon as you finish taking your lecture notes, take a few minutes to review them.

© wavebreakmedia/Shutterstock.com

To be most effective, immediate review needs to occur as soon as possible or at least within the first 20 minutes of learning something.

- **Intermediate review.** After you have finished reading and reviewing a new chapter in your textbook, spend a few minutes reviewing an earlier one. This step will help you to master the material and to recall it easily for the midterm or final exam. Another way to do intermediate review is to set up time periodically in your study schedule for reviewing previous chapters and classroom notes. Doing intermediate reviews helps to access the materials you have stored in long-term memory.

- **Final review.** Before a major exam, organize your notes, materials, and assignments. Estimate how long it will take you to review the material. Break the material into manageable chunks. For an essay exam, use mind maps or summary sheets to write down the main points that you need to remember and recite these ideas frequently. For objective tests, use flash cards or lists to remember details and concepts that you expect to be on the test. Here is a sample seven-day plan for reviewing 10 chapters for a final exam:

Day 1 Gather materials and study Chapters 1 and 2 by writing key points on summary sheets or mind maps. Make flash cards of details you need to remember. Review and highlight lecture notes and handouts on these chapters.

Day 2 Review Chapters 1 and 2. Study Chapters 3 and 4 and the corresponding lecture notes.

Day 3 Review Chapters 1 to 4. Study Chapters 5 and 6 and the corresponding lecture notes.

Day 4 Review Chapters 1 to 6. Study Chapters 7 and 8 along with the corresponding lecture notes.

Day 5 Review Chapters 1 to 8. Study Chapters 9 and 10 along with corresponding lecture notes.

Day 6 Review notes, summary sheets, mind maps, and flash cards for Chapters 1 to 10. Relax and get a good night's sleep. You are well prepared.

Day 7 Do one last quick review of Chapters 1 to 10 and walk into the test with the confidence that you will be successful on the exam.

Predicting Test Questions

There are many ways to predict the questions that will be on the test. Here are some ideas that might be helpful:

- Look for clues from the professor about what will be on the test. Many times professors put information about the tests on the course syllabus. During lectures, they often give hints about what will be important to know. If a professor repeats something more than once, make note of it as a possible test question. Anything written on the board is likely to be on the test. Sometimes the professor will even say, "This will be on the test." Write these important points in your notes and review them.
- College textbooks are usually written in short sections with bold headings. Turn each bold-faced heading into a question and read to answer the question. Understand and review the main idea in each section. The test questions will generally address the main ideas in the text.
- Don't forget to study and review the handouts that the professor distributes to the class. If the professor has taken the time and effort to provide extra material, it is probably important and may be on the test.
- Form a study group and divide up the material to be reviewed. Have each member of the group write some test questions based on the important points in each main section of the text. When the study group meets, take turns asking likely test questions and providing the answers.
- When the professor announces the test, make sure to ask what material is to be covered on the test and what kind of test it is. If necessary, ask the professor which concepts are most important. Know what kinds of test questions will be asked (essay, true-false, multiple-choice, matching, or short-answer). Some professors may provide sample exams or math problems.
- Use the first test to understand what is expected and how to study for future tests.

> "The will to win is not nearly as important as the will to prepare to win."
> Bobby Knight

Journal Entry # 1

Write one paragraph about the ideal way to prepare for a major exam such as a midterm or final. Consider these factors while thinking about your answer: attendance, distribute the practice, time management, review tools, predicting test questions and the most efficient way to review.

Preparing for an Open-Book Test

In college, you may have some open-book tests. Open-book tests are often used in very technical subjects where specific material from the book is needed to answer questions. For example, in an engineering course, tables and formulas in the book may be needed to solve engineering problems on an exam. To study for an open-book test, focus on understanding the material and being able to locate key information for the exam. Consider making index tabs for your book so that you can locate needed information quickly. Be sure to bring your book, calculator, and other needed material to the exam.

Emergency Procedures

If it is a day or two before the test and you have not followed the above procedures, it is time for the college practice known as "cramming." There are two main problems that result from this practice. First, you cannot take advantage of distributed practice, so it

© Mike Elliott/Shutterstock.com

will be difficult to remember large amounts of material. Within a week, you are likely to forget 75% of the material you learned while cramming.[1] It requires much effort and results in little benefit. Second, it is not fun and, if done often, will result in anxiety and a dislike of education. Because of these problems, some students who rely on cramming wrongly conclude that they are not capable of finishing their education.

If you must cram for a test, here are some emergency procedures that may be helpful in getting the best grade possible under difficult circumstances:

- When cramming, **it is most important to be selective.** Try to identify the main points and recite and review them.
- Focus on reviewing and reciting the lecture notes. In this way, you will cover the main ideas the professor thinks are important.
- If you have not read the text, skim and search each chapter looking for the main points. Highlight and review these main points. Read the chapter summaries. In a math textbook, practice sample problems.
- Make summary sheets containing the main ideas from the notes and the text. Recite and review the summary sheets.
- For objective tests, focus on learning new terms and vocabulary related to the subject. These terms are likely to be on the test. Flash cards are helpful.
- For essay tests, develop an outline of major topics and review the outline so you can write an essay.
- Get enough rest. Staying up all night to review for the test can result in confusion, reduced mental ability, and test anxiety.
- Hope for the best.
- Plan ahead next time so that you can get a better grade.

If you have very little time to review for a test, you will probably experience information overload. One strategy for dealing with this problem is based on the work of George Miller of Harvard University. He found that the optimum number of chunks of information we can remember is seven plus or minus two (or five to nine chunks of information).[2] This is also known as the Magical Number Seven Theory. For this last-minute review technique, start with five sheets of paper. Next, identify five key concepts that are likely to be on the test. Write one concept on the top of each sheet of paper. Then check your notes and text to write an explanation, definition, or answer for each of these topics. If you have more time, find two to four more concepts and research them, writing the information on additional sheets. You should have no more than nine sheets of paper. Arrange the sheets in order of importance. Review and recite the key ideas on these sheets. Get a regular night's sleep before the test and do some relaxation exercises right before the test.

© YanLev/Shutterstock.com

Ideas That Don't Work

Some students do poorly on tests for the following reasons.

- Attending a party or social event the evening before a major test rather than doing the final review will adversely affect your test score. Study in advance and reward yourself with the party after the test.
- Skipping the major review before the test may cause you to forget some important material.
- Taking drugs or drinking alcohol before a test may give you the impression that you are relaxed and doing well on the test, but the results are disastrous to your success on the exam and your good health.
- Not knowing the date of the test can cause you to get a low grade because you are not prepared.
- Not checking or knowing about the final exam schedule can cause you to miss the final.
- Missing the final exam can result in a lower grade or failing the class.
- Arriving late for the exam puts you at a disadvantage if you don't have time to finish or have to rush through the test.
- Deciding not to buy or read the textbook will cause low performance or failure.
- Having a fight, disagreement, or argument with parents, friends, or significant others before the test will make it difficult to focus on the exam.
- Sacrificing sleep, exercise, or food to prepare for the exam makes it difficult to do your best.
- Cheating on an exam can cause embarrassment, a lower grade, or failure. It can even lead to expulsion from college.
- Missing the exam because you are not prepared and asking the professor to let you make up the exam later is a tactic that many students try. Most professors will not permit you to take an exam late.
- Inventing a creative excuse for missing an exam is so common that some professors have a collection of these stories that they share with colleagues. Creative excuses don't work with most professors.
- Arriving at the exam without the proper materials such as a pencil, Scantron, paper, calculator, or book (for open-book exams) can cause you to miss the exam or start the exam late.

> "Failure is simply the opportunity to begin again more intelligently."
> Henry Ford

QUIZ

Test Preparation

Test what you have learned by selecting the correct answers to the following questions.

1. In test preparation, it is important to use this memory technique:

    a. Distribute the practice.
    b. Read every chapter just before the test.
    c. Do most of the review right before the test to minimize forgetting.

2. To take advantage of distributed practice, it is important to develop a:

    a. summary sheet.
    b. study schedule.
    c. mind map.

3. Effective tools to learn facts and details are

    a. mind maps.
    b. summary sheets.
    c. flash cards.

4. The best way to review is

    a. to start early and break it into small parts.
    b. immediately before the test.
    c. in large blocks of time.

5. If you have to cram for an exam, it is most important to

    a. stay up all night studying for the exam
    b. focus on the lecture notes and forget about reading the text
    c. be selective and review and recite the main points

How did you do on the quiz? Check your answers: 1. a, 2. b, 3. c, 4. a, 5. c

Ten Rules for Success

Here are 10 rules for success on any test. Are there any new ideas you can put into practice?

1. **Make sure to set your alarm,** and consider having a backup in case your alarm doesn't go off. Set a second alarm or have someone call to make sure you are awake on time.

2. **Arrive a little early for your exam.** If you are taking a standardized test like the Scholastic Aptitude Test (SAT) or Graduate Record Exam (GRE), familiarize yourself with the location of the exam. If you arrive early, you can take a quick walk around the building to relax or spend a few minutes doing a review so that your brain will be tuned up and ready.

3. **Eat a light breakfast including some carbohydrates and protein.** Be careful about eating sugar and caffeine before a test, because this can contribute to greater anxiety and low blood sugar by the time you take the test. The worst breakfast would be something like a doughnut and coffee or a soda and candy bar. Examples of good breakfasts are eggs, toast, and juice or cereal with milk and fruit.

4. **Think positively about the exam.** Tell yourself that you are well prepared and the exam is an opportunity to show what you know.

5. **Make sure you have the proper materials:** Scantrons, paper, pencil or pen, calculator, books and notes (for open-book exams).

6. **Manage your time.** Know how long you have for the test and then scan the test to make a time management plan. For example, if you have one hour and there are 50 objective questions, you have about a minute for each question. Halfway through the time, you should have completed 25 questions. If there are three essay questions in an hour, you have less than 20 minutes for each question. Save some time to look over the test and make corrections.

7. **Neatness is important.** If your paper looks neat, the professor is more likely to have a positive attitude about the paper before it is even read. If the paper is hard to read, the professor will start reading your paper with a negative attitude, possibly resulting in a lower grade.

8. **Read the test directions carefully.** On essay exams, it is common for the professor to give you a choice of questions to answer. If you do not read the directions, you may try to answer all of the questions and then run out of time or give incomplete answers to them.

9. **If you get stuck on a difficult question, don't worry about it.** Just mark it and find an easier question. You may find clues on the rest of the test that will aid your recall, or you may be more relaxed later on and think of the answer.

10. **Be careful not to give any impression that you might be cheating.** Keep your eyes on your own paper. If you have memory aids or outlines memorized, write them directly on the test paper rather than a separate sheet so that you are not suspected of using cheat notes.

Journal Entry #2

Write one paragraph about the most common mistakes students make while getting ready for an exam.

Dealing with Test Anxiety

Some anxiety is a good thing. It can provide motivation to study and prepare for exams. However, it is common for college students to suffer from test anxiety. Too much anxiety can lower your performance on tests. Some symptoms of test anxiety include:

- Fear of failing a test even though you are well prepared
- Physical symptoms such as perspiring, increased heart rate, shortness of breath, upset stomach, tense muscles, or headache
- Negative thoughts about the test and your grade
- Mental blocking of material you know and remembering it once you leave the exam

> "Luck is what happens when preparation meets opportunity."
> Darrell Royal

You can minimize your test anxiety by being well prepared and by applying the memory strategies described in earlier chapters. Prepare for your exams by attending every class, keeping up with your reading assignments, and reviewing during the semester. These steps will help increase your self-confidence and reduce anxiety. Apply the principles of memory improvement to your studying. As you are reading, find the important points and highlight them. Review these points so that they are stored in your long-term memory. Use distributed practice and spread out learning over time rather than trying to learn it all at once. Visualize and organize what you need to remember. Trust in your abilities and intend to remember what you have studied.

© Stuart Miles/Shutterstock.com

If you find that you are anxious, here are some ideas you can try to cope with the anxiety. Experiment with these techniques to see which ones work best for you.

- **Do some physical exercise.** Physical exercise helps to use up stress hormones. Make physical activity a part of your daily routine. Arrive for your test a little early and walk briskly around campus for about 20 minutes. This exercise will help you to feel relaxed and energized.
- **Get a good night's sleep before the test.** Lack of sleep can interfere with memory and cause irritability, anxiety, and confusion.
- **Take deep breaths.** Immediately before the test, take a few deep breaths; hold them for three to five seconds and let them out slowly. These deep breaths will help you to relax and keep a sufficient supply of oxygen in your blood. Oxygen is needed for proper brain function.
- **Visualize and rehearse your success.** Begin by getting as comfortable and relaxed as possible in your favorite chair or lying down in bed. Visualize yourself walking into the exam room. Try to imagine the room in as much detail as possible. If possible, visit the exam room before the test so that you can get a good picture of it. See yourself taking the exam calmly and confidently. You know most of the answers. If you find a question you do not know, see yourself circling it and coming back to it later. Imagine that you find a clue on the test that triggers your recall of the answers to the difficult questions. Picture yourself handing in the exam with a good feeling about doing well on the test. Then imagine you are getting the test back and you get a good grade on the test. You congratulate yourself for a job well done. If you suffer from test anxiety, you may need to rehearse this scene several times. When you enter the exam room, the visual picture that you have rehearsed will help you to relax.
- **Acknowledge your anxiety.** The first step in dealing with anxiety is to admit that you are anxious rather than trying to fight it or deny it. Say to yourself, "I am feeling anxious." Take a few deep breaths and then focus your attention on the test.
- **Do the easy questions first and mark the ones that may be difficult.** This will help you to relax. Once you are relaxed, the difficult questions become more manageable.

Tips to Minimize Anxiety

- Exercise
- Sleep
- Take deep breaths
- Visualize success
- Acknowledge anxiety
- Easy questions first
- Yell, "Stop!"
- Daydream
- Practice perspective
- Give yourself time
- Get help

- **Yell, "Stop!"** Negative and frightening thoughts can cause anxiety. Here are some examples of negative thoughts:

    I'm going to fail this test.

    I don't know the answer to number 10!

    I never do well on tests.

    Essays! I have a hard time with those.

    I'll never make it through college.

    I was never any good in math!

    These types of thoughts don't help you do better on the test, so stop saying them. They cause you to become anxious and to freeze up during the test. If you find yourself with similar thoughts, yell, "Stop!" to yourself. This will cause you to interrupt your train of thought so that you can think about the task at hand rather than becoming more anxious. Replace negative thoughts with more positive ones such as these:

    I'm doing the best I can.

    I am well prepared and know most of the answers.

    I don't know the answer to number 10, so I'll just circle it and come back to it later.

    I'll make an outline in the margin for the essay question.

    College is difficult, but I'll make it!

    Math is a challenge, but I can do it!

- **Daydream.** Think about being in your favorite place. Take time to think about the details. Allow yourself to be there for a while until you feel more relaxed.
- **Practice perspective.** Remember, one poor grade is not the end of the world. It does not define who you are. If you do not do well, think about how you can improve your preparation and performance the next time.
- **Give yourself time.** Test anxiety develops over a period of time. It will take some time to get over it. Learn the best ways to prepare for the exam and practice saying positive thoughts to yourself.
- **Get help.** If these techniques do not work for you, seek help from your college health or counseling center.

Journal Entry #3

You have a friend who prepares for exams, but suffers from test anxiety. Review the section on test anxiety and write a one paragraph e-mail to your friend with some ideas on dealing with test anxiety. Consider both physical and mental preparation as well as some relaxation techniques that can be helpful.

I am taking a college success course and the book has some ideas on dealing with test anxiety. The book suggests . . .

Dealing with Math Anxiety

Math anxiety is a negative physical and/or emotional reaction toward math. It can lead to avoidance of math and procrastination in doing your math homework. It is often caused by negative experiences with math in elementary school or at home with parents helping with homework. Often students were embarrassed by being asked to solve a problem on the board and not being successful. Perhaps teachers, parents, siblings, or friends made negative comments about your math ability. It is important to think about the source of your math anxiety and then move on to new possibilities.

© Creativa Images/Shutterstock.com

Math anxiety is often related to low confidence in math. To build self-confidence, begin with positive thinking. You may have had difficulty with math in the past, but with a positive attitude and the proper study techniques, you can meet the challenge. The first step to success in math is to put in the effort required. Attend class, do your homework, and get help if needed. It is important to experience success, even in small steps, and build on your success. If you put in the effort and hard work, you will gain experience in math. If you gain experience with math, you will become more confident in your ability to do math. If you have confidence, you will gain satisfaction in doing math. You may even learn to like it! If you like the subject, you can gain competence. The process looks like this:

"Do not worry about your difficulties in mathematics. I can assure you mine are still greater."
— Albert Einstein

Hard work → Experience → Confidence → Satisfaction → Competence

If you suffer from math anxiety, you can make an appointment to talk with your instructor, advisor, or counselor to find out what resources may be available to you. Although you may have had difficulty with math in the past, you can become successful by following these steps. Your reward is self-satisfaction and increased opportunity in technical, scientific, and professional careers. Math is required for graduation too.

Math Tests

Taking a math test involves some different strategies:

Tips for Avoiding Common Math Errors[2]

- Any quantity multiplied by zero is zero
- Any quantity raised to the zero power is one
- Any fraction multiplied by its reciprocal is one
- Only like algebraic terms may be combined
- Break down to the simplest form in algebra
- In algebra, multiply and divide before adding and subtracting
- If an algebraic expression has more than one set of parentheses, get rid of the inner parenthesis first and work outward
- Any operation performed on one side of the equation must be performed on the other side

1. Some instructors will let you write down formulas on an index card or a small crib sheet. Prepare these notes carefully, writing down the key formulas you will need for the exam.
2. If you have to memorize formulas, review them right before the test and write them on the test immediately.
3. As a first step, quickly look over the test. Find a problem you can solve easily and do this problem first.
4. Manage your time. Find out how many problems you have to solve and how much time is available for each problem. Do the problems worth the most points first. Stay on track.
5. Try this four-step process:
   a. Understand the problem.
   b. Devise a plan to solve the problem. Write down the information that is given. Think about the skills and techniques you have learned in class that can help you to solve the problem.
   c. Carry out the plan.
   d. Look back to see if your answer is reasonable.
6. If you cannot work a problem, go on to the next question. Come back later when you are more relaxed. If you spend too much time on a problem you cannot work, you will not have time for the problems that you can work.
7. Even if you think an answer is wrong, turn it in. You may get partial credit.
8. Show all the steps in your work and label your answer. On long and complex problems, it is helpful to use short sentences to explain your steps in solving the problem.
9. Estimate your answer and see if it makes sense or is logical.
10. Write your numbers as neatly as possible to avoid mistakes and to make them legible for the professor.
11. Leave space between your answers in case you need to add to them later.
12. Check for careless errors. Forgetting a plus or a minus sign or adding or subtracting incorrectly can have a big impact on your grade. Be sure to use all the time allowed for the test. Save at least five minutes at the end of your test to read over your test.
13. Build your confidence and reinforce your memory by doing a final review of the most important concepts and formulas right before you go to sleep. Do not learn new material right before sleeping since this could cause math anxiety.
14. Get enough sleep before the math test. Remember that you are missing 30% of your IQ points if you miss sleeping the night before the test. If you are mentally sharp, the test will be easier.

Journal Entry #4

You are enrolled in a math course that is required for graduation and want to make sure that you are successful in this course. List and briefly explain five ideas that will help you to be successful in this math course.

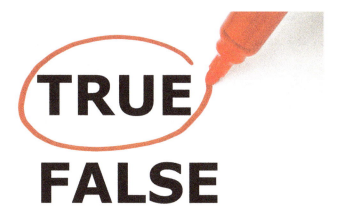

Taking Tests

True-False Tests

Many professors use objective tests such as true-false and multiple-choice because they are easy to grade. The best way to prepare for these types of tests is to study the key points in the textbook, lecture notes, and class handouts. In the textbook, take each bold-faced topic and turn it into a question. If you can answer the questions, you will be successful on objective tests.

In addition to studying for the test, it is helpful to understand some basic test-taking techniques that will help you to determine the correct answer. Many of the techniques used to determine whether a statement is true or false can also be used to eliminate wrong answers on multiple-choice tests.

To develop strategies for success on true-false exams, it is important to understand how a teacher writes the questions. For a true-false question, the teacher identifies a key point in the book or lecture notes. Then he or she has two choices. For a true statement, the key idea is often written exactly as it appears in the text or notes. For a false statement, the key idea is changed in some way to make it false.

One way to make a statement false is to add a **qualifier** to the statement. **Absolute** qualifiers often make a statement false. **General** qualifiers are often found in true statements.

Absolute Qualifiers (false)		General Qualifiers (true)	
all	none	usually	frequently
always	never	often	sometimes
only	nobody	some	seldom
invariably	no one	many	much
best	worst	most	generally
everybody	everyone	few	ordinarily
absolutely	absolutely not	probably	a majority
certainly	certainly not	might	a few
no	every	may	apt to

Seven Tips for Success on True-False Tests

1. **Identify the key ideas in the text and class notes and review them.**

2. **Accept the question at face value.** Don't overanalyze or create wild exceptions in your mind.

3. **If you don't know the answer, assume it is true.** There are generally more true statements because we all like the truth (especially teachers) and true questions are easier to write. However, some teachers like to test students by writing all false statements.

4. **If any part of a true-false statement is false, the whole statement is false.** Carefully read each statement to determine if any part of it is false. Students sometimes assume a statement is true if most of it is true. This is not correct.

    Example: Good relaxation techniques include deep breathing, exercise, and visualizing your failure on the exam.

    This statement is false because visualizing failure can lead to test anxiety and failure.

5. **Notice any absolute or general qualifiers.** Remember that absolute qualifiers often make a statement false. General qualifiers often make a statement true.

    Example: The student who crams **always** does poorly on the exam.

    This statement is false because **some** students are successful at cramming for an exam.

    Be careful with this rule. Sometimes the answer can be absolute.

    Example: The grade point average is always calculated by dividing the number of units attempted by the grade points. (true)

6. **Notice words such as *because, therefore, consequently,* and *as a result*.** They may connect two things that are true but result in a false statement.

    Example: Martha does not have test anxiety. (true)

    Martha makes good grades on tests. (true)

    Martha does not have test anxiety and therefore makes good grades on tests.

    This statement is false because she also has to prepare for the exam. Not having test anxiety could even cause her to lack motivation to study and do poorly on a test.

7. **Watch for double negatives.** Two nos equal a yes. If you see two negatives in a sentence, read them as a positive. Be careful with negative prefixes such as un-, im-, mis-, dis-, il-, and ir-. For example, the phrase "not uncommon" actually means "common." Notice that the word "not" and the prefix "un-" when used together form a double negative that equals a positive.

    Example: Not being **un**prepared for the test is the best way to earn good grades.

    The above sentence is confusing. To make it clearer, change both of the negatives into a positive:

    Being prepared for the test is the best way to earn good grades.

> ### ACTIVITY
>
> ## Practice True-False Test
>
> Answer the following questions by applying the tips for success in the previous section. Place a T or an F in the blanks.
>
> _____ 1. If a statement has an absolute qualifier, it is always false.
>
> _____ 2. Statements with general qualifiers are frequently true.
>
> _____ 3. If you don't know the answer, you should guess true.
>
> _____ 4. Studying the key points for true-false tests is not unimportant.
>
> _____ 5. Good test-taking strategies include eating a light breakfast that includes carbohydrates and protein and drinking plenty of coffee to stay alert.
>
> _____ 6. Ryan attended every class this semester and therefore earned an A in the class.
>
> How did you do on the test? Answers: 1. F, 2. T, 3. T, 4. T, 5. F, 6. F

Multiple-Choice Tests

College exams often include multiple-choice questions rather than true-false questions because it is more difficult to guess the correct answer. On a true-false question, the student has a 50 percent chance of guessing the correct answer, while on a multiple-choice question, the odds of guessing correctly are only 25 percent. You can think of a multiple-choice question as four true-false questions in a row. First, read the question and try to answer it without looking at the options. This will help you to focus on the question and determine the correct answer. Look at each option and determine if it is true or false. Then choose the **best** answer.

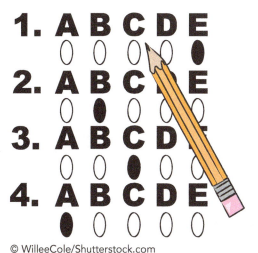
© WilleeCole/Shutterstock.com

To choose the best option, it is helpful to understand how a teacher writes a multiple-choice question. Here are the steps a teacher uses to write a multiple-choice exam:

1. Find an important point in the lecture notes, text, or handouts.
2. Write a **stem**. This is an incomplete statement or a question.
3. Write the correct answer as one of the options.
4. Write three or four plausible but incorrect options that might be chosen by students who are not prepared. These incorrect options are called **decoys**. Here is an example:

   Stem: If you are anxious about taking math tests, it is helpful to:
   a. Stay up the night before the test to review thoroughly. (**decoy**)
   b. Visualize yourself doing poorly on the test so you will be motivated to study. (**decoy**)
   c. Practice math problems regularly during the semester. (**correct answer**)
   d. Do the most difficult problem first. (**decoy**)

Test Taking 215

Being well prepared for the test is the most reliable way of recognizing the correct answer and the decoys. In addition, becoming familiar with the following rules for recognizing decoys can help you determine the correct answer or improve your chances of guessing the correct answer on an exam. If you can at least eliminate some of the wrong answers, you will improve your odds of selecting the correct answer.

Rules for recognizing a decoy or wrong answer:

1. **The decoys are all true or all false statements.** Read each option and determine which options are false and which statements are true. This will help you to find the correct answer.

    Example: To manage your time on a test, it is important to:
    a. Skip the directions and work as quickly as possible. (false)
    b. Skim through the test to see how much time you have for each section. (true)
    c. Do the most difficult sections first. (false)
    d. Just start writing as quickly as possible. (false)

    Read the stem carefully, because sometimes you will be asked to identify one false statement in a group of true statements.

2. **The decoy may contain an absolute qualifier.** The option with the absolute qualifier (e.g., always, only, every) is likely to be false because few things in life are absolute. There are generally exceptions to any rule.

3. **The decoy can be partly true.** However, if one part of the statement is false, the whole statement is false and an incorrect answer.

    Example: Memory techniques include visualization, organization, and telling yourself you won't remember.

    In this example, the first two techniques are true and the last part is false, which makes the whole statement false.

4. **The decoy may have a conjunction or other linking words that makes it false.** Watch for words and phrases such as *because, consequently, therefore,* and *as a result.*

5. **The decoy may have a double negative.** Having two negatives in a sentence makes it difficult to understand. Read the two negatives as a positive.

6. **The decoy may be a foolish option.** Writing multiple decoys is difficult, so test writers sometimes throw in foolish or humorous options.

    Example: In a multiple-choice test, a decoy is:
    a. a type of duck.
    b. an incorrect answer.

216 Chapter 8

c. a type of missile used in air defense.
   d. a type of fish.

   The correct answer is b. Sometimes students are tempted by the foolish answers.

7. **The decoy is often a low or high number.** If you have a multiple-choice question with numbers, and you are not sure of the correct answer, choose the number in the middle range. It is often more likely to be correct.

   Example: George Miller of Harvard University theorized that the optimum number of chunks of material that we can remember is:
   a. 1–2 (This low number is a decoy.)
   b. 5–9 (This is the correct answer.)
   c. 10–12 (This is close to the correct answer.)
   d. 20–25 (This high number is a decoy.)

   There is an exception to this rule when the number is much higher or lower than the average person thinks is possible.

8. **The decoy may look like the correct answer.** When two options look alike, one is incorrect and the other may be the correct answer. Test writers often use words that look alike as decoys.

   Example: In false statements, the qualifier is often:
   a. absolute.
   b. resolute.
   c. general.
   d. exaggerated.

   The correct answer is a. Answer b is an incorrect look-alike option.

9. **Decoys are often shorter than the correct answer.** Longer answers are more likely to be correct because they are more complete. Avoid choosing the first answer that seems to be correct. There may be a better and more complete answer.

   Example: Good test preparation involves:
   a. doing the proper review for the test.
   b. good time management.
   c. a positive attitude.
   d. having good attendance, studying and reviewing regularly, being able to deal with test anxiety, and having a positive mental attitude.

   Option d is correct because it is the most complete and thus the best answer.

10. **Decoys may be grammatically incorrect.** The correct answer will fit the grammar of the stem. A stem ending with "a" will match an answer beginning with a consonant; stems ending with "an" will match a word beginning with a vowel. The answer will agree in gender, number, and person with the stem.

    Example: In test taking, a decoy is an:
    a. incorrect answer.
    b. correct answer.
    c. false answer.
    d. true answer.

    The correct answer is A. It is also the only answer that grammatically fits with the stem. Also note that decoys can be all true or all false. In standardized tests, the grammar is usually correct. On teacher-made tests, the grammar can be a clue to the correct answer.

11. **A decoy is sometimes an opposite.** When two options are opposites, one is incorrect and the other is sometimes, but not always, correct.

    Example: A decoy is:
    a. a right answer.
    b. a wrong answer.
    c. a general qualifier.
    d. a true statement.

    The two opposites are answers a and b. The correct answer is b.

12. **A decoy may be the same as another answer.** If two answers say the same thing in different ways, they are both decoys and incorrect.

    Example: A true statement is likely to have this type of qualifier:
    a. extreme
    b. absolute
    c. general
    d. factual

    Notice that answers a and b are the same and are incorrect. The correct answer is c.

    Example: How much does a gallon of water weigh?
    a. 8.34 pounds
    b. 5.5 pounds
    c. 5 pounds 8 ounces
    d. 20 pounds

    B and c are the same and are therefore incorrect answers. Answer d is a high number. The correct answer is a.

If you are unable to identify any decoys, these suggestions may be helpful:

- Mark the question and come back to it later. You may find the answer elsewhere on the test, or some words that help you remember the answer. After answering some easier questions, you may be able to relax and remember the answer.
- Trust your intuition and choose something that sounds familiar.
- Do not change your first answer unless you have misread the question or are sure that the answer is incorrect. Sometimes students overanalyze a question and then choose the wrong answer.
- The option "All of the above" is often correct because it is easier to write true statements rather than false ones. Options like A and B, B and D, or other combinations are also likely to be correct for the same reason.
- If you have no idea about the correct answer, guess option B or C. Most correct answers are in the middle.

© Peter Gyure/Shutterstock.com

ACTIVITY

Practice Multiple-Choice Test

Circle the letters of the correct answers. Then check your answers using the key at the end of this section.

1. The correct answer in a multiple-choice question is likely to be
   a. the shortest answer.
   b. the longest and most complete answer.
   c. the answer with an absolute qualifier.
   d. the answer that has some truth in it.

2. When guessing on a question involving numbers, it is generally best to
   a. choose the highest number.
   b. choose the lowest number.
   c. choose the mid-range number.
   d. always choose the first option.

3. If you have test anxiety, what questions should you answer first on the test?
   a. The most difficult questions
   b. The easiest questions
   c. The questions at the beginning
   d. The questions worth the least number of points

4. When taking a multiple-choice test, you should
   a. pick the first choice that is true.
   b. read all the choices and select the best one.
   c. pick the first choice that is false.
   d. choose the extreme answer.

5. A good method for guessing is to
   a. identify which choices are true and false.
   b. use the process of elimination.
   c. notice absolute qualifiers and conjunctions.
   d. all of the above.

6. The key to success when taking a multiple-choice test is
   a. cheating.
   b. good preparation.
   c. knowing how to guess.
   d. being able to recognize a qualifier.

7. The following rule about decoys is correct:
    a. A decoy is always absolute.
    b. A decoy can be partly true.
    c. Every decoy has a qualifier.
    d. Decoys are invariably false statements.

8. An example of an absolute qualifier is
    a. generally.
    b. never.
    c. sometimes.
    d. frequently.

9. Statements with absolute qualifiers are generally
    a. true.
    b. false.
    c. irrelevant.
    d. confusing.

10. If two multiple-choice options are the same or very similar, they are most likely
    a. a decoy and a correct answer.
    b. a correct answer.
    c. a true answer.
    d. a mistake on the test.

11. It is generally not a good idea to change your answer unless
    a. you are very anxious about the test.
    b. you do not have good intuition.
    c. you notice that your intelligent friend has a different answer.
    d. you have misread the question and you are sure that the answer is incorrect.

How did you do on the quiz? Check your answers: 1. b, 2. c, 3. b, 4. b, 5. d, 6. b, 7. b (Notice the absolute qualifiers in the decoys), 8. b, 9. b (Notice the opposites), 10. a (Notice the grammar), 11. d

Matching Tests

A matching test involves two lists of facts or definitions that must be matched together. Here are some tips to help you successfully complete a matching exam:

1. Read through both lists to discover the pattern or relationship between the lists. The lists might give words and definitions, people and accomplishments, or other paired facts.

2. Count the items on the list of answers to see if there is only one match for each item or if there are some extra answer choices.

3. Start with one list and match the items that you know. In this way, you have a better chance of guessing on the items that you do not know.

4. If you have difficulty with some of the items, leave them blank and return later. You may find the answers or clues on the rest of the test.

ACTIVITY

Practice Matching Test

Match the items in the first column with the items in the second column. Write the letter of the matching item in the blank at the left.

_____ 1. Meaningful organization A. Learn small amounts and review frequently.

_____ 2. Visualization B. The more you know, the easier it is to remember.

_____ 3. Recitation C. Tell yourself you will remember.

_____ 4. Develop an interest D. Pretend you like it.

_____ 5. See the big picture E. Make a mental picture.

_____ 6. Intend to remember F. Rehearse and review.

_____ 7. Distribute the practice G. Focus on the main points first.

_____ 8. Create a basic background H. Personal organization.

Answers: 1. H, 2. E, 3. F, 4. D, 5. G, 6. C, 7. A, 8. B

Sentence-Completion or Fill-in-the-Blank Tests

Fill-in-the-blank and sentence-completion tests are more difficult than true-false or multiple-choice tests because they require the **recall** of specific information rather than the **recognition** of the correct answer. To prepare for this type of test, focus on facts such as definitions, names, dates, and places. Using flash cards to prepare can be helpful. For example, to memorize names, place each name on one side of a card and some identifying words on the other side. Practice looking at the names on one side of the card and then recalling the identifying words on the other side of the card. Then turn the cards over and look at the identifying words to recall the names.

Sometimes the test has clues that will help you to fill in the blank. Clues can include the length of the blanks and the number of blanks. Find an answer that makes sense in the sentence and matches the grammar of the sentence. If you cannot think of an answer, write a general description and you may get partial credit. Look for clues on the rest of the test that may trigger your recall.

ACTIVITY

Practice Fill-in-the-Blank Test

Complete each sentence with the appropriate word or words.

1. Fill-in-the-blank tests are more difficult because they depend on the _____ of specific information.

2. On a true-false test, a statement is likely to be false if it contains an _____ qualifier.

3. Test review tools include _____, _____, and _____.

4. When studying for tests, visualize your _____.

Answers: 1. recall, 2. absolute, 3. flash cards, summary sheets, and mind maps (also study groups and highlighters), 4. success

Essay Tests

Many professors choose essay questions because they are the best way to show what you have learned in the class. Essay questions can be challenging because you not only have to know the material, but must be able to organize it and use good writing techniques in your answer.

© Lucky Business/Shutterstock.com

Essay questions contain key words that will guide you in writing your answer. One of the keys to success in writing answers to essay questions is to note these key words and then structure your essay accordingly. As you read through an essay question, look for these words:

Analyze	Break into separate parts and discuss, examine, or interpret each part.
Argue	State an opinion and give reasons for the opinion.
Comment	Give your opinion.
Compare	Identify two or more ideas and identify similarities and differences.
Contrast	Show how the components are the same or different.
Criticize	Give your opinion and make judgments.
Defend	State reasons.
Define	Give the meaning of the word or concept as used within the course of study.
Describe	Give a detailed account or provide information.
Demonstrate	Provide evidence.
Diagram	Make a drawing, chart, graph, sketch, or plan.
Differentiate	Tell how the ideas are the same and how they are different.
Describe	Make a picture with words. List the characteristics, qualities, and parts.
Discuss	Describe the pros and cons of the issues. Compare and contrast.
Enumerate	Make a list of ideas, events, qualities, reasons, and so on.
Explain	Make an idea clear. Show how and why.
Evaluate	Describe it and give your opinion about something.
Illustrate	Give concrete examples and explain them. Draw a diagram.
Interpret	Say what something means. Describe and then evaluate.
Justify	Prove a point. Give the reasons why.
Outline	Describe the main ideas.
Prove	Support with facts. Give evidence or reasons.
Relate	Show the connections between ideas or events.
State	Explain precisely. Provide the main points.
Summarize	Give a brief, condensed account. Draw a conclusion.
Trace	Show the order of events.

Here are some tips on writing essays:

1. To prepare for an essay test, use a mind map or summary sheet to summarize the main ideas. Organize the material in the form of an outline or mental pictures that you can use in writing.

2. The first step in writing an essay is to quickly survey the test and read the directions carefully. Many times you are offered a choice of which and how many questions to answer.

3. Manage your time. Note how many questions need to be answered and how many points each question is worth. For example, if you have three questions to answer in one hour, you will have less than 20 minutes for each question. Save some time to check over your work.

    If the questions are worth different numbers of points, divide up your time proportionately. In the above example with three questions, if one question is worth 50 points and the other two are worth 25 points, spend half the time on the 50-point question (less than 30 minutes) and divide the remaining time between the 25-point questions (less than 15 minutes each).

4. If you are anxious about the test, start with an easy question in order to relax and build your confidence. If you are confident in your test-taking abilities, start with the question that is worth the most points.

5. Get organized. Write a brief outline in the margin of your test paper. Do not write your outline on a separate sheet of paper because you may be accused of using cheat notes.

6. In the first sentence of your essay, rephrase the question and provide a direct answer. Rephrasing the question keeps you on track and a direct answer becomes the thesis statement or main idea of the essay.

   Example: (Question:) Describe a system for reading a college textbook.
   (Answer:) A system for reading a college textbook is Survey, Question, Read, Review, Recite, and Reflect (SQ4R). (Then you would go on to expand on each part of the topic.)

7. Use the principles of good composition. Start with a thesis statement or main idea. Provide supporting ideas and examples to support your thesis. Provide a brief summary at the end.

8. Write your answer clearly and neatly so it is easy to grade. Grading an essay involves an element of subjectivity. If your paper looks neat and is easy to read, the professor is likely to read your essay with a positive attitude. If your paper is difficult to read, the professor will probably read your paper with a negative attitude.

9. Determine the length of your essay by the number of points it is worth. For example, a five-point essay might be a paragraph with five key points. A 25-point essay would probably be a five-paragraph essay with at least 25 key points.

10. Save some time at the end to read over your essays. Make corrections, make sure your answers make sense, and add any key information you may have forgotten to include.

What to Do When Your Test Is Returned

When your test is returned, use it as feedback for future test preparation in the course. Look at your errors and try to determine how to prevent these errors in the future.

- Did you study correctly?
- Did you study the proper materials?
- Did you use the proper test-taking techniques?
- Was the test more difficult than you expected?
- Did you run out of time to take the test?
- Was the test focused on details and facts or on general ideas and principles?
- Did you have problems with test anxiety?

© Matthew Benoit/Shutterstock.com

Analyzing your test performance can help you to do better in the future.

© airdone/Shutterstock.com

> **Journal Entry #5**
>
> Of course it is a good idea to be well prepared for exams, but there are times when you will have to figure out the answer or even make a guess on the correct answer. Review the section on "Taking Tests" and list five ideas for guessing that you can try in the future.

KEYS TO SUCCESS

Be Prepared

The key idea in this chapter is to be prepared. Good preparation is essential for success in test taking as well as in many other areas of life. Being successful begins with having a vision of the future and then taking steps to achieve your dream.

Sometimes people think of success in terms of good luck. Thomas Jefferson said, "I'm a great believer in luck, and I find the harder I work, the more I have of it." Don't depend on good luck. Work to create your success.

You can reach your dream of attaining a college education through preparation and hard work. Use the ideas in this chapter to ensure your success. Remember that preparation begins on the first day of class: it does not begin when the professor announces a test. On the first day of class, the professor provides an overview, or outline, of what you will learn. Attend every class. The main points covered in the class will be on the test. Read your assignments a little at a time starting from the first day. If you distribute your practice, you will find it easier to learn and to remember.

When it comes time to review for the test, you will already know what to expect on the test, and you will have learned the material by attending the lectures and reading your text. Reviewing for the test is just review; it is not original learning. It is a chance to strengthen what you have learned so that you can relax and do your best on the test. Review is one of the final steps in learning. With review, you will gain a sense of confidence and satisfaction in your studies.

If you are not prepared, you will need to cram for the test and you may not be as successful on the test as you could be. If you are not successful, you may get the mistaken idea that you cannot be successful in college. Cramming for the test produces stress, since you will need to learn a great deal of information in a short time. Stress can interfere with memory and cause you to freeze up on exams. It is also difficult to remember if you have to cram. The memory works best if you do a small amount of learning regularly over a period of time. Cramming is hard work and no fun. The worst problem with cramming is that it causes you to dislike education. It is difficult to continue to do something that you have learned to dislike.

Good preparation is the key to success in many areas of life. Whether you are taking a college course, playing a basketball game, going on vacation, planning a wedding, or building a house, good preparation will help to guarantee your success. Begin with your vision of the future and boldly take the first steps. The best preparation for the future is the good use of your time today.

> "The secret of getting ahead is getting started. The secret of getting started is breaking your complex, overwhelming tasks into small manageable tasks, and then starting on the first one."
> Mark Twain

> "The future starts today, not tomorrow."
> Pope John Paul II

Appreciating Island Cultures: How Maui Slowed the Sun (Maori)

One day, Maui and his brothers were making a hangi, or underground oven, to make their dinner. They finished heating up the stones and the sun went down so quickly that it became too dark to even see! Maui got so mad because he had to eat his food in the dark, that he stood in the light of the fire and spoke to his people in anger, "We have to rush to do our chores EVERY DAY! We rush to gather our food before the sun sets! Why are we slaves to the sun? I know what I'm going to do. I am going to catch the sun before it rises and teach it to travel slowly across the sky!!"

One of his brothers said "It would be IMPOSSIBLE to catch the sun, Maui. He's bigger and stronger than anything you have ever caught!" His other brother said "The heat would SURELY kill you. It will be so hot that it will burn you to death!" They all sat around laughing at him. When they were all quiet, Maui took the sacred jaw bone that he received from his ancestor Murirangawhenua and waved it in the air shouting, "With this magic jawbone, I will conquer the sun!"

Most of the people were behind Maui because of all the other things he had accomplished, like gaining fire from Mahuika or catching the greatest fish in the world. So, they decided to help Maui conquer the sun. Maui and his whanau, or family, collected flax and he taught them all how to make flax ropes. He learned how to do this when he was in the underworld. They made square-shaped ropes called tuamaka, flat ropes called paharahara and twisted the flax to make the ropes round. This took them five days to accomplish.

During the night, Maui and his brothers took their ropes and traveled east whence the sun would first rise. They hid under the plants and trees during the day so the sun couldn't see them coming. They collected water in bowls for travel. On the twelfth night, Maui and his brothers arrived at the edge of a giant hot pit dug deep into the ground. Inside the pit, Tamanuitera, the sun, was fast asleep. The brothers were silent . . . afraid of what would happen if Tamanuitera woke up. Maui told his brothers to build four huts around the edges of the pit and hide their long ropes there. In front of the huts, they used the water they had gathered to soften the clay and build a wall to shelter them. Next, they spread their flax ropes into a noose and finished just before the sun woke up at dawn.

Dawn over Maui © Pierre Leclerc/Shutterstock.com

Maui told them "When Tamanuitera wakes up and his head and shoulders are in the noose, I'll call you to pull tight on the ropes." One of his brothers started to get worried and wanted to run while he still could. He told one of his other brothers "Why are we doing this? It's crazy!" His brother responded "I know, we will be burnt alive if we don't escape now!" They tried to sneak away together until Maui saw them from a corner of his eye and brought them back. He said "If you run now, the sun will see you when he rises out of the pit. You will be the first to die if that happens!"

Just then, the sun had started to wake and rise from the pit. They quickly ran back to their hut and grabbed their ropes to hide behind their walls of clay. Scared, they awaited Maui's orders. Maui hid and watched as Tamanuitera slowly came out of the deep pit, not knowing of the trap. His head went through the noose and next, his shoulders. Maui jumped up and yelled "Pull now! Pull now!!" The brothers were scared and didn't want to come out. Maui yelled "If you don't pull now, it will be too late! Pull now!"

Tamanuitera was furious as he saw Maui there standing before him. He started to hurl balls of fire toward Maui, but Maui evaded them and held tightly to his rope, chanting "Tauranui (Big Rope), tauraroa (long rope), taurakaha (Strong rope), taratoa (warrior rope), taura here (rope that fastens) I Tamanuitera (to the sun), whakamaua (fix/hold) kiamau (hold fast) kiaita (fix onto)!" Just then, the brothers jumped from their hiding places and grabbed their ropes just before Tamanuitera could get free!

The sun screamed in rage! Maui fought the intense heat of the giant sun and moved to the edge of the pit, raising the magic jawbone above his head, bringing it down on the sun. The jawbone flashed like a lightning bolt as it hit the sun. Tamanuitera cried "Why are you doing this to me?" Maui said "From this day forward, you will travel slowly across the sky, never again will the length of our day be dictated by you!" The sun struggled to free himself, but the power from the magic jawbone did not allow him to be free, so he gave up the fight and surrendered.

Finally, Maui told his brothers to let go of the ropes. Tamanuitera slowly traveled up into the sky, knowing his defeat. From that day on, the days became longer for Maui and his people to have more time to fish, gather food, and do what needed to get done throughout the day. The people never questioned Maui's ability and strength again because he had championed the sun and tamed him. Now, Tamanuitera travels slowly across the sky each day.

- Hangi: Underground oven
- Kia Ita: Fix onto
- Kia Mau: Hold fast
- Murirangawhenua: Maui's ancestor
- Paharahara: Flat ropes
- Tamanuitera: The sun
- Taura Here: Rope that fastens
- TauraKaha: Strong rope
- Taura Nui: Big rope
- TauraRoa: Long rope
- Tara Toa: Warrior rope
- Tuamaka: Square-shaped ropes
- Whakamaua: Fix/hold
- Whanau: Family

Questions

1. What was the focus of Maui's anger? Was he angry only for himself or for his community?
2. Like Maui, how would your success throughout college benefit the community around you?
3. How did this task show Maui's leadership skills? What were Maui's strengths?
4. What are some challenges that you have faced when you were placed in a leadership role and why?
5. What are the strengths that you have when you are placed in a leadership role and why?

© Lyudmyla Kharlamova/Shutterstock.com

College Success 1

The College Success 1 website is continually updated with supplementary material for each chapter including Word documents of the journal entries, classroom activities, handouts, videos, links to related materials, and much more. See http://www.collegesuccess1.com/.

Notes

1. Terry Doyle and Todd Zakrajsek. The New Science of Learning (Sterling, Virginia: Stylus) 2013, 75.
2. G. A. Miller, "The Magical Number Seven, Plus or Minus Two: Some Limits on Our Capacity for Processing Information," *Psychological Review* 63 (March 1956): 81–97.

Test-Taking Checklist

Name _____   Date _____

Place checkmarks next to the test-taking skills you have now.

_____ Attend every class (or almost every class)

_____ Have a copy of the course syllabus with test dates

_____ Start test preparation early and study a little at a time

_____ Do not generally cram for exams

_____ Have a place to study (not the kitchen, TV room, or bedroom)

_____ Participate in a study group

_____ Review immediately after learning something

_____ Review previous notes and reading assignments on a regular basis

_____ Schedule a major review before the exam

_____ Know how to predict the test questions

_____ Get enough rest before a test

_____ Visualize my success on the exam

_____ Eat a light but nutritious meal before the exam

_____ Maintain a regular exercise program

_____ Read all my textbook assignments before the exam

_____ Review my classroom notes before the exam

_____ Skim through the test and read all directions carefully before starting the test

_____ Answer the easy questions first and return later to answer the difficult questions

_____ Check over my test before handing it in

_____ Write an outline before beginning my essay answer

_____ Manage my study time to adequately prepare for the test

_____ Review my returned tests to improve future test preparation

_____ Write the test neatly and make sure my writing is legible

_____ Avoid test anxiety by being well prepared and practicing relaxation techniques

_____ Prepare adequately for tests

Analyze Your Test-Taking Skills

Name _____ Date _____

Use the test-taking checklist on the previous page to answer the following questions.

1. My strengths in test-taking skills are

2. Some areas I need to improve are

3. Write three intention statements about improving your test-taking skills.

Math Success Checklist

Name _____ Date _____

Highlight or place a checkmark next to the items you regularly do in your math course.

_____ I spend about 10 hours a week or more studying for my math course.

_____ My goal is to make an A or a B on my first math test.

_____ I have confidence that I can succeed in my math course.

_____ If I don't understand something in my math course, I ask questions or get help.

_____ I take notes in my math course and review them as soon as possible after class.

_____ I write as neatly as possible in my math homework and exams.

_____ I make note cards on important information and review them frequently.

_____ I learn the definition of math terms in my class.

_____ I preview the chapter in my math text before the lecture.

_____ I practice math problems until I feel comfortable with them.

_____ I study math and do my math homework when I am most alert during the day.

_____ I make it a priority to attend all my math classes.

_____ I have a weekly study schedule for studying math.

_____ I know about some relaxation techniques I can use if I become anxious during the exam.

_____ I use practice tests to prepare for math exams.

_____ The night before math exams, I do a quick review and then get a good night's sleep.

_____ On math exams, I quickly survey the test and do the easy questions first.

_____ On math exams, I estimate the answer and see if it makes sense and is logical.

To improve my success in math, I intend to:

Practice with Short Essays

Name _____ Date _____

Your professor may ask you to do this as a classroom exercise. Review the section in the text on how to write a short essay. Answer the following short essay question worth five points.

1. Explain how you can improve your chances of success when preparing for exams. Include the physical, mental, and emotional preparation necessary for success.

2. Rate your essay. Did you do the following?

   _____ I read the directions and the essay question thoroughly before I began.

   _____ I organized my thoughts or made a brief outline before starting.

   _____ The first sentence was a direct answer and rephrased the question.

   _____ My thesis statement or main idea was clear.

   _____ The remaining sentences in the essay supported my main idea.

   _____ Since this is a five-point essay, I made at least five key points in the essay.

   _____ My answer was written clearly and neatly. My handwriting was legible.

   _____ I spelled the words correctly and used good grammar.

   _____ I read over my essay to make sure it made sense.

3. For essay exams, I need to work on

CHAPTER 9

Thinking Positively about the Future

Learning Objectives

Read to answer these key questions:

- What is my life stage?

- How does positive thinking affect my future success?

- What are some beliefs of successful people?

- What are some secrets to achieving happiness?

From *College & Career Success, Concise Version*, Seventh Edition, by Marsha Fralick. Copyright © 2016 by Kendall Hunt Publishing Company. Reprinted by permission.

Psychologists have identified life stages that we all go through. Knowing about life stages can help you to understand where you are now and where you might be in the future. Positive thinking is also a powerful tool for achieving life goals. Learn to use your attitudes and beliefs to enhance your future success. Many of you have happiness as one of your lifetime goals. This chapter ends with some useful ideas about how to achieve happiness in your life.

Life Stages

> "Philosophy is perfectly right in saying that life must be understood backward. But one forgets the other clause—that it must be lived forward."
> Soren Kierkegaard

A number of researchers believe that adults progress through a series of orderly and predictable stages in which success or failure at each stage has an influence on later stages. Understanding these stages can help you to understand where you are now and where you are headed in the future. Life stage theorists include Erik Erikson and Daniel Levinson. Gail Sheehy, author of *Passages* and *New Passages*, is a journalist who has summarized and popularized current research on life stages.[1] As you read through these theories, think about how they apply to you at the present and in your future life.

© arbit/Shutterstock.com

Erik Erikson

Erik Erikson proposes that human beings progress through eight stages of psychosocial development in a fixed order.[2] These stages are turning points, or crises, and the outcome of each turning point will determine future personality development. Erickson identifies eight stages, which range from birth to age 65 and beyond.

1. **Basic trust vs. mistrust (age 0–1).** Based on the parents' care, the infant learns to trust others and feel comfortable in the world or learns to distrust a world that is perceived to be unsafe.

2. **Autonomy vs. shame and doubt (age 1–3).** Between the ages of one and three, children learn to feel competent by feeding themselves, learning to use the toilet, and playing alone. If they do not accomplish these tasks successfully, children learn to doubt their own abilities.

3. **Initiative vs. guilt (age 3–5).** During this stage, children learn to plan their own activities within the parents' guidelines. If the children do not learn these tasks, they develop guilt over their misbehavior.

4. **Industry vs. inferiority (age 5–11).** In this stage children learn to meet the demands of parents, teachers, and peers. They learn to clean their rooms, do their homework, and ride a bike, for example. If they accomplish these tasks successfully, they learn that their effort (industry) leads to success. If they do not learn these tasks, Erikson believes that they develop a lifelong feeling of inferiority.

5. **Identity vs. role confusion (age 11–18).** During this stage, the child develops his or her identity. It is also during this stage that the child starts to prepare for work by gaining insights into personality, interests, and values as well as learning about the world of work. If these tasks are not successfully accomplished, the result is confusion over his or her role in life.

6. **Intimacy vs. isolation (age 18–40).** This is an adult stage of development in which relationships are formed with a partner. The task is to develop loving and committed relationships with others that partially replace the bonds with parents. If this task is not completed, the adult remains isolated from others and has difficulty establishing meaningful relationships. He or she is less capable of full emotional development.

7. **Generativity vs. stagnation (age 40–65).** During this adult stage, the person contributes to future generations through raising children, helping others, developing products, or coming up with creative new ideas. At this time, the person continues to grow and produce, but puts unfulfilled dreams aside and finds meaning in work and family. If this task is not accomplished, growth is stopped and the person becomes stagnant and self-centered.

8. **Integrity vs. despair (age 65-plus).** At this stage, people reap the benefits of all that they have done during their lives and accept the fact that life is temporary. If this task is not accomplished, the individual is in despair and struggles to find meaning in life.

Daniel Levinson

The research and writing by Daniel Levinson has been very useful in understanding adult development and career development.[3] Levinson proposes four stages in adult development:

1. Pre-adulthood
2. Early adulthood (age 17–45)
3. Middle adulthood (age 40–60)
4. Late adulthood (age 60–65)

Each of these stages of adulthood alternates between stable and transitional periods. Stable periods last six to seven years, during which people pursue their goals and create a desired structure in their lives. Transitional periods last four to five years, during which people question and reappraise the structure and consider making changes. These transitional periods provide the opportunity for growth and reflection.

These stable and transitional periods are related to age. Levinson's research showed that people do vary a little on the onset or termination of each stage, but generally by not more than two years. He also believes that people go through these stages in a fixed sequence during which certain developmental tasks present themselves in a fixed order. How a person deals with these developmental tasks has a big impact on later life. Transitional and stable periods, including developmental tasks, are summarized below. As you read each description, think about your life stage and where you may be headed in the future.

- **Age 17–22 Transitional Period.** The task here is to move from adolescence to young adulthood and to separate from parents.

- **Age 22–28 Stable Period.** This is a period of settling down and creating life structure, while still keeping the options open to explore jobs and relationships.
- **Age 28–33 Transitional Period.** During this period, adults reappraise their current life structure. There is the feeling that if a change is to be made, it must be made before it is too late.
- **Age 33–40 Stable Period.** During this time, adults build clear work, family, and leisure roles. The need to attain one's dream is powerful and intense. Levinson says that this stage ends with BOOP (Becoming One's Own Person). Women often have the challenge of balancing work and family roles at this time.
- **Age 40–45 Transitional Period.** This is a time of turmoil. Up to 80 percent of men and 85 percent of women experience a moderate to severe crisis at this time.[4] At this point there is an awareness of human mortality and the feeling that half of life is now over. There is often a generational shift at this point; adults may have teenage children, and their parents are getting old or have passed away. At this point adults assess their progress toward accomplishing their dream. If the dream has not been accomplished, there is a sense of failure. If the dream has been accomplished, the person considers whether it was worth the effort and wonders, "Is this all there is?" Women are often juggling three roles: career, marriage, and motherhood. Only 4 percent of women manage to have it all: marriage, motherhood, and a full-time career.[5] Efforts to combine these roles often do not provide the satisfaction that women expect.
- **Age 45–50 Stable Period.** During this period, adults work on stable life structures for the middle years. They often have more autonomy and flexibility in choosing roles.
- **Age 50–55 Transitional Period.** Adults continue to work on questions raised during the midlife crisis.
- **Age 55–60 Stable Period.** Adults work on stable life structures.
- **Age 60–65 Transitional Period.** Adults deal with retirement transitions.

Gail Sheehy

Journalist Gail Sheehy, author of New Passages, notes that because of increasing life spans, earlier theories of life stages need to be updated because they assume a lifespan of 65 years. Sheehy notes that women today who reach 50 (without developing cancer or heart disease) can expect to live to be 92 years old. Men who are healthy and live to age 65 can expect to live until the age of 81.[6] The good news is that we will all be living longer and healthier lives in the years to come. In terms of life stages, Sheehy states that "the territory of the mid-forties, fifties and sixties and beyond is changing so fundamentally it now opens up whole new passages and stages of life." She asks us to "stop and recalculate. Imagine the day you turn 45 as the infancy of another life . . .a second adulthood in middle life."[7] She divides adult life stages into these time periods:

- **Provisional Adulthood and the Try-Out 20s (Ages 18-20).** This stage is traditionally characterized by two opposing goals: a desire for exploration and a desire for stability. Historically, this was a time to finish one's education and move away from the parents' home to start a career and family. Young people are now living at home longer, and the period of adolescence has been extended. She describes a dramatic shift that occurs around the age of 30. Before the age of 30, many are still expecting help from their parents; after the age of 30 people feel confident enough to make their own choices and become more independent from parents.
- **First Adulthood: The Turbulent 30s and the Flourishing 40s (Ages 30-45).** Thirty-year-olds step into first adulthood with questions about who they are and what life is all about. They pay the rent or mortgage, make the car payment, and take care of the children. They become conscious of becoming older, and at age 35, they take inventory and ask, "Is half of my life over? Is this what it is all about?"

© Paul Vasarhelyi/Shutterstock.com

These questions are the beginning of a mid-life crisis. Since people are living longer, half of their life is not over at age 35. The mid-life crisis used to happen around age 38–43. It is now often delayed until the mid-40's.

The midlife crisis is a major transition in life in which we question what we did during the first half of life. The central issue in midlife is dealing with growing older and our own mortality. During this time, adults make major changes in their lives. They may start a new hobby, change careers, go back to school, start a new business, get a divorce, or buy a new sports car. It is like adolescence a second time around. While the midlife crisis can be dangerous, it can have some positive outcomes. Adults look at their lives and make changes that lead to continued growth and enjoyment of life. The midlife crisis is a gateway to a new beginning or second adulthood. Half of life is not over; half of life lies ahead, and adults can take advantage of their experiences in the first half to find exciting opportunities in the second half.

- **Second Adulthood: The Ages of Mastery and Integrity (Ages 45–85 and beyond).** The second adulthood is divided into the Ages of Mastery (Ages 45–65) and the Age of Integrity (ages 65–85 and beyond).[8]

The Age of Mastery (ages 45-65) is the apex of life, in which people are stable and have a psychological sense of mastery. People face the second half of life with 45 years of experience in living. People in their 50s are more serene about their mortality. At age 35, our mortality becomes a realization and at age 40, it becomes a terrifying idea. At age 50, we are better able to accept the aging process. We have had experience with life and have successfully dealt with many challenges. At this age, many may feel physically fit and devote time to exercise and better health. The question becomes, "How long do I want to live and how can I invest my time in my mental and physical health?"

Successful aging does not happen automatically. To age successfully, people need to look at their priorities and determine what is most important in life. Successful aging means taking an active part in life rather than being sedentary and inactive. The central question of this age is a search for the meaning of life. People find meaning by searching for their passion. They need to find what they really enjoy and do it.

The Age of Integrity (ages 65-85 and beyond) is a new life stage resulting from the average extended life span. In the "serene 60s," only 10 percent of Americans 65 and older have a chronic health problem that restricts them from carrying on a major activity. Those who do have chronic health problems are often suffering as a result of neglecting their health at earlier ages.[9] In the sixties, most people are healthy and looking forward to using their experience with life to make contributions to their families and communities. People who have lived to The Age of Integrity have learned to deal with life. They have passed through many stages and dealt with many crises. They have learned how to put life into perspective.

Retirement is one of the most difficult transitions in the Age of Integrity. It used to be that people worked for about 30 years and then retired. However, if a person retires at age 65, there are still 20–30 years of life to live. A new idea is serial retirement. A person retires from one career and enters a new career and retires again. This happens because of the need to stay active and involved as well as the need to extend financial resources over a longer life span. It is difficult to predict how much money will be needed to retire 20 or 30 years into the future. To successfully move through the retirement transition, people need to continue to grow and learn how to play after a life of work.

Gail Sheehy summarizes some of the research on factors contributing to health and well-being in the 60s and beyond:[10]

- Having mature love (a wife, husband, or partner) is more important than money or power.
- Continued growth experiences and feeling an excitement about life help people to feel happy.
- It is important to find your passion and pursue it.
- Exercise is the most important factor in retarding the aging process. It was found that men and women who walk a half-hour a day cut their mortality rates in half.[11]

© Julie Campbell/Shutterstock.com

- **Healthy Centenarians.** Many people are living to the age of 90-100. Gail Sheehy describes the characteristics of successful centenarians based on a number of studies:

"Most have a high native intelligence, a keen interest in current events, a good memory, and few illnesses. They tend to be early risers, sleeping on average between six and seven hours. Most drink coffee, follow no special diets, but generally prefer diets high in protein, low in fat. There is no uniformity in their drinking habits, but they use less medication in their lifetimes than many old people use in a week. They prefer living in the present, with changes, and are usually religious in the broad sense. All have a degree of optimism and a marked sense of humor. Life seems to have been a great adventure" [12]

> "Learn from yesterday, hope for tomorrow. The important thing is not to stop questioning."
> Albert Einstein

Writer F. Scott Fitzgerald said that we need to learn "to accept life not as a series of random events but as a path of awakening."[13] We learn and grow and develop over a lifetime. Knowing about the stages of our lives helps us to realize that as long as we continue to grow and develop, we can awaken to each new day with the prospect of continued satisfaction and enjoyment of life.

Journal Entry #1

Consider the life stage theories of Erik Erikson, Daniel Levinson, and Gail Sheehy, and then write a paragraph about your current life stage and whether you agree or disagree with their theories. Here is an easy outline:

According to Erik Erikson, my life stage is . . .
According to Daniel Levinson, my life stage is . . .
According to Gail Sheehy, my life stage is . . .
I agree with or I disagree with . . . . . .

QUIZ

Understanding Life Stages

Test what you have learned by selecting the correct answers to the following questions.

1. Erik Erikson believes that all human beings pass through eight stages of development
    a. that last 10 years for each stage.
    b. in a random pattern.
    c. in a fixed order.

2. According to Erikson, the main task of the identity vs. role confusion stage (age 11–18) is
    a. learning to follow the rules of society.
    b. discovering personality and interests in preparation for work.
    c. forming intimate relationships.

3. Daniel Levinson says that stages of adult development alternate between
    a. stable and transitional periods.
    b. calm and stressful periods.
    c. integrity and despair.

4. The midlife crisis is defined as
    a. a brief period of insanity.
    b. a major transition in which we question what we did in the first half of life.
    c. the realization that half of life is over.

5. One of the most important factors contributing to successful aging is
    a. increasing time for relaxation.
    b. continuing exercise throughout life.
    c. reflecting on past accomplishments.

How did you do on the quiz? Check your answers: 1. c, 2. b, 3. a, 4. b, 5. b

Thinking Positively about Your Life

Thinking positively about yourself and your life is one of the most important skills you can learn for your future success. Following are some ways to practice positive thinking.

"Hope arouses, as nothing else can arouse, a passion for the possible."
Rev. William Coffin Jr.

"Three grand essentials to happiness in this life are something to do, something to love, and something to hope for."
Joseph Addison

© kentoh/Shutterstock.com

Optimism, Hope, and Future-Mindedness

You can increase your chances of success by using three powerful tools: optimism, hope, and future-mindedness. These character traits lead to achievement in athletics, academics, careers, and even politics. They also have positive mental and physical effects. They reduce anxiety and depression as well as contributing to physical well-being. In addition, they aid in problem solving and searching out resources to solve problems. A simple definition of optimism is expecting good events to happen in the future and working to make them happen. Optimism leads to continued efforts to accomplish goals, whereas pessimism leads to giving up on accomplishing goals. A person who sets no goals for the future cannot be optimistic or hopeful.

Being hopeful is another way of thinking positively about the future. One research study showed for entering college freshmen, level of hope was a better predictor of college grades than standardized tests or high school grade point average.[14] Students who have a high level of hope set higher goals and work to attain these goals. If they are not successful, they change goals and move in a new direction with a renewed sense of hope for a positive future.

Future-mindedness is thinking about the future, expecting that desired events and outcomes will occur, and then acting in a way that makes the positive outcomes come true. It involves setting goals for the future and taking action to accomplish these goals as well as being confident in accomplishing these goals. Individuals with future-mindedness are conscientious and hardworking and can delay gratification. They make to-do lists and use schedules and day planners. Individuals who are future-minded would agree with these statements:[15]

- Despite challenges, I always remain hopeful about the future.
- I always look on the bright side.
- I believe that good will always triumph over evil.
- I expect the best.
- I have a clear picture in mind about what I want to happen in the future.
- I have a plan for what I want to be doing five years from now.
- If I get a bad grade or evaluation, I focus on the next opportunity and plan to do better.

Believe in Yourself

Anthony Robbins defines belief as "any guiding principle, dictum, faith, or passion that can provide meaning and direction in life . . . Beliefs are the compass and maps that guide us toward our goals and give us the surety to know we'll get there."[16] The beliefs that we have about ourselves determine how much of our potential we will use and how successful we will be in the future. If we have positive beliefs about ourselves, we will feel confident and accomplish our goals in life. Negative beliefs get in the way of our success. Robbins reminds us that we can change our beliefs and choose new ones if necessary.

> "The birth of excellence begins with our awareness that our beliefs are a choice. We usually do not think of it that way, but belief can be a conscious choice. You can choose beliefs that limit you, or you can choose beliefs that support you. The trick is to choose the beliefs that are conducive to success and the results you want and to discard the ones that hold you back."[17]

The Self-Fulfilling Prophecy

The first step in thinking positively is to examine your beliefs about yourself, your life, and the world around you. Personal beliefs are influenced by our environment, significant events that have happened in life, what we have learned in the past, and our picture of the future. Beliefs cause us to have certain expectations about the world and ourselves. These expectations are such a powerful influence on behavior that psychologists use the term "self-fulfilling prophecy" to describe what happens when our expectations come true.

For example, if I believe that I am not good in math (my expectation), I may not try to do the assignment or may avoid taking a math class (my behavior). As a result, I am not good in math. My expectations have been fulfilled. Expectations can also have a positive effect. If I believe that I am a good student, I will take steps to enroll in college and complete my assignments. I will then become a good student. The prophecy will again come true.

To think positively, it is necessary to recognize your negative beliefs and turn them into positive beliefs. Some negative beliefs commonly heard from college students include the following:

I don't have the money for college.
English was never my best subject.
I was never any good at math.

When you hear yourself saying these negative thoughts, remember that these thoughts can become self-fulfilling prophecies. First of all, notice the thought. Then see if you can change the statement into a positive statement such as:

I can find the money for college.
English has been a challenge for me in the past, but I will do better this time.
I can learn to be good at math.

If you believe that you can find money for college, you can go to the financial aid office and the scholarship office to begin your search for money to attend school. You can look for a better job or improve your money management. If you believe that you will do better in English, you will keep up with your assignments and go to the tutoring center or ask the professor for help. If you believe that you can learn to be good at math, you will attend every math class and seek tutoring when you do not understand. Your positive thoughts will help you to be successful.

"Attitude is the librarian of our past, the speaker of our present and the prophet of our future."
— John Maxwell

"¡Sí, se puede!" (Yes, you can!)
— César Chavez

"If I believe I cannot do something, it makes me incapable of doing it. But when I believe I can, then I acquire the ability to do it, even if I did not have the ability in the beginning."
— Mahatma Gandhi

"Human beings can alter their lives by altering their attitude of mind."
— William James

Positive Self-Talk and Affirmations

Self-talk refers to the silent inner voice in our heads. This voice is often negative, especially when we are frustrated or trying to learn something new. Have you ever had thoughts about yourself that are similar to these:

How could you be so stupid!
That was dumb!
You idiot!

> **ACTIVITY**
>
> What do you say to yourself when you are angry or frustrated? Write several examples of your negative self-talk.

> "We are what we think.
> All that we are arises
> With our thoughts.
> With our thoughts
> we make the world."
> — Buddha

Negative thoughts can actually be toxic to your body. They can cause biochemical changes that can lead to depression and negatively affect the immune system.[18] Negative self-talk causes anxiety and poor performance and is damaging to self-esteem. It can also lead to a negative self-fulfilling prophecy. Positive thoughts can help us build self-esteem, become confident in our abilities, and achieve our goals. These positive thoughts are called affirmations.

If we make the world with our thoughts, it is important to become aware of the thoughts about ourselves that are continuously running through our heads. Are your thoughts positive or negative? Negative thoughts lead to failure. What we hear over and over again shapes our beliefs. If you say over and over to yourself such things as, "I am stupid," "I am ugly," or "I am fat," you will start to believe these things and act in a way that supports your beliefs. Positive thoughts help to build success. If you say to yourself, "I'm a good person," "I'm doing my best," or "I'm doing fine," you will begin to believe these things about yourself and act in a way that supports these beliefs. Here are some guidelines for increasing your positive self-talk and making affirmations:

> "The most common way people give up their power is by thinking they don't have any."
> — Alice Walker

1. Monitor your thoughts about yourself and become aware of them. Are they positive or negative?

2. When you notice a negative thought about yourself, imagine creating a new video with a positive message.

3. Start the positive message with "I" and use the present tense. Using an "I" statement shows you are in charge. Using the present tense shows you are ready for action now.

4. Focus on the positive. Think about what you want to achieve and what you can do rather than what you do not want to do. For example, instead of saying, "I will not eat junk food," say, "I will eat a healthy diet."

5. Make your affirmation stronger by adding an emotion to it.

6. Form a mental picture of what it is that you want to achieve. See yourself doing it successfully.

7. You may need to say the positive thoughts over and over again until you believe them and they become a habit. You can also write them down and put them in a place where you will see them often.

Here are some examples of negative self-talk and contrasting positive affirmations:

Negative: I'm always broke.

Affirmation: I feel really good when I manage my finances. See yourself taking steps to manage finances. For example, a budget or savings plan.

Negative: I'm too fat. It just runs in the family.

Affirmation: I feel good about myself when I exercise and eat a healthy diet. See yourself exercising and eating a healthy diet.

Negative: I can't do this. I must be stupid.

Affirmation: I can do this. I am capable. I feel a sense of accomplishment when I accomplish something challenging. See yourself making your best attempt and taking the first step to accomplish the project.

ACTIVITY

Select one example of negative self-talk that you wrote earlier. Use the examples above to turn your negative message into a positive one and write it here.

Visualize Your Success

Visualization is a powerful tool for using your brain to improve memory, deal with stress, and think positively. Coaches and athletes study sports psychology to learn how to use visualization along with physical practice to improve athletic performance. College students can use the same techniques to enhance college success.

If you are familiar with sports or are an athlete, you can probably think of times when your coach asked you to use visualization to improve your performance. In baseball, the coach reminds players to keep their eye on the ball and visualize hitting it. In swimming, the coach asks swimmers to visualize reaching their arms out to touch the edge of the pool at the end of the race. Pole-vaulters visualize clearing the pole and sometimes even go through the motions before making the jump. Using imagery lets you practice for future events and pre-experience achieving your goals. Athletes imagine winning the race or completing the perfect jump in figure skating. In this way they prepare mentally and physically and develop confidence in their abilities. It still takes practice to excel.

© Sergey Nivens/Shutterstock.com

> "The future first exists in imagination, then planning, then reality."
> — R.A. Wilson

Just as the athlete visualizes and then performs, the college student can do the same. It is said that we create all things twice. First we make a mental picture, and then we create the physical reality by taking action. For example, if we are building a house, first we get the idea; then we begin to design the house we want. We start with a blueprint and then build the house. The blueprint determines what kind of house we construct. The same thing happens in any project we undertake. First we have a mental picture, and then we complete the project. Visualize what you would like to accomplish in your life as if you were creating a blueprint. Then take the steps to accomplish what you want.

As a college student, you might visualize yourself in your graduation robe walking across the stage to receive your diploma. You might visualize yourself in the exam room confidently taking the exam. You might see yourself on the job enjoying your future career. You can make a mental picture of what you would like your life to be and then work toward accomplishing your goal.

Successful Beliefs

Stephen Covey's book *The 7 Habits of Highly Effective People* has been described as one of the most influential books of the 20th century.[19] In 2004, he released a new book called *The 8th Habit: From Effectiveness to Greatness*.[20] These habits are based on beliefs that lead to success.

1. **Be proactive.** Being proactive means accepting responsibility for your life. Covey uses the word "response-ability" for the ability to choose responses. The quality of your life is based on the decisions and responses that you make. Proactive people make things happen through responsibility and initiative. They do not blame circumstances or conditions for their behavior.

2. **Begin with the end in mind.** Know what is important and what you wish to accomplish in your life. To be able to do this, you will need to know your values and goals in life. You will need a clear vision of what you want your life to be and where you are headed.

3. **Put first things first.** Once you have established your goals and vision for the future, you will need to manage yourself to do what is important first. Set priorities so that you can accomplish the tasks that are important to you.

4. **Think win-win.** In human interactions, seek solutions that benefit everyone. Focus on cooperation rather than competition. If everyone feels good about the decision, there is cooperation and harmony. If one person wins and the other loses, the loser becomes angry and resentful and sabotages the outcome.

5. **First seek to understand, then to be understood.** Too often in our personal communications, we try to talk first and listen later. Often we don't really listen: we use this time to think of our reply. It is best to listen and understand before speaking. Effective communication is one of the most important skills in life.

6. **Synergize.** A simple definition of synergy is that the whole is greater than the sum of its parts. If people can cooperate and have good communication, they can work together as a team to accomplish more than each individual could do separately. Synergy is also part of the creative process.

7. **Sharpen the saw.** Covey shares the story of a man who was trying to cut down a tree with a dull saw. As he struggled to cut the tree, someone suggested that he stop and sharpen the saw. The man said that he did not have time to sharpen the saw, so he continued to struggle. Covey suggests that we need to take time to stop and sharpen the saw. We need to stop working and invest some time in ourselves by staying healthy physically, mentally, spiritually, and socially. We need to take time for self-renewal.

Successful Beliefs

- Be proactive
- Begin with the end in mind
- Put first things first
- Think win-win
- First seek to understand, then to be understood
- Synergize
- Sharpen the saw
- Find your voice, and inspire others to find theirs

8. **Find your voice, and inspire others to find theirs.** Believe that you can make a positive difference in the world and inspire others to do the same. Covey says that leaders "deal with people in a way that will communicate to them their worth and potential so clearly that they will come to see it in themselves." Accomplishing this ideal begins with developing one's own voice or "unique personal significance."[21]

QUIZ

Positive Thinking

Test what you have learned by selecting the correct answers to the following questions.

1. The self-fulfilling prophecy refers to
   a. the power of belief in determining your future.
   b. good fortune in the future.
   c. being able to foretell the future.

2. Positive self-talk results in
   a. lower self-esteem.
   b. overconfidence.
   c. higher self-esteem.

3. The statement "We create all things twice" refers to
   a. doing the task twice to make sure it is done right.
   b. creating and refining.
   c. first making a mental picture and then taking action.

4. A win-win solution means
   a. winning at any cost.
   b. seeking a solution that benefits everyone.
   c. focusing on competition.

5. The statement by Stephen Covey, "Sharpen the saw," refers to
   a. proper tool maintenance.
   b. studying hard to sharpen thinking skills.
   c. investing time to maintain physical and mental health.

How did you do on the quiz? Check your answers: 1. a, 2. c, 3. c, 4. b, 5. c

Journal Entry #2

Write five intention statements about thinking positively about your life. In thinking about your statements, consider these factors: optimism, hope, future-mindedness, belief in yourself, the self-fulfilling prophecy, positive self-talk, affirmations, visualizing your success, and successful beliefs.

Secrets to Happiness

Many of you probably have happiness on your list of lifetime goals. It sounds easy, right? But what is happiness, anyway?

Psychologist Martin Seligman says that real happiness comes from identifying, cultivating, and using your personal strengths in work, love, play, and parenting.[22] You have identified these strengths by learning about your personality type, multiple intelligences, and interests.

It means living the good life in the present and increasing your longevity. These factors are associated with happiness: expressing gratitude, being optimistic, being employed, having positive self-esteem, enjoying leisure activity, having good health, and enjoying friendships.[23] Happy individuals have better marriages, friendships, and mental health. They have better work performance, and higher levels of employment and income.

Seligman contrasts authentic happiness with hedonism. He states that a hedonist "wants as many good moments and as few bad moments as possible in life."[24] Hedonism is a shortcut to happiness that leaves us feeling empty. For example, we often assume that more material possessions will make us happy. However, the more material possessions we have, the greater the expectations, and we no longer appreciate what we have.

> *"Suppose you could be hooked up to a hypothetical 'experience machine' that, for the rest of your life, would stimulate your brain and give you any positive feelings you desire. Most people to whom I offer this imaginary choice refuse the machine. It is not just positive feelings we want, we want to be entitled to our positive feelings. Yet we have invented myriad shortcuts to feeling good: drugs, chocolate, loveless sex, shopping, masturbation, and television are all examples. (I am not, however, suggesting that you should drop these shortcuts altogether.) The belief that we can rely on shortcuts to happiness, joy, rapture, comfort, and ecstasy, rather than be entitled to these feelings by the exercise of personal strengths and virtues, leads to the legions of people who in the middle of great wealth are starving spiritually. Positive emotion alienated from the exercise of character leads to emptiness, to inauthenticity, to depression, and as we age, to the gnawing realization that we are fidgeting until we die."*[25]

Most people assume that happiness is increased by having more money to buy that new car or HDTV. However, a process called hedonistic adaptation occurs that makes this type of happiness short-lived. Once you have purchased the new car or TV, you get used to it quickly. Soon you will start to think about a better car and a bigger TV to continue to feel happy. Seligman provides a formula for happiness:[26]

$$Happiness = S + C + V$$

In the formula S stands for set range. Psychologists believe that 50 percent of happiness is determined by heredity. In other words, half of your level of happiness is determined by the genes inherited from your ancestors. In good times or bad times, people generally return to their set range of happiness. Six months after receiving a piece of good fortune such as a raise or promotion or winning the lottery, unhappy people are still unhappy. Six months after a tragedy, naturally happy people return to being happy.

The letter C in the equation stands for circumstances such as money, marriage, social life, health, education, climate, race, gender, and religion. These circumstances account for 8 to 15 percent of happiness. Here is what psychologists know about how these circumstances affect happiness:

- Once basic needs are met, greater wealth does not increase happiness.
- Having a good marriage is related to increased happiness.
- Happy people are more social.
- Moderate ill health does not bring unhappiness, but severe illness does.
- Educated people are slightly happier.
- Climate, race, and gender do not affect level of happiness.
- Religious people are somewhat happier than nonreligious people.

> *"Most folks are about as happy as they make up their minds to be."*
> Abraham Lincoln

Checklist for Achieving Happiness

- Express gratitude.
- Be an optimist.
- Think positively.
- Use your personal strengths.
- Practice kindness.
- Increase flow activities.
- Savor life's joys.
- Accomplish your goals.
- Take care of your body.

> *Success is getting what you want; happiness is wanting what you get.*
> Dale Carnegie

The letter *V* in the equation stands for factors under your voluntary control. These factors account for approximately 40 percent of happiness. Factors under voluntary control include positive emotions and optimism about the future. Positive emotions include hope, faith, trust, joy, ecstasy, calm, zest, ebullience, pleasure, flow, satisfaction, contentment, fulfillment, pride, and serenity. Seligman suggests the following ideas to increase your positive emotions:

> "Happiness is not something ready made. It comes from your own actions."
>
> Dalai Lama

- Realize that the past does not determine your future. The future is open to new possibilities.
- Be grateful for the good events of the past and place less emphasis on the bad events.
- Build positive emotions through forgiving and forgetting.
- Work on increasing optimism and hope for the future.
- Find out what activities make you happy and engage in them. Spread these activities out over time so that you will not get tired of them.
- Take the time to savor the happy times. Make mental photographs of happy times so that you can think of them later.
- Take time to enjoy the present moment.
- Build more flow into your life. Flow is the state of gratification we feel when totally absorbed in an activity that matches our strengths.

© nasirkhan/Shutterstock.com

Are you interested in taking steps to increase your happiness? Here are some activities proposed by Sonya Lyubomirsky, a leading researcher on happiness and author of *The How of Happiness*.[27] Choose the ones that seem like a natural fit for you and vary them so that they do not become routine or boring. After putting in some effort to practice these activities, they can become a habit.

1. **Express gratitude.** Expressing gratitude is a way of thinking positively and appreciating good circumstances rather than focusing on the bad ones. It is about appreciating and thanking the people who have made positive contributions to your life. It is feeling grateful for the good things you have in life. Create a gratitude journal and at the end of each day write down things for which you are grateful or thankful. Regularly tell those around you how grateful you are to have them in your life. You can do this in person, by phone, in a letter, or by email. Being grateful helps us to savor positive life experiences.

2. **Cultivate optimism.** Make a habit of looking at the bright side of life. If you think positively about the future, you are more likely to take the effort to reach your goals in life. Spend some time thinking or writing about your best possible future. Make a mental picture of your future goals as a first step toward achieving them. Thinking positively boosts your mood and promotes high morale. Most importantly, thinking

> "Finish each day and be done with it. You have done what you could; some blunders and absurdities have crept in; forget them as soon as you can. Tomorrow is a new day; you shall begin it serenely and with too high a spirit to be encumbered with your old nonsense."
> Ralph Waldo Emerson

positively can become a self-fulfilling prophecy. If you see your positive goals as attainable, you are more likely to work toward accomplishing them and invest the energy needed to deal with obstacles and setbacks along the way.

3. **Avoid overthinking and social comparison.** Overthinking is focusing on yourself and your problems endlessly, needlessly, and excessively. Examples of overthinking include "Why am I so unhappy?" "Why is life so unfair?" and "Why did he/she say that?" Overthinking increases sadness, fosters biased thinking, decreases motivation, and makes it difficult to solve problems and take action to make life better.

Social comparison is a type of overthinking. In our daily lives, we encounter people who are more intelligent, beautiful, richer, healthier, or happier. The media fosters images of people with impossibly perfect lives. Making social comparisons can lead to feelings of inferiority and loss of self-esteem.

Notice when your are overthinking or making comparisons with others and stop doing it. Use the "Yell, 'Stop!'" technique to refocus your attention. This technique involves yelling, "Stop!" to yourself or out loud to change your thinking. Another way to stop overthinking is to distract yourself with more positive thoughts or activities. Watch a funny movie, listen to music, or arrange a social activity with a friend. If these activities are not effective, try writing down your worries in a journal. Writing helps to organize thoughts and to make sense of them. Begin to take some small steps to resolve your worries and problems.

4. **Practice acts of kindness.** Doing something kind for others increases your own personal happiness and satisfies your basic need for human connection. Opportunities for helping others surround us each day. How about being courteous on the freeway, helping a child with homework, or helping your elderly neighbor with yard work? A simple act of kindness makes you feel good and often sets off a chain of events in which the person who receives the kindness does something kind for someone else.

5. **Increase flow activities.** Flow is defined as intense involvement in an activity so that you do not notice the passage of time. Musicians are in the flow when they are totally involved in their music. Athletes are in the flow when they are totally focused on their sport. Writers are in the flow when they are totally absorbed in writing down their ideas. The key to achieving flow is balancing skills and challenges. If your skills are not sufficient for the activity, you will become frustrated. If your skills are greater than what is demanded for the activity, you will become bored. Work often provides an opportunity to experience flow if you are in a situation in which your work activities are matched to your skills and talents.

As our skills increase, it becomes more difficult to maintain flow. We must be continually testing ourselves in ever more challenging activities to maintain flow. You can take some action to increase the flow in your life by learning to fully focus your attention on the activity you are doing. It is important to be open to new and different experiences. To maintain the flow in your life, make a commitment to lifelong learning.

6. **Savor life's joys.** Savoring is the repetitive replaying of the positive experiences in life and is one of the most important ingredients of happiness. Savoring happens in the past, present, and future. Think often about the good things that have happened in the past. Savor the present by relishing the present moment. Savor the future by anticipating and visualizing positive events or outcomes in the future.

There are many ways to savor life's joys. Replay in your mind happy days or events from the past. Create a photo album of your favorite people, places, and events and look at it often. This prolongs the happiness. Take a few minutes each day to appreciate ordinary activities such as taking a shower or walking to work. Engage the senses to notice your environment. Is it a sunny day? Take some time to look at the sky, the trees, and the plants. Landscape architects incorporate artwork, trees, and flowers along the freeways to help drivers to relax on the road. Notice art and objects of beauty. Be attentive to the present moment and be aware of your surroundings. Picture in your mind positive events you anticipate in the future. All of these activities will increase your "psychological bank account" of happy times and will help deal with times that are not so happy.

> "Happiness consists more in small conveniences or pleasures that occur every day, than in great pieces of good fortune that happen but seldom."
> Benjamin Franklin

7. **Commit to accomplishing your goals.** Working toward a meaningful life goal is one of the most important things that you can do to have a happy life. Goals provide structure and meaning to our lives and improve self-esteem. Working on goals provides something to look forward to in the future.

The types of goals that you pursue have an impact on your happiness. The goals that have the most potential for long-term happiness involve changing your activities rather than changing your circumstances. Examples of goals that change your circumstances are moving to the beach or buying a new stereo. These goals make you happy for a short time. Then you get used to your new circumstances and no longer feel as happy as when you made the initial change. Examples of goals that change your activities are returning to school or taking up a new sport or hobby. These activities allow you to take on new challenges that keep life interesting for a longer period of time. Choose intrinsic goals that help you to develop your competence and autonomy. These goals should match your most important values and interests.

> "An aim in life is the only fortune worth finding."
> Robert Louis Stevenson

8. **Take care of your body.** Engaging in physical activity provides many opportunities for increasing happiness. Physical activity helps to:
   - Increase longevity and improve the quality of life.
   - Improve sleep and protect the body from disease.

© Efired/Shutterstock.com

   - Keep brains healthy and avoid cognitive impairments.
   - Increase self-esteem.
   - Increase the opportunity to engage in flow.
   - Provide a distraction from worries and overthinking.

9. Take the time to think about the good things in your life. As an exercise, at the end of each day, pause to think about the good things that happened.

Journal Entry #3

Psychologists Martin Seligman and Sonya Lyubomirsky write about the secrets to happiness. Write about four of their ideas with which you agree or disagree.

David Myers, a professor of psychology at Hope College in Michigan, is a leading researcher on happiness. He says that 90 percent of us are naturally happy. He adds that if most of us "were characteristically unhappy, the emotional pain would lose its ability to alert us to an unusual and possibly harmful condition."[28]

Just as you have made a decision to get a college degree, make a decision to be happy. Make a decision to be happy by altering your internal outlook and choosing to change your behavior. Here are some suggestions for consciously choosing happiness.

1. Find small things that make you happy and sprinkle your life with them. A glorious sunset, a pat on the back, a well-manicured yard, an unexpected gift, a round of tennis, a favorite sandwich, a fishing line cast on a quiet lake, the wagging tail of the family dog, or your child finally taking some responsibility—these are things that will help to create a continual climate of happiness.

2. Smile and stand up straight. Michael Mercer and Maryann Troiani, authors of *Spontaneous Optimism: Proven Strategies for Health, Prosperity and Happiness,* say that "unhappy people tend to slouch, happy people don't. . . . Happy people even take bigger steps when they walk."[29]

3. Learn to think like an optimist. "Pessimists tend to complain; optimists focus on solving their problems."[30] Never use the word "try"; this word is for pessimists. Assume you will succeed.

4. Replace negative thoughts with positive ones.

5. Fill your life with things you like to do.

6. Get enough rest. If you do not get enough sleep, you will feel tired and gloomy. Sleep deprivation can lead to depression.

7. Learn from your elders. Psychologist Daniel Mroczek says that "people in their sixties and seventies who are in good health are among the happiest people in our society. . . . They may be better able to regulate their emotions, they've developed perspective, they don't get so worried about little things, and they've often achieved their goals and aren't trying to prove themselves."[31]

8. Reduce stress.

9. Take charge of your time by doing first things first.

10. Close relationships are important. Myers and Mroczek report higher levels of happiness among married men and women.[32]

11. Keep things in perspective. Will it matter in six months to a year?

12. Laugh more. Laughter produces a relaxation response.

Journal Entry # 4

Write five intention statements about increasing your future happiness.
I intend to . . .

KEYS TO SUCCESS

You Are What You Think

"Whether you think you can, or think you can't . . . you're right." Henry Ford

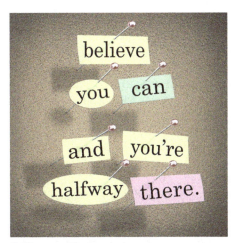

© iQoncept/Shutterstock.com

Sometimes students enter college with the fear of failure. This belief leads to anxiety and behavior that leads to failure. If you have doubts about your ability to succeed in college, you might not go to class or attempt the challenging work required in college. It is difficult to make the effort if you cannot see positive results ahead. Unfortunately, failure in college can lead to a loss of confidence and lack of success in other areas of life as well.

Henry Ford said, "What we believe is true, comes true. What we believe is possible, becomes possible." If you believe that you will succeed, you will be more likely to take actions that lead to your success. Once you have experienced some small part of success, you will have confidence in your abilities and will continue on the road to success. Success leads to more success. It becomes a habit. You will be motivated to make the effort necessary to accomplish your goals. You might even become excited and energized along the way. You will use your gifts and talents to reach your potential and achieve happiness. It all begins with the thoughts you choose.

*"Watch your thoughts; they become words.
Watch your words; they become actions.
Watch your actions; they become habits.
Watch your habits; they become character.
Watch your character; it becomes your destiny."*[33]

—Frank Outlaw

To help you choose positive beliefs, picture in your mind how you want your life to be. Imagine it is here now. See all the details and experience the feelings associated with this picture. Pretend it is true until you believe it. Then take action to make your dreams come true.

Journal Entry #5

Henry Ford said, "Whether you think you can, or think you can't . . . you're right." Based on this quote, how can your thoughts help you to be successful in college and in your career?

Appreciating Island Cultures: Maui and His Magic Fish Hook

Maui, the demi-god, was the smallest in his family, but he had the sharpest mind and was always playing tricks on people, especially his brothers. His brothers were great fishermen, but it was said that Maui was not good at fishing and they would laugh at him because of it. So, in return, Maui would play tricks on them and distract the fish so he

© browndogstudios/Shutterstock.com

could fill his own boat, but his brothers soon caught on to what he was doing and decided not to take him fishing with them.

One day Maui made a magical fishing hook carved from bone. When he made it, he prayed and prayed for the hook to have a mighty power. He named the hook "Manaiakalani." The next morning, Maui asked his brothers to take him fishing again, but they refused. "No!" they said as they launched their wa'a (canoe) out. Maui tried to jump on the Wa'a, but they pushed him off and paddled away.

When they came back, Maui asked them "How many fish did you guys catch?" They answered him, "None! We caught a shark that we cannot eat, but we didn't catch any fish." Maui told them, "You should've taken me! I would've helped you catch fish." The brothers said "You can catch fish when the sea is empty?" Maui said "Take me tomorrow and you'll see!"

So the next day they allowed Maui to get into the wa'a and go with them. They paddled deep into the sea and dropped their line down. They caught nothing. Maui tied his hook, Manaiakalani, and held it until the right time. The brothers started saying "I thought you said we would catch lots of fish if you came with us. Why don't you catch fish!" Maui said, "Not here! You have to paddle farther out. So the brothers paddled and stopped. They started to throw their line out but Maui said "No, paddle farther." The brothers told them "This is far enough. This is where we are going to stop."

Maui said, "If I'm gonna catch fish, you have to paddle farther out." So they listened to him and paddled so far from their island they couldn't see it anymore. That's when Maui said "This is far enough." So they stopped. Maui told them to follow specific directions. "Listen carefully. You have to turn the wa'a around and paddle back toward home. You'll know when I have caught fish, you'll feel it. Once you feel that, paddle faster with all of your strength, but DON'T LOOK BACK!"

The brothers listened, turned the canoe toward their moku, land, and started to paddle. Maui threw his hook out and the brothers knew when Maui caught something; they felt its mighty pull. So they began to paddle faster and harder with all their strength. When it began to get harder, Maui yelled, "Paddle faster!! DO NOT LOOK BACK!"

The brothers were all wondering what kind of fish it was that Maui caught because it was pulling so strong. Curiosity got the better of one of his brothers and he turned around to look. He shouted at his brothers, "Maui is pulling up islands!!!" Just then, everyone turned to see and stopped paddling. Just then, the line of the hook broke! Maui said "See what you have done! I was pulling a giant land out of the sea, but you looked back!!! Now, I only have these islands!"

Questions

1. Maui's brothers did not want to take him fishing, why?
2. How can some of your habits hinder you from being successful?
3. What were some challenges Maui faced?
4. How did Maui overcome them?
5. How did positive thinking and persistence help Maui to be successful?

Manaiakalani: Name of Maui's magic fish hook
Moku: Land mass
Wa'a: Canoe

College Success 1

© Lyudmyla Kharlamova/
Shutterstock.com

The College Success 1 website is continually updated with supplementary material for each chapter including Word documents of the journal entries, classroom activities, handouts, videos, links to related materials, and much more. See http://www.collegesuccess1.com/.

"You become what you believe."

Oprah Winfrey

Notes

1. Gail Sheehy, *Passages* (New York: E.P. Dutton, 1976) and *New Passages* (New York: Random House, 1995).

2. Erik H. Erikson, *Childhood and Society* (New York: W.W. Norton, 1963).

3. D. J. Levinson and J. D. Levinson, *Seasons of a Woman's Life* (New York: Knopf, 1996). D. J. Levinson, C. N. Darrow, E. B. Klein, M. H. Levinson, and B. McKee, *Seasons of a Man's Life* (New York: Knopf, 1978).

4. D. J. Levinson, "A Conception of Adult Development," *American Psychologist* 41 (1986): 107.

5. Levinson and Levinson, *Seasons of a Woman's Life*, 372.

6. Sheehy, *New Passages*, 5–6.

7. Ibid., 6.

8. Ibid., 145.

9. Ibid., 351.

10. Ibid., 384.

11. Ibid., 426.

12. Ibid., 427.

13. Ibid., 429.

14. Daniel Goleman, "Hope Emerges as a Key to Success in Life," *New York Times*, December 24, 1991.

15. Peterson and Seligman, *Character Strengths and Virtues*, 570. Goleman "Hope Emerges as a Key to Success in Life."

16. Anthony Robbins, Unlimited Power (New York: Fawcett Columbine, 1986), 54-55.

17. Ibid., 54-55.

18. Joan Smith, "Nineteen Habits of Happy Women," *Redbook Magazine*, August 1999, 68.

19. Stephen R. Covey, *The 7 Habits of Highly Effective People* (New York: Simon and Schuster, 1989).

20. Stephen R. Covey, *The 8th Habit: From Effectiveness to Greatness* (New York: Free Press, 2004).

21. Ibid.

22. Christopher Peterson, A Primer in Positive Psychology (Oxford: University Press, 2006), 92.
23. Martin Seligman, Authentic Happiness: Using the New Positive Psychology to Realize Your Potential for Lasting Fulfillment (New York: The Penguin Press, 2008).
24. Ibid., 6.
25. Ibid., 8.
26. Ibid., 45.
27. Sonya Lyubomirsky, *The How of Happiness* (New York: The Penguin Press, 2008).
28. Quoted in Joan Smith, "Nineteen Habits of Happy Women," *Redbook Magazine*, August 1999, 66.
29. Quoted in Smith, "Nineteen Habits of Happy Women."
31. Ibid.
32. Ibid.
33. Rob Gilbert, ed., *Bits and Pieces* (Fairfield, NJ: The Economics Press), Vol. R, No. 40, p. 7, copyright 1998.

Measure Your Success

Name _____ Date _____

Now that you have finished the text, complete the following assessment to measure your improvement. Compare your results to the assessment taken at the beginning of class.

Read the following statements and rate how true they are for you at the present time.

5 Definitely true
4 Mostly true
3 Somewhat true
2 Seldom true
1 Never true

_____ I am motivated to be successful in college.

_____ I know the value of a college education.

_____ I know how to establish successful patterns of behavior.

_____ I can concentrate on an important task until it is completed.

_____ I am attending college to accomplish my own personal goals.

_____ I believe to a great extent that my actions determine my future.

_____ I am persistent in achieving my goals.

_____ **Total points for Motivation**

_____ I can describe my personality type.

_____ I can list careers that match my personality type.

_____ I can describe my personal strengths and talents based on my personality type.

_____ I understand how my personality type affects how I manage my time and money.

_____ I know what college majors are most in demand.

_____ I am confident that I have chosen the best major for myself.

_____ Courses related to my major are interesting and exciting to me.

_____ **Total points for Personality and Major**

_____ I have a list or mental picture of my lifetime goals.

_____ I know what I would like to accomplish in the next four years.

_____ I spend my time on activities that help me accomplish my lifetime goals.

_____ I effectively use priorities in managing my time.

© Kenishirotie/Shutterstock.com

Thinking Positively about the Future

_____ I can balance study, work, and recreation time.

_____ I generally avoid procrastination on important tasks.

_____ I am good at managing my money.

_____ **Total points for Managing Time and Money**

_____ I understand the difference between short-term and long-term memory.

_____ I use effective study techniques for storing information in long-term memory.

_____ I can apply memory techniques to remember what I am studying.

_____ I know how to minimize forgetting.

_____ I know how to use mnemonics and other memory tricks.

_____ I know how to keep my brain healthy throughout life.

_____ I use positive thinking to be successful in my studies.

_____ **Total points for Brain Science and Memory**

_____ I understand the latest findings in brain science and can apply them to studying.

_____ I use a reading study system based on memory strategies.

_____ I am familiar with e-learning strategies for reading and learning online.

_____ I know how to effectively mark my textbook.

_____ I understand how math is different from studying other subjects.

_____ I have the math study skills needed to be successful in my math courses.

_____ I take responsibility for my own success in college and in life.

_____ **Total points for Brain Science and Study Skills**

_____ I know how to listen for the main points in a college lecture.

_____ I am familiar with note-taking systems for college lectures.

_____ I know how to review my lecture notes.

_____ I feel comfortable with writing.

_____ I know the steps in writing a college term paper.

_____ I know how to prepare a speech.

_____ I am comfortable with public speaking.

_____ **Total points for Taking Notes, Writing, and Speaking**

_____ I know how to adequately prepare for a test.

_____ I can predict the questions that are likely to be on the test.

_____ I know how to deal with test anxiety.

_____ I am successful on math exams.

_____ I know how to make a reasonable guess if I am uncertain about the answer.

_____ I am confident of my ability to take objective tests.

_____ I can write a good essay answer.

_____ **Total points for Test Taking**

_____ I understand the theories of life stages.

_____ I can describe my present developmental stage in life.

_____ I have self-confidence.

_____ I use positive self-talk and affirmations.

_____ I have a visual picture of my future success.

_____ I have a clear idea of what happiness means to me.

_____ I usually practice positive thinking.

_____ **Total points for Future**

_____ I am confident of my ability to succeed in college.

_____ I am confident of my ability to succeed in my career.

_____ **Total additional points**

Total your points:

_____ Motivation

_____ Personality and Major

_____ Managing Time and Money

_____ Brain Science and Memory

_____ Brain Science and Study Skills

_____ Taking Notes, Writing, and Speaking

_____ Test Taking

_____ Future

_____ Additional Points

_____ **Grand total points**

If you scored

290–261   You are very confident of your skills for success in college and your career.

260–232   You have good skills for success in college. You can always improve.

231–203   You have average skills for success in college.

Below 202   You need some help to survive in college. Visit your college counselor for further assistance or re-read some of the chapters in this text.

Use these scores to complete the exercise "Chart Your Success" as in Chapter 1. Note that the additional points are not used in the chart.

Success Wheel

Name _____ Date _____

Use your scores from "Measure Your Success" to complete the following success wheel. Use different colored markers to shade in each section of the wheel.

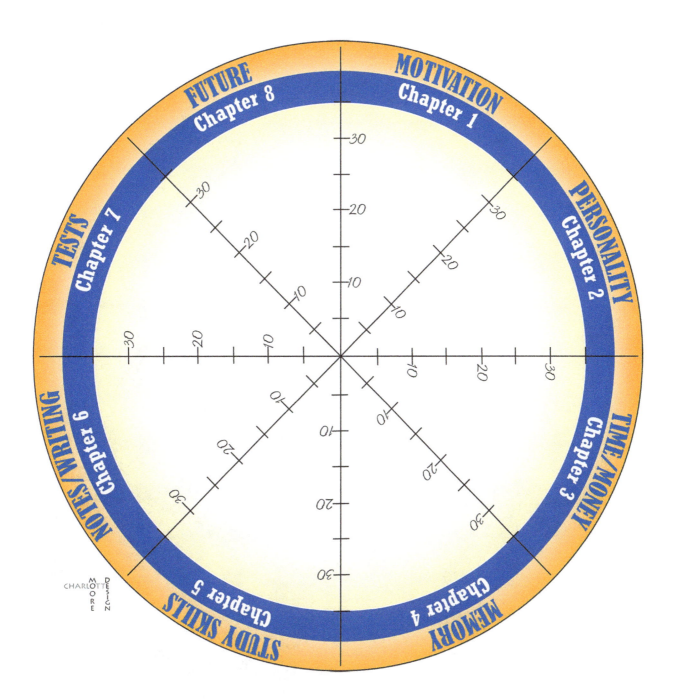

Compare your results to those on this same assessment in Chapter 1. How much did you improve?

Thinking Positively about the Future

Visualize Your Success

Name _____   Date _____

To be successful, you will need a clear mental picture of what success means to you. Take a few minutes to create a mental picture of what success means to you. Include your education, career, family life, lifestyle, finances, and anything else that is important to you. Make your picture as specific and detailed as possible. Write about this picture or draw it in the space below. You may wish to use a mind map, list, outline, or sentences to describe your picture of success.

Happiness Is . . .

Name _____ Date _____

Think of small things and big things that make you happy. List or draw them in the space below.

Thinking Positively about the Future

Intentions for the Future

Name _____   Date _____

Look over the table of contents of this book and think about what you have learned and how you will put it into practice. Write 10 intention statements about how you will use the material you have learned in this class to be successful in the future.

1.

2.

3.

4.

5.

6.

7.

8.

9.

10.

GLOSSARY

Acronym   Acronyms are short cuts in our language using the first letter of each word in the phrase to create a new word. For example, NASA stands for National Aeronautics and Space Administration.

Acrostic   This is a creative rhyme, song, poem or sentence that helps you to remember. For example, you can remember the oceans with the acrostic "I Am a Person" (Indian, Arctic, Atlantic, Pacific)

Affirmation   This is a true statement. Making positive statements increases success.

Aloha   This term is the basis of all Hawaiian values. It means love for the land, family, people, and culture. It leads to success in life, education, and careers. It is also used to say hello or goodbye.

Auditory learning strategies   This is learning through listening and talking.

Brain science   This is another word for neuroscience which is the branch of science dealing with how the brain works, including how we learn.

Chronotype   Chronotype in this textbook refers to your time preference and when you are most alert. It is your prime time for accomplishing challenging tasks.

Cornell format   This is a note taking system for taking organized notes consisting of a recall column and a section for taking notes.

Cramming   In college, this is the practice of waiting until the last minute to study for exams and then studying for a long period of time just before the test. This practice often leads to test anxiety and poor performance.

Critical thinking   One of the goals of higher education is learning critical thinking which includes questioning established ideas, creating new ideas, and using information to solve problems. It includes respect for the ideas of others.

Decoy   In this textbook, a decoy is an incorrect answer on a test. The text provides rules for recognizing a decoy, or incorrect answer.

Distribute the practice   This memory technique involves learning small amounts of material and reviewing it frequently.

Elaboration   This is a memory technique that involves adding details and connections to enhance memory. For example, you can increase elaboration by writing the material in your own words, rewriting your notes, using flash cards or creating a mind map.

E-learning strategies   These are strategies for learning or studying online.

Existential intelligence   This is one of the multiple intelligences and is defined as the capacity to ask profound questions about the meaning of life and death.

Extrinsic motivation   Extrinsic motivation comes as a result of a reward from someone else. For example, money is an extrinsic motivation for working.

Extrovert   This personality type is energized by social interaction and enjoys occupations with much social contact.

Fear of failure   This is a major reason for procrastination.

Fear of success   Fear of success is not taking the last step needed to be successful because success would require major life changes. It is another reason for procrastination.

Feeling type   This personality type makes decisions based on personal values and excels at occupations dealing with people.

Future-mindedness   This is thinking about the future, expecting that desired events and outcomes will occur, and then acting in a way that makes the positive outcomes come true.

Gustatory learning strategies This involves learning through taste.

Hawai'iloa This is the second voyaging canoe that followed the Hokule'a. It was named after a Hawaiian voyager who, according to tradition, was the first discoverer of Hawai'i.

Hedonist This refers to a person who wants as many good moments and as few bad moments as possible in life.

Hedonistic adaptation Some people assume that having more money or possessions leads to happiness, but the more you have, the more you want.

Hokule'a This Hawaiian word means "star of joy" referring to the star Arcturus which guided ancient navigators. It is a double-hulled canoe that has been navigating the world as a symbol of the renaissance of Pacific Island culture.

Interpersonal intelligence This is one of the multiple intelligences and is defined as understanding people.

Intrapersonal intelligence This is one of the multiple intelligences and is defined as the ability to understand oneself and how to best use your natural talents and abilities.

Intrinsic motivation This means that you do an activity because you enjoy it and it has personal meaning for you. College students are more likely to be successful if they use intrinsic motivation.

Introvert This personality type prefers more limited social contacts. They are often described as quiet or reserved. Their personal strengths are helpful in complex occupations requiring quiet for concentration.

Immediate review This is a powerful memory technique that involves reviewing immediately after learning something to prevent forgetting.

Intermediate review This is a short review done periodically to minimize forgetting.

Intuitive type This personality type focuses on possibilities, meanings and implications and enjoys creative occupations.

Judging type This personality type is orderly and organized and often excels in business. Note that it does not mean to judge other people, as the term implies.

Kinesthetic learning strategies This involves learning through movement, as in learning to ride a bicycle.

Life stages Psychologists believe that we all progress through a series of orderly and predictable stages in which success or failure at each stage has an influence on later stages.

Loci systems This is a memory technique that uses familiar places to aid in memory. For example, in a speech, imagine the entryway of a building and associate it with the introduction to the speech.

Locus of control The locus of control is where you place the responsibility for control over your life. In other words, "Who is in control?" Students using internal locus of control believe that they are in control of their lives and take the steps needed to be successful. Students with an external locus of control blame others and may not take action to be successful.

Long-term memory This type of memory involves storage of memories over a long period of time as contrasted with short-term memory which quickly disappears.

Magical Number 7 Theory George Miller of Harvard University found that the optimum number of chunks or bits of information we can hold in short-term memory is five to nine. It is frequently recommended to group information into 7 categories for the most efficient recall.

Malama Honua This Hawaiian phrase means taking care of Island Earth to improve the lives and futures of all the earth's inhabitants.

Math anxiety You have math anxiety when you have a negative physical or emotional reaction toward math.

Mind map This is a system for taking notes that shows the relationship between ideas in a visual way.

Mindset   A mindset is a mental attitude that influences a person's responses and attitudes. A growth mindset involves positive thinking that leads a person to put in the effort needed to be successful. A fixed mindset is based on negative thinking and can be an obstacle to success.

Mnemonic   This word comes from the Greek word mneme which means to remember. Mnemonics include memory techniques such as acrostics, acronyms, and loci systems.

Modified three column note-taking method   This note-taking method is suggested for taking notes in math and includes a column for key words, examples and explanations.

Multiple Intelligences   This is the human ability to design or compose something valued in at least one culture. This definition broadens the scope of human intelligence.

Multisensory integration   This means using all the senses to learn more efficiently.

Naturalist intelligence   This is one of the multiple intellegences and is defined as the ability to recognize, classify and analyze plants, animals, and cultural artifacts.

Neuroscience   This is the science that deals with the structure and function of the brain, including how we learn.

Ohana   This word means family and represents an important Hawaiian value.

Olfactory learning strategies   This involves learning by using the sense of smell.

Outline method   This is a system for taking notes using an outline format.

Peg systems   This is a memory device that uses words or numbers and associations to remember lists of words.

Perceptive type   This personality type likes to live life in a spontaneous and flexible way and is good at dealing with change. This type may need to work on time management to be successful.

Positive self-talk   This means using positive thoughts that influence behavior and increase personal success.

Power writing   This system for writing a college term paper includes prepare, organize, write, edit and revise.

Prime time   In this textbook, prime time is the time that you are most alert. Use this time to accomplish challenging academic tasks.

Procrastination   When you habitually delay or postpone doing important tasks, you are procrastinating.

Self-fulfilling prophecy   Beliefs that we have about ourselves have such a powerful influence on behavior that the expectations become true.

Sensing type   This personality type learns through experience and trusts information that is concrete and observable. They excel in careers that require detailed work.

Short-term memory   This is often called the working memory which is like a temporary space or desktop used to process information. Information stored in short-term memory quickly disappears.

Signal words   These words are clues to understanding the structure and content of a lecture. Some examples include: in addition, next, first, and most important.

Smart goal   Smart goals are specific, measurable, achievable, realistic and timely.

Spatial intelligence   This is one of the multiple intelligences. It is defined as the ability to manipulate objects in space.

SQ4R   This study system for reading a college textbook includes survey, question, read, recite, review and reflect.

Tactile learning strategies   This is learning through touching the material or using a "hands on" approach to learning.

Telegraphic sentences These sentences are used in note taking and are shortened and abbreviated similar to text messages.

Test anxiety This is the fear of failing a test which can cause students to have difficulty with recall when taking tests. It is often caused by lack of proper test preparation.

Time bandit In this textbook, the term refers to the many things that keep us from spending time on important goals.

Thinking type This personality type prefers logical thinking and excels in scientific, business and technical occupations.

Transculturation This process involves adapting to a different culture without sacrificing individual cultural identity.

Values Values are defined as what we think is important and what we feel is right and good.

Visual clue This is a memory device that involves using a memory jogger to improve memory. For example, place your keys on your books to remember to take your books to class.

Visual learning strategies This involves learning through reading, observing or seeing things.

Wishful thinking In this fallacy in reasoning, an extremely positive outcome is proposed to distract from logical thinking. It is often involved in "get rich quick" scams.

Writer's block This happens when you cannot think of what to write or how to begin. It is often caused by anxiety about writing.

INDEX

A

Aaron, Hank, 150
Achievement, 28
Acrostics, memory tricks, 128–129
Affiliation motivation, 27
Aguilar, Mario E., 9
Audio learning, 143–144
Authentic Happiness (Seligman), 73

B

Ban Ki-moon, 9
Brain, memory and, 132–133
Budget, 100–101, 103, 104
    for college, 117
    money management and, 100–101
Bureau of Labor Statistics, 69

C

Career
    choice, 62
    choosing, 18
College
    budget for, 117
    habit of students, 30
    lecture, 169
    major and career, choosing, 18
    schedule, 87
    succeeding in, 16, 43–44
    value of education, 16–17
College textbook
    read and recite, 146–147
    review and reflect, 147–148
    survey and question, 146
Concentration
    external environment, 23
    improving, 19, 22–24
    internal distractions, 23–24
    reading, 150–151
Cornell note-taking system, 171–173, 178
Course
    behavioral sciences, social, 150
    foreign language, 150
    literature, 150
    math, 154–156
    science, 149–150
Covey, Stephen, 104, 244–245
Cramming, 204–205, 225
Cultures
    appreciating island, 10–11
    finding a safe place, 9–10
    navigating different, 9–10
    Pacific island culture, 7–9
    pride in Hawaiian, revival of, 7–9
    for success, 10
    taking pride in, 2

D

Decision making, 63–64
Diet, 29
Distractions
    internal, managing, 23–24
    while reading, 151
Diversity, 4

E

Ebbinghaus, Herman, 121
Educational attainment, 4
Education, earnings based on, 16–17
Education, Hawai'i history of, 6–7
The 8th Habit: From Effectiveness to Greatness (Covey), 244
E-learning, 151–152
Emotions, 127, 247
Essay test, 205, 222–224
Excitement, procrastination and, 96
Exercise, 29
Extraversion, 51–53
Extrinsic motivation, 24–25

F

Fear
    of failure, 96, 251
    of success, 96
Feeling, personality type, 56–57, 63
Financial security, ideas for, 103
Flash cards, 202
Ford, Henry, 251
Foreign language courses, 150
Free Application for Federal Student Aid (FAFSA), 102

G

Goals
    definition, 82
    vs. fantasy, 83–84, 99
    lifetime, 82–83, 107–110
Goal setting, 82–83, 111–112
Gustatory learning, 142, 144–145

H

Happiness, 246–250, 261
Hawai'i
    education in, history of, 6–7
    Hawaiian values, 4–5
Hawaiian
    pride in, revival of, 7–9
    values, 4–5
The Hokule'a, 7–9
The How of Happiness (Lyubomirsky), 247

I

Interest
    beware of, 101
    developing, 123
    in studies, 22
Intrinsic motivation, 24–25
Introversion, 51–53
Intuition, personality type, 54–55

J

James, William, 191
Jefferson, Thomas, 225
Judging, personality type, 58–59
Jung, Carl, 50

K

Kahuli shells, 10–11
Kane, Herb, 7–8
Kinesthetic learning, 142, 144
Kroeger, Otto, 65

L

Learning
    distributed practice, 126–127
    techniques, 123–128
Learning style
    e-learning, 151–152
    success, 158–159
Left brain *vs.* right brain, learning strategies, 142
Leonard, Frances, 99
Lili'uokalani, 7
Listening, 169–170
Literature courses, 150
Loci/location systems, 130
Locus of control, 25–27

Long-term memory (LTM), 120, 202–203
Lyubomirsky, Sonya, 247

M

Magical Number Seven Theory, 124, 205
Maillot, Byron, 9
Major
    choosing, 18, 50, 69–73
    earnings and, 70
Management
    money, 65, 99–103
    time, 64–65, 85–86, 91–94
Master schedule, 89, 115
Math
    anxiety, 211–212
    courses, 149, 154–156
Memory
    brain power, 132–133
    forgetting, 120–121
    long-term, 120
    memory test, 139
    memory tricks, 128–131
    Note-taking, 168
    positive thinking, 134
    reading, 124, 137–138
    short-term, 120, 122
    technique, 123–128
Miller, George, 124, 205
Miller, Gerald R, 128
A Millionaire's Notebook (Scott), 82
Mind maps, 174–175, 174f, 178, 202
Mnemonics
    acrostics, 128–129
    aloud, repeating, 131
    loci/location systems, 130
    peg systems, 129–130
    routine, 131
    visual clues, 130–131
    writing and, 131
Money management, 65, 99–103
    budget and, 100–101
    goals setting, 82–83, 104
    tips, 103
Motivation, 19
    achievement, 28
    affiliation, 27
    concentration, improving, 22–24
    extrinsic, 24–25
    interest in studies, 22
    intrinsic, 24–25
    locus of control, 25–27
    positive thinking, 20–21
    reward, using, 28

Mroczek, Daniel, 250
Multi-sensory integration, 142, 155–156
Myers, David, 250

N

Neuroscience learning, 142–145
Nieto, Sonia, 2
Note-taking
    abbreviations, 171
    checklist, 194
    Cornell format, 171–173
    efficiency, 176–178
    good listening, 169–170
    mind map format, 174–175, 174f
    outline format, 173, 173f
    reason for, 168
    review methods, 178
    signal words, 176–177
    skills, 195
    telegraphic sentences, 176
    tips for, 170–171, 191

O

Objective tests, 202, 203, 205
Olfactory learning, 144
Online reading, 151–152
Open-book tests, 204
Optimism, 20–21
organization, 124
Outline note-taking system, 173, 178

P

Pacific Island culture, 7–9
Pacific Islanders, 2
Peg systems, 129–130
Perceptive, personality type, 58–59
Perfectionism, 93, 96
Persistence, 31–32
Personality
    decision making, 63–64
    extraversion, 51–52
    introversion, 51–52
    intuition, 54–55, 63
    judging, 58
    money, 65
    passion, 72–73
    perceiving, 58–59
    preferences, 76
    scenarios, 78–79
    sensing, 54–55
    strengths, 51
    thinking, 56–57

    time management, 64–65
    work environment, prefiguration, 62–63
Pessimism, 20–21
Piailug, Mau, 8
Picasso, Pablo, 72
Positive self-talk, 242–243
Positive thinking, 134
    about your life, 239–241
    affirmations, 242–243
    beliefs, 241, 244–245, 251
    optimism, hope, and future-mindedness, 240
    positive self-talk, 242–243
    secrets to happiness, 246–250, 261
    self-fulfilling prophecy, 241
Power writing
    editing and revising, 185–187
    organization, 182–183
    preparation, 180–182
Practical learning, 142–145
Priority, ABCs of time management, 85–86
Procrastination
    dealing with, 95–97
    definition, 95
    psychological reasons for, 95
Public speaking, 187–189
Pukui, Mary Abigail, 7

Q

Qualifiers, 213

R

Reading
    college textbook, 145–149
    concentration, 150–151
    distractions while, 151
    e-learning, 151–152
    marking textbook, 152–153, 191
    memory and, 125–128, 137–138
    online strategies, 151–152
    positive thinking, 134
    skimming and, 191
    SQ4R system, 145–153, 145f
    strategies for different subjects, 149–150
    textbook guidelines, 152–153
    textbook reading skills, 162
Relaxation
    techniques, 188
    while studying, 128

Reward, 28
The Ritual of Kindness, 9
Robbins, Anthony, 241

S

SAFMEDS technique, 147
Say All Fast for one Minute Each Day and Shuffle (SAFMEDS), 127
Say All Fast in one Minute Each Day Shuffle. *See* SAFMEDS
Schedule, 104
    master, 89, 115–116
    studying, 87–88, 201
    for success, 88–91, 113
    work, 87–88
Science courses, 149–150
Self-assessment, 37–40
Self-fulfilling prophecy, 241
Self-talk
    negative, 242
    positive, 242–243
Seligman, Martin, 73, 246–247
Sensing, personality type, 54–55
The 7 Habits of Highly Effective People (Covey), 244
Short-term memory, 120–133
Skimming, 22, 47, 191
Speaking
    preparing and delivering, 188–189
    public, 187–189
    relaxation techniques, 188
SQ4R system. *See* Survey, QuestionRead, Recite, Review, Reflect (SQ4R) system
Stress, 225
Studying
    groups, 202
    relax while, 128
    schedule, 201
    time estimation, 87–88
Success
    beliefs, 241, 244–245, 251
    circumstance, 158–159
    cultures, 10
    fear of, 96
    habits and, 29–30
    measuring, 37–40, 255–256, 259
    optimism, hope, and future-mindedness, 240
    roadblocks and pathways to, 45–46
    rules for, 208
    schedule for, 88–91, 113
    self-fulfilling prophecy, 241
    visualization your, 243–244, 260
Summary sheets, 202
Survey, QuestionRead, Recite, Review, Reflect (SQ4R) system
    for reading college textbook, 145–149, 145*f*
    speed and purpose, 148, 148*f*
    techniques, 149

T

Tactile learning, 144
Talents, 51
Telegraphic sentences, 176
Test preparation
    attending class, 200
    distributed practice, 200–201
    emergency procedures, 204–205
    predicting questions, 204
    prevent future errors, 224–225
    reviewing effectively, 202–203
    studying schedule, 201
Tests
    anxiety, 211–213
    math, 212
    objective, 202, 203, 205
    open-book, 204
    predicting questions, 204
    reasons for poor grade, 206
    review tools, 202
    rules for success, 208
Test-taking
    checklist, 228, 229
    essay tests, 222–224
    matching tests, 220–221
    multiple-choice tests, 215–220
    sentence-completion/fill-in-the-blank, 221–222
    true-false tests, 213–214
Textbook
    guidelines for marking, 152–153
    reading skills, 162
    skimming, 22, 47, 149, 191
The How of Happiness (Lyubomirsky), 247
Thinking, 56–57
    wishful, 21
Thompson, Nainoa, 8
Thuesen, Janet, 65
Time bandits, 94–95
Time Is Money (Leonard), 99
Time management, 64–65
    ABCs priority, 85–86
    goals setting, 82–83, 104
    study *vs.* work, 87–88
    tricks, 91–94
    with web application, 91
Transculturation, 9
Twain, Mark, 72

V

Value, college education, 16–17
Visualization, 125, 130
    your success, 243–244, 260
Visual learning, 142–143

W

Wishful thinking, 21
Work
    environment, 62–63
    time estimation, 87–88
Writer's block, 184–185
Writing
    essays, 223–224
    references, 183–184
    skills, 185, 196, 197
    tips for, 183
    writer's block, 184–185